Shroom

TO TWO OF MY FAVORITE BEINGS THAT ARE WITH ME NOW
IN SPIRIT, IF NOT SUBSTANCE: GUMMY, WHO TAUGHT ME TO LOVE NATURE,
AND BUBBA (I KNEW I SHOULD HAVE TRAINED YOU TO BE
A TRUFFLE DOG. YOU WOULD HAVE BEEN A CHAMP).

Mind-bendingly

Good Recipes

for Cultivated and

Wild Mushrooms

Shroom

BECKY SELENGUT

Foreword by Langdon Cook
Wine pairings by sommelier April Pogue
Photography by Clare Barboza

Andrews McMeel
Publishing
Kansas City • Sydney • London

Contents

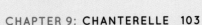

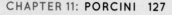

Acknowledgments

I should probably first thank the Grand Union supermarket in Landing, New Jersey, for selling my father that hideous can of watery button mushrooms in 1976. That sad can was my childhood entrée into the world of culinary shroomery, and the truth is that I had no other choice but to learn how to cook (and choose) mushrooms well, if for no other reason than to wipe that taste out of my culinary memory bank.

Mushrooms have always been one of my favorite foods, and I have The Herbfarm restaurant, specifically Chef Jerry Traunfeld (who provides a recipe on page 145) and owners Ron and Carrie Zimmerman, to thank for allowing me to cook in their kitchen for three years, but especially during

their famous Menu for a Mycologist's Dream. It was there that I got to cook with more edible mushrooms than I even knew existed in the world.

I owe much gratitude to Jeremy Faber, who, along with Christina Choi and their business, Foraged and Found Edibles, brought those mushrooms through the restaurant's back door and into my consciousness. Jeremy has sold me incredible mushrooms over the years and has been a tremendous source of expertise and guidance. This book has the wisdom of his forager's fingerprints all over it.

A gentle and appreciative head bump to my agent, Sally Ekus. She got my sense of humor from the very beginning and taught me how to write a great proposal that really represented my voice and vision. Thank you also to Lisa Ekus and staff.

My editor Jean Lucas was a pleasure to work with. She allowed me endless freedom while also carefully corralling my kookiness. Many thanks to all the staff at Andrews McMeel, especially production editors Dave Shaw and Maureen Sullivan, production coordinator Carol Coe, copy editor Valerie Cimino, proofreader Ann Cahn and my fabulous book designer Diane Marsh.

And then there are those who took me into the woods: Amy Grondin continues to trust me with the exact whereabouts of her secret patches. Following the trail of food by her side is one of my favorite pastimes. Langdon Cook has always inspired me with his childlike enthusiasm for all things that the woods, lakes, rivers, and oceans provide, not to mention his brilliant ability to capture that enthusiasm and knowledge with just the right turn of phrase. Thanks also to Grace Sparks for lighting a mycological fire under me so many years ago—I still have daydreams of that mushroom paradise you introduced me to. Thank you to Connie Green for writing such a kick-ass book in *The Wild Table*; it inspired me endlessly.

My talented crew of cooking advisers must be thanked for their recipe advice and friendship, especially Marc "Poodle" Schermerhorn and Jeanette "Jet" Smith. My two-week writer's retreat at Chef Ashlyn Forshner's fantastic island oasis (Whidbey Island Bed and Breakfast) and the focus it allowed me is one of the main reasons I am so proud of this book. Her B and B's delicious breakfasts and the wide open spaces to throw the ball for her dog, Tabasco, and feed huckleberries to Phyllis Diller, the transexual rooster, and Hedy Lamarr and Goldie Hawn (aka the best chickens ever) fed me in more ways than one.

Thank you to Chefs Raghavan Iyer, Virginia Willis, and Lynne Vea for their recipe contributions; they were asked because I'm one of their biggest fans. Thank you to ThuyLieu Hoang (I'm throwing an appreciative head of garlic in her general direction). Jenifer Ward: Best. Biscuit. Ever.

Justin Marx and all the staff at Marx Foods are an exceptionally fun group to work with; their fabulous ingredients inspired many of the recipes in this book. Matthew Amster-Burton and I started a writing group of two a few years ago that quickly morphed into a ridiculous podcast. Being on "air" with our many guests on Closed for Logging got my creative juices going in ways never previously imagined; I have him and our wacky friendship to thank for that. Whether she signed up for it willingly or not, Jill Lightner makes me a better writer all the time. (I tried to work the word *gopher* into this book in her honor, but it just didn't work out—or did it?) Thanks to the ECI editors Terri Taylor, Jen Ede, Melissa Petersen, and Natalie Russell for giving me the scoop on the availability of mushrooms across the country.

Thank you so much to my Shroomtastic Recipe Testing Team. Because of their diligence, these recipes are now ready for prime time: Victoria Trimmer, Dan Gulden, Joan Mudget, Shannon and Cathy Lyons-McBride, Malia Kawaguchi, Lina Miller Furst and Marc Furst, Courtney Smith, Lee Tostevin, Katie Owsley, Katie Sherrill, Jenny Hartin, Jenny Neill, Zephyr Dunnicliffe, Pam Capone, Erica Kerwien, Koriann and Alex Cox, Alan Draper, Lisa Costantino, Cheryl Miller, Meredith Fanning, Claire Howard, Kirk Peterson, Kevin and Janice Ward, Chris Duval, Karen Rosenzweig, Tamara Kaplan, Adaire O'Brien, Suzanne Parcells, Darren Toshi, Maddie Spiller, Jeff Stallman, John Herschell Taghap, Liana Lau, Brenda Vassau,

Ellen Marett, Kaya Hoffman, Kevin Oliver, Nancy Harvey, Larry and Kristen Liang, Bonnie Collett, Jennifer Harris, Anna R Hurwitz, and Rhianon and Aaron Wood-Snyderman.

An extra portion of shrooms with a side of my gratitude to my taste testers and other givers of advice and wisdom: Carrie Kincaid, Heather Diller, Jesse Selengut, Deborah Hardt, Caroline Gibson, Walt Trisdale, Harry and Kathleen Love, Heather Weiner, Davide Kane, Mandeja, Jen Todd, Mel Watson, Eric Little, Sherri Knight, CJ Tomlinson, Nadia Flusche, Lindsay "Leek" Grimm, Bill and Nancy Gloye, Brian Dunnicliffe, Lisa Liefke, David Wiley, Brandi Henderson, Birgit and Lauri Jokela, and Jeremy Selengut and family (because if they lived closer they would have happily eaten every dish I offered up for testing).

Thank you to the students and the staff at PCC, Bastyr University, and The Pantry for keeping the lights on at home and allowing me to continue doing this thing less fortunate people call "work."

I have endless respect and appreciation for my photographer and dear friend Clare Barboza. We're a team, and I can only hope this is the second of many more books to come.

To my wife, April: Thank you for putting up with my book-writing absences and being there for me always. If you weren't a contributor to this book, I would have dedicated it to you.

Langdon Cook

Don't be afraid . . . step a little closer . . . a strange and wonderful world awaits: the kingdom of fungi.

It's a disorienting kingdom. Mushrooms are the stuff of fairy tales and folklore. Neither plant nor animal, they seem almost extraterrestrial. A few are deadly, others mind-altering. But mostly they're just beguiling blooms in the forest—and, it turns out, welcome additions to our table.

Here in North America, we are only just beginning to understand what much of the world has known for centuries: Mushrooms make good dinner companions. They come in a dizzying array of shapes, hues, and textures, not to mention taste profiles. They can be a side, or a centerpiece, or a nearly invisible secret ingredient to add depth and complexity to soups, stews, and sauces. For vegetarians and vegans, they're an ideal meat substitute. Perhaps this diversity is part of the problem for some home cooks—where to start?

Enter Becky Selengut to demystify the fungus among us! Inside these pages we learn about the many varieties of cultivated and wild fungi available today; their individual charms and strengths; tips for cleaning and preserving; and how to make them shine in a final dish. There are recipes here for everyone, with an emphasis on seasonal pairings, as in Roasted Chanterelles and Bacon with Sweet Corn Sauce, a perfect salute to summer.

The first time I took Becky foraging for mushrooms, many years ago, she made dirty jokes about morels and then had the audacity to find all the nicest porcini. I wasn't surprised. Becky is a quick study and an inspired cook. I knew right away that this brief introduction to the art and joy of the mushroom hunt would one day yield a bountiful harvest: the lovely, approachable, and indispensable *Shroom*.

—LANGDON COOK,
AUTHOR OF *THE MUSHROOM HUNTERS: ON THE TRAIL OF AN UNDERGROUND AMERICA*

Introduction

Mushrooms amaze me, and if you don't mind me saying, I think they should amaze you, too. Bewitching and beguiling, they have without doubt captured the attention of every culture that has been exposed to them. They can push up stones, appear overnight (seemingly out of nowhere), repair soils by removing toxins and heavy metals, cover areas as vast as 1,665 football fields (currently the largest living organism), come in every shape and color, and have as varied a range of flavor, aroma, and texture as a roasted peanut has to a piece of salmon. Full of protein, mushrooms contain the most vitamin D of any non-meat food. They have inspired poetry, graced the finest tables of kings and queens, and, to unlucky and misguided foragers, been the cause of their last breath in this world.

Humans have more in common genetically with fungus than plants, and yet we understand very little about what precise combination of factors makes them tick. Or more accurately, what makes them fruit. Mushrooms, themselves, are just the tip of the iceberg. What we see aboveground after a good rain is merely the fruiting body of a much larger organism. The "body" of a mushroom (known as mycelium) exists largely in secret masses of white threads beneath our feet, staying in deep cover. Then, only when the conditions are just right, the mycelia make a seemingly overnight attempt to capture our attention, sending up the mushroom to entice wind or animal to distribute its spores and carry on its fungal lineage. If trees are the protective overlords of the forest, mushrooms are clearly the drama queens.

Some types of mushrooms work in concert with plants and trees. It turns out that what we might have learned as children—that tree roots, and tree roots alone, provide water to the tree—is not the entire story. The mushrooms' mycelia extend the roots of the trees and provide life-supporting water and nutrients to their symbiotic partner. The trees also help the mushrooms. Lacking in chlorophyll, mushrooms (not to mention humans) are unable to photosynthesize, depending instead upon the trees or plants to convert the sun's energy into food. This is known as a mycorrhizal relationship, and I think of these cross-kingdom unions as one would a quirky but solid marriage.

Other mushrooms get their nutrients from dead trees and plants—they are known as saprobes and are typically the easiest mushrooms to cultivate (some examples: shiitake, button, beech, oyster, lion's mane, and maitake). Commercial growers provide the organic matter the mushroom needs to live, inoculate the medium with spores, and provide ideal growing conditions. A third type of mushroom survives by altering or attempting to suck the life force out of their chosen host (lobster mushrooms are one example). These parasitic mushrooms sound remarkably like some people I've dated.

While there are debates within mushroom circles between what I'll call the "pluckers" (those who pick the mushroom completely out of the ground) and the "cutters" (those who cut the mushroom off at the base), it's generally agreed upon that removing a mushroom from the woods is comparable to picking an apple off a tree. All things being equal, you will most likely see the same mushrooms year after year in the same patch.

At the end of the day, we still have much to learn about mushrooms. There are so many types, in fact, that there is a whole class of unidentified mushrooms called lbm (little brown mushrooms). One thing we do know about mushrooms, however, is that for those with an appreciation for their flavor, there is so much to love. And yet, so many people hate them. "They're mushy and dirty," they say; "Yuck! They smell like wet socks!" cry others. "It's a texture thing," reason the rest. And with downturned cap, the remarkable mushroom sits, forlorn, in a self-help support group next to an eggplant and some okra. A runny egg yolk leads the group. Cilantro takes meeting minutes. But what if a lot of this bias were due to poor cooking technique and bad recipes? What if the often maligned mushroom was ready for its day in the sun, its stroll down the forest catwalk? What if we judged a mushroom not by the reputation of its poorly cooked brothers and sisters but on its individual merits and endless potential?

Before I discuss what *Shroom* is all about, let's first talk about what it's not: This is not a foraging book, not a guidebook, not a book on hallucinatory mushrooms (despite its title—sorry for the bait and switch); nor is this a book that will reveal the best spots for you to pick mushrooms or how to tell if they will kill you or not. There are plenty of books out there for those things, so I have delegated all responsibility for your welfare to those authors. Perhaps I should inform them.

So what, then, is this book about? *Shroom* is a lighthearted take on one of my favorite subjects: how to cook and eat the world's best mushrooms. There are other mushroom cookbooks out there, some of them quite excellent, and I encourage you to check out the bibliography for my favorites. Others, however, feature mushrooms in mostly European-centric recipes: bathed in cream and butter, swimming in sauce, never having been giving a direct flavor-generating tour of the bottom of a good hot skillet. There is nothing wrong with cream and butter, mind you, and I do use them, but I wanted to write a different kind of cookbook, one that celebrates a multicultural culinary America with mushroom-accented dishes inspired by places all over the world; a book where mushrooms are sometimes driving the dish and other times taking a spot in the back seat; a book that could convert mushroom haters and subtly, devilishly, subvert their biases through one delicious bite after another; a book for you, the mushroom lover, to inspire you with dishes that I think all mycophile gourmands should know how to make; a book that teaches you the fundamentals of good cooking so that even if I ultimately fail to convert your mushroom-hating brother or spouse, mother or friend, you will have learned something invaluable about culinary technique and mushroom cookery.

The best edible mushrooms have vastly different personalities, no different than your friends: Some are dark and moody, while others are cheerful and fruity, subtle and mysterious, or bold and grounded. The purpose of this book is to introduce you to these colorful characters and take you on a global culinary journey that highlights their unique gifts to the world. Follow me.

How to Use This Book

My number-one qualification for choosing the fifteen mushrooms featured in this book is that I had to love the flavor of them. Enoki? In my humble opinion, they're kind of a snooze-fest of a fungus. Call them the dental floss of the mushroom kingdom. Sure they're pretty, but back to my number-one qualification: flavor. Second qualification? I wanted you to have a fighting chance of finding these mushrooms in either your local grocery store (button/cremini/portobello/shiitake/oyster), specialty market (chanterelle, morel, lion's mane, maitake, truffle), farmer's market or mail-order site (lobster, porcini, black trumpet, hedgehog) or Asian market (king trumpet, beech, matsutake). In the back of the book (page 193), you'll find a description of some other mushrooms worth eating, but to try them you'll most likely have to grab a basket and a knife and hit the woods, as I've rarely seen them sold in markets.

Worth noting right from the get-go: I'm a meat eater working on eating less meat; perhaps you are too. Of the seventy-five recipes in this book, two-thirds of them are straight-up vegetarian. If you are gluten-free, I encourage you to make almost all of these recipes substituting in your favorite gluten-free equivalent (gluten-free tamari for soy sauce, gluten-free noodles of your choice, and so forth). That being said, for the tart recipe (page 163), bahn mi on baguette (page 10) and the homemade fettuccine (page 174) I would encourage you to look online at Jeanne Sauvage's Web site www.theartofglutenfreebaking.com for some well-tested gluten-free dough and pasta recipes.

FROM 1 TO 5: EASY, INTERMEDIATE, AND ADVANCED RECIPES

For each of the fifteen types of mushrooms, there are five recipes, organized from simplest (1, 2) to intermediate (3, 4) to most challenging (5).

- **EASY RECIPES:** The first two recipes in each chapter are designed for a beginner who is eager to learn how to cook with mushrooms but may be intimidated by the idea, or the home cook who wants a recipe that can be prepared in 45 minutes or less on a weeknight. I'm a cooking teacher by profession, and I love

How-To Videos

To help you with some of the techniques I talk about in the book, I recorded some how-to videos for you. Check out www.shroomthecookbook.com or the ShroomTheCookbook Channel on YouTube, where you'll see videos for the following:

- Storing shrooms
- Cleaning shrooms
- Prepping shrooms
- Rehydrating shrooms
- Sautéing shrooms
- Roasting shrooms
- Making porcini powder
- Making shroom stock

helping novice cooks (especially intimidated novice cooks) learn how to work with foods that may be unfamiliar to them. In these recipes, I gently hold your hand throughout the cooking process and, I hope, anticipate any questions you might have. I tell this to all my students, but it's especially important for inexperienced cooks: Make sure to read the recipe through at least twice before starting. Pay special attention to the information in the front of the book (Basics, Cleaning Shrooms, and Drying, Rehydrating, and Freezing Shrooms). Check out the videos at www.shroomthecookbook.com to help guide you.

- **INTERMEDIATE RECIPES:** The next two recipes are written for a more experienced home cook. These recipes can be prepared in about an hour, might expose you to slightly more unusual ingredients, have multiple steps, and require some special equipment or a little advanced prep time.

- **ADVANCED RECIPES:** The last recipe of the five is designed for the adventurous and involved cook, perhaps a self-described "weekend warrior"—someone who is happy spending several hours in the kitchen and likes a challenge. It is also meant to appeal to professional chefs who want to flip directly to recipes that involve more advanced techniques, sub-recipes, multiple components, and/or garnishes. My friend Marc and I always joke that he won't make a recipe at home unless it starts with the words "Day 1."

- **WINE (AND OTHER BEVERAGE) PAIRINGS:** Beverage pairings were selected by my wife, the talented (no bias here) sommelier April Pogue. It was a tough job testing recipes and buying multiple bottles of wine to figure out the best food and wine pairings with her, but someone had to do it.

A NOTE ON SUBSTITUTIONS

There are substitutes listed for each kind of mushroom in the Fact Sheet preceding the recipes in each chapter. While part of me wants to say that each of the fifteen types of mushrooms in this book are distinctly different and impossible to substitute, I'm both a realist (maybe 5 percent of readers have easy access to lion's mane mushrooms) and an opportunist (if a recipe sounds good and I don't have all the ingredients, I won't let that stop me). Maybe you are the same way, so I will guide you toward a mushroom substitution that will most closely approximate the mushroom featured in the chapter.

FRESH VS. DRIED

I will specify in an ingredients list when fresh is better than dried or vice-versa—though in many recipes either can be used with no problem. If I don't specify anything, you can assume that dried and fresh will both work.

SIZE MATTERS
- **SMALL DICE:** ¼ by ¼ by ¼ inch

- **MEDIUM DICE:** ½ by ½ by ½ inch

- **LARGE DICE:** ¾ by ¾ by ¾ inch

Basics

Seven really important things that need to go in a box so you will be sure to read it:

1. Memorize this: 2 ounces of dried mushrooms = 1 pound fresh mushrooms.

2. Mushrooms are roughly 90 percent water. Humans are roughly 50 to 65 percent water. We don't worry about absorbing water when we bathe and neither should you worry about mushrooms doing so if they get wet. Wild mushrooms are already getting rained on, on a fairly regular basis. In conclusion, if you are filthy, take a bath; if your mushrooms are filthy, give them a bath. For more detailed mushroom washing instructions, go to page xxvi; and also check out www.shroomthecookbook.com.

3. I'm including a recipe for mushroom stock on page xxiii. It's painfully simple, so there are no excuses not to make a double batch and store it in quart-size containers in your freezer. A lot of the recipes in this book will be all the more delicious if you use this very simple stock.

4. If a mushroom were murdered, the plastic bag would be considered the deadly weapon. Plastic is Kryptonite to a mushroom. And just in case I haven't yet made my point, if you store mushrooms in a plastic bag coffin, you will have stumbled upon the most efficient way to render them slimy and gross. They can't breathe in plastic, and mushrooms really need to breathe, so do them a favor and put them in either a brown paper bag or a basket with a dry piece of newspaper or paper towel on top and store them in your refrigerator (but not in the humid crisper drawer). There are a few exceptions to the no-plastic rule: Mushrooms can be vacuum sealed in plastic (or stored in a freezer bag, pressing as much air out as you can) and stored in the freezer for later use (see Freezing Mushrooms 101 on page xxxi for more information). You can also vacuum-seal dried mushrooms (or use zip-top bags, as directed on page xxix) and store in the freezer to ensure that no critter contamination issues arise (see Drying Mushrooms 101 on page xxix for more information). Some manufacturers package their mushrooms in special plastic bags that can breathe (you are likely to find maitake and beech mushrooms in these special bags). My expert-forager friend advises that you should still take them out of these "breathable" plastic bags and put them in brown paper bags no matter what the manufacturer says. I have found them to be fine in the special bags for up to a week or two, but no more.

5. Caramelization equals flavor. Browning mushrooms, whether in the oven, in a sauté pan, or on a grill, is one of the best things you can do to increase the Umami Awesomeness Flavor Quotient™ (UAFQ). I just made that acronym up. An equation to remember: plenty of room + plenty of heat = high UAFQ.

6. I don't recommend eating raw mushrooms. Cooking makes most mushrooms taste a lot better. Truffles are the exception to the rule. Don't just take my word for it. Here's Dr. Andrew Weil on why you shouldn't eat raw mushrooms: "Mushrooms have very tough cell walls and are essentially indigestible if you don't cook them. Thoroughly heating them releases the nutrients they contain, including protein, B vitamins, and minerals, as well as a wide range of novel compounds not found in other foods. But there are other reasons to cook your mushrooms. Raw mushrooms contain small amounts of toxins, including some compounds that are considered carcinogens. These are destroyed by cooking them thoroughly."

7. Mushrooms, when eaten in quantity, can have a similar effect on the body as cabbage, beans, or broccoli. I tell you this only so you will feel empathetic toward my wife, as I tested all seventy-five of these recipes in a one-month period.

Ingredients and Basic Recipes

CHILI-PEANUT OIL: You can find many varieties of bottled chili oil in Asian markets or online, but it's ridiculously easy to make a batch from scratch and store it in your fridge. Plus, your homemade oil contains none of the additives and preservatives that are commonly added to the bottled versions.

To make your own, in a small saucepan set over medium heat, combine 1 cup peanut or coconut oil, along with 3 to 5 tablespoons red pepper flakes (see Note). (The quantity will depend on how hot you want the oil to be.) Heat the oil to 300°F on an instant-read thermometer. Remove the pan from the heat and try not to breathe in the fumes! Let the oil cool to 250°F, and then add 1 tablespoon toasted sesame oil and 2 tablespoons minced roasted unsalted peanuts. Transfer to a clean glass jar with a tight-fitting lid. Add 1 teaspoon salt and 1 teaspoon sugar. Seal the jar, shake it a few times to distribute the ingredients, and leave at room temperature for 2 days. Refrigerate. It will keep for at least 1 month, if not longer, in the fridge.

NOTE: You can purchase whole dried chiles, toast them in a dry pan until flexible and fragrant, and then buzz them in the food processor, or just use regular bottled red pepper flakes.

DUXELLES: Developed by the seventeenth-century French chef François Pierre La Varenne and named after his employer, the French Marquis d'Uxelles, duxelles are a mushroom condiment that stores wonderfully in the freezer. Essentially they are a simple way to remove the water from mushrooms and preserve them to use as a flavor enhancer in all manner of dishes at a later date. If you have a pound of any type of mushroom sitting around, with no idea what to do with them, make duxelles.

To make duxelles, simply chuck the cleaned, trimmed mushrooms into a food processor, and pulse them until they are finely chopped. Heat a few tablespoons of vegetable oil in a large sauté pan over high heat, and add the mushrooms and some salt. Cook, stirring occasionally, until most of the water has been released and the volume of the mushrooms has really shrunk down. When the mushrooms start to brown, toss in some minced shallot or garlic, if you like. Add a splash of wine or cognac, or not. You can freeze the duxelles in an ice-cube tray and then pop them out into a freezer bag to use in a million things, or you can just freeze the whole batch in a bigger container for making beef Wellington at a later date. Or forget the whole preservation thing and spread the duxelles on crostini and call it a day.

FATS AND OILS: I cook with only a few kinds. I use butter and extra-virgin olive oil for all medium-heat and low-heat cooking. I use coconut oil, avocado oil, duck or bacon fat, and ghee (clarified butter) for medium-heat to high-heat cooking. (You can use the flavorless kind of coconut oil when you don't want to taste coconut in the dish. I like the flavor, so I just use the extra-virgin kind all the time.) And for the occasional deep-fat frying, I use a high-heat oil such as peanut oil or rice bran oil. (A few recipes in the book call for frying.)

FISH SAUCE: I really love Red Boat brand. It's made with high-quality anchovies on the island of Phu Quoc, in Vietnam. It's the only fish sauce that I can taste right out of the bottle and not make a face.

MUSHROOM STOCK: You will not be sorry you took the time to make your own. As you cook and are busy prepping vegetables and such, e.g., carrots, celery, onions, mushrooms, parsley, and thyme, rather than toss or compost the carrot tops and peels, celery ends and leaves, onion ends and cores, shiitake and button stems, thyme and parsley stems, and any other produce bits you collect, save them. (Skip vegetables like kale, cabbage, broccoli, or anything with a dominating flavor or color that you wouldn't want in a mushroom stock—no beets!)

To make the stock, add these vegetable scraps to a quart-size resealable plastic bag that lives in the freezer. When the bag is full, you are ready to make your stock. At the market, pick up a small onion, some dried porcini, and a handful of fresh shiitake mushrooms. Preheat the oven to 400°F. Drizzle a little high-heat oil on a rimmed baking pan. Throw the shiitakes, along with the chopped-up onion, onto the pan, and toss with the oil. Roast until caramelized, about 20 minutes. Deglaze the pan with a little wine or water, scraping up any brown bits stuck to the pan. Dump the mushrooms and onions, along with the liquid, into a stockpot along with the contents of that freezer bag (no need to thaw) and a few rehydrated pieces of dried porcini (along with the strained soaking liquid). Cover with 3 quarts water, chuck in about 5 peppercorns, bring to a boil, lower to a simmer, and cook, uncovered, for 45 minutes. Pour the contents of the pot through a fine-mesh strainer set over a large bowl, pressing on the solids to extract as much liquid as possible. You should end up with about 2 quarts mushroom stock. Want to make vegetable stock? Do the same thing, but just use fewer mushrooms and more vegetables (and a big flavor bonus if you roast some of the vegetables as you would the shiitake and onion). If you want to make mushroom stock but don't have a full bag of

trimmings in the freezer, just use an assortment of vegetables and mushrooms (equaling roughly 1 quart) and follow the same general procedure. See the video on making shroom stock at www.shroomthecookbook.com.

> **NOTE:** If you end up purchasing mushroom stock for the recipes in the book that call for homemade, you'll want to start with less salt in your recipe and adjust as you go so that you don't oversalt the dish.

MUSHROOM DASHI: Dashi is a type of Japanese soup and stock, typically based on kelp and dried bonito (tuna) flakes. In this mushroom-based dashi, I'm forgoing the tuna, which keeps it vegetarian and focused on the mushroom flavor. Wipe off 2 roughly 4-inch square pieces of kombu (kelp) with a damp paper towel. Add the kombu to a saucepan, along with 4 cups homemade mushroom stock. Turn the heat to medium and slowly bring the soup to just below a boil. Simmer for about 10 minutes. (If your stock is already hot, infuse the kombu in the hot stock, covered, off the heat for 10 minutes prior to simmering over medium-high heat for about 5 minutes.) Remove the kombu. The dashi is now ready to use. (I will sometimes finely dice this kombu and use it as an ingredient in the dish, or if you like green smoothies, you can reserve it for up to 1 week in the fridge and use a small amount for that. Otherwise, pitch it into your compost.)

PORCINI POWDER: Break high-quality dried porcini (avoid buying really dark, dusty, broken, or worm-eaten pieces) into small pieces and buzz to a fine powder in an electric spice grinder. Store in a plastic freezer bag or glass jar in the freezer for up to 6 months. There are several ways to use this powder. You can mix it with hot water and then cook it into a soup or stew, or use it along with salt and pepper as a crust for beef or fish, or add it to boost the earthiness in a vegetarian dish. I use it for extra umami in the recipe for Grilled Porcini with Toasted Shallot and Balsamic Vinaigrette (page 132) and to crust the hanger steak on page 134. See www.shroomthecookbook.com for a video demonstration of how to make porcini powder. Please note that the porcini powder you make will be uncooked. You will want to cook this powder, by simmering it into the soup or stew, by searing the meat in the pan, and so forth. Keep in mind that you can't really remove the gritty sediment from porcini when you are making porcini powder (as you would when rehydrating). Make sure you choose clean-looking high-quality dried porcini and grind to a very fine powder. Do that, and you shouldn't have any grit problems.

TOASTING NUTS: There are a few ways to toast nuts. If you watch carefully, you can do it in a skillet on the stovetop, but I find the easiest and safest way to go is to preheat your oven to 350°F. Spread the nuts on a baking sheet and pop them into the oven. Pine nuts really enjoy burning (they're evil), so keep a close eye on those and check after 4 to 5 minutes. Ditto for sliced almonds. For the bigger nuts (whole almonds, walnuts, and others), take a peek at them after 8 to 10 minutes.

USING WINE IN RECIPES: A long time ago, my friend Susan gave me a tip about cooking with wine. She said she used dry (white) vermouth whenever a recipe called for white wine because she didn't drink a lot of white wine at home. To waste practically a whole bottle of white wine down the drain just for the ½ cup you need in a recipe is a travesty. Now perhaps some of you can't relate, but for those who can, dry vermouth has a nice long shelf life, is made with botanicals that complement most recipes, and has more alcohol (bonus!). Since learning that tip, I've completely moved away from cooking with white wine. But red wine? I have no problem making that go away if I only use a little in a recipe. Always cook with a wine you wouldn't mind drinking. It's simple, really: Reducing bad wine makes for an even worse sauce. A quaffable wine that's reduced in a sauce can be magical. That being said, you probably shouldn't cook with a precious or expensive wine, because you will lose the nuances of it once it's cooked. Find something enjoyable and affordable and cook with that.

Recommended Cooking Equipment

CAST-IRON SKILLETS: Almost all of the pans in my kitchen are cast iron. (I especially love the old brand Griswold—if you can find one at a garage sale, grab it!) Cast iron can be inexpensive, last several lifetimes, sear foods beautifully, and, when well cared for, can even fry an egg just like a nonstick pan. Try not to stress too much over proper care. I've used and abused my pans over the years, and they always bounce back. To determine how seasoned (that is, nonstick) your pan is, I do what I call "the fried egg test." Try to cook an egg in the cast-iron skillet, after first heating it and adding a slick of oil on the bottom. If the egg sticks and you are not able to remove it easily, you'll need to season the pan. Heat the oven to 350°F, and coat the pan inside and out with a neutral-flavored oil. (Flaxseed oil is very good for this.) Bake it for 1 hour, with aluminum foil on the rack underneath to catch any drips. Only use that pan for foods that are high in fat or are cooked with a lot of oil. If you love bacon, make that your bacon pan. During this seasoning period, clean the pan by sprinkling a small handful of kosher salt in the pan and then scrubbing it with a wadded-up piece of paper towel. Make sure that all the salt is wiped out and then store the pan in a dry place until the next time you want to cook something fatty. Don't use soap or water on the pan during the seasoning period. Once you can fry an egg successfully in the pan (with no sticking), your pan has graduated. Now you can wash it with water and a stiff non-metal scrub brush (only very occasionally with a drop of soap, if needed). Wipe the pan dry with a paper towel and then heat until dry on top of the stove or place in a still-hot oven. Follow this by wiping a little neutral-flavored oil into the pan to shine it up and protect it between uses. This keeps your cast-iron pans nice and rust-free. Rust is the enemy of cast iron.

SPICE GRINDER: Some people insist on calling it a coffee grinder, but I buy them purely for grinding spices. I'm talking about the electric ones that won't set you back more than $25. Don't get too attached to a brand, because I've found through the years that they all seem to have a 1- to 2-year life span. You can break up cinnamon sticks and grind those; ditto for nuts, herbs like rosemary and thyme, and all manner of small spices. I also have a backup mortar and pestle (my favorite is the Mexican *molcajete*) for the inevitable moment when your spice grinder croaks mid-recipe.

KITCHEN SCALE: I recommend you get a digital scale for your kitchen. More and more recipes are using weight rather than the far less accurate volume measurements. It's really difficult—not to mention inaccurate—to instruct someone to use 1 cup of morel mushrooms, knowing the variability on how many someone could place or wedge into 1 cup. If this helps convince you at all, when it comes to pastry recipes, you use far fewer dishes, making for way less cleanup, because you simply tare (zero) the scale and keep adding the ingredients, one by one. With a kitchen scale, gone are the days of liquid and dry measuring cups. It's a one- or two-bowl cooking or baking operation.

Cleaning Really Dirty Shrooms

While many purists will tell you to always use a damp paper towel or a brush to clean mushrooms, and to never let them come in contact with water, I reserve the plunge-and-slosh technique for mushrooms that are filthy, covered in pine needles and mud, and most likely already a little saturated with water from a rainy fall day. That being said, I haven't washed or brushed buttons, creminis, portobellos, or any of the other cultivated mushrooms featured in this book (shiitake, beech, lion's mane, maitake, oyster, king oyster) since, well, ever. If there is a bit of dirt on them, I'll wipe it off with a towel. But honestly, it's well within my comfort level to trust that a searing-hot pan will render inert any dirt or bacteria that came on board my cultivated mushrooms—but that's me, and maybe not you. So, if you have really dirty mushrooms (or you're not convinced by my reticence to wash cultivated mushrooms), please refer to the washing instructions that follow. If you are a mushroom forager, keep in mind that brushing and trimming in the field saves a lot of work later. Refer to www.shroomthecookbook.com for a video demonstration of cleaning mushrooms.

1. Fill a large bowl with cool water. Lay out a large, absorbent kitchen towel on a baking pan or on your counter.

2. Plunge a handful of mushrooms into the water (not too many) and slosh them around with your fingertips, loosening the dirt and pine needles. Be quick about it.

3. Scoop the mushrooms out of the bowl with your fingers (the dirt will settle to the bottom, but any needles and leaves tend to float, so be careful as you pull them up and out of the water). Lay them out on the towel. Lay another towel on top and gently press to pull out extra moisture, then pull off the top towel and allow the mushrooms to air-dry. Thirty minutes later they will be ready to use. You can help the process along by gently rolling them in the towel, or even spinning them in a towel-lined salad spinner.

   NOTE: For rain-soaked mushrooms or ones that you've washed in this fashion, it is even more crucial to cook them in a large, wide sauté pan over high heat to quickly evaporate the moisture (or, alternatively, spread them out on a baking pan and roast in a hot oven). If you bunch them up, they will steam and get mushy.

4. The trick for sautéing wet mushrooms (or honestly, any mushroom, as they consist mostly of water) is high heat and lots of elbow room around each mushroom. I can't stress this enough.

This mushroom needs a bath.

This one just needs a wipe with a lightly damp cloth or a quick brushing.

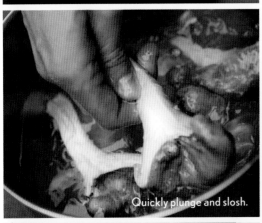

Quickly plunge and slosh.

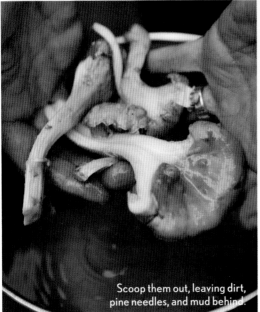

Scoop them out, leaving dirt, pine needles, and mud behind.

If you can avoid washing mushrooms, do.

Drying Mushrooms 101

First, a note on purchasing dried mushrooms: Keep in mind that they are likely to be the ones that didn't pass muster to sell fresh, so they tend to be the older, wormier, or less aesthetically pleasing ones. This is not always the case, of course, but it's a safe generalization. This is not to say there is anything necessarily wrong with them flavorwise, but if your intention was to rehydrate them into faux-fresh pristine lookalikes, you might be disappointed. The one exception to this rule are dried morel mushrooms. Man, do those rehydrate beautifully. I'd be hard-pressed to tell the difference between a rehydrated fresh cooked and a never dried fresh cooked.

There are three ways to dry mushrooms—well, I bet there are more, but I think you might find these three helpful. No matter which way you ultimately dry your mushrooms, make sure they are really bone dry. Drying times vary depending on the mushroom, method, and conditions in your house. Your mushrooms can dry in as quickly as an afternoon or as long as several days. I've listed the various methods here, in order of what I recommend for achieving the best results.

METHOD #1: USE A DEHYDRATOR. First, clean the mushrooms (see page xxvi). Cut the caps and stems into thin slices (¼ inch or less), or tear them into thin pieces. Arrange them on the drying racks, leaving a little space between them, then follow the manufacturer's directions for dehydrating them. It will typically take 6 to 10 hours at 110°F, but I've dried them at higher temperatures for shorter periods with success. Much depends on how wet they are and what type of mushroom you are working with. Don't consider them dry until they audibly snap in half. If they bend, back in they go.

METHOD #2: AIR-DRY THEM. First, clean the mushrooms (see page xxvi). Cut the caps and stems into thin slices (¼ inch or less) or tear them into thin pieces. Lay them out on a large cooling rack or, even better, a window screen in a sunny location with good airflow. Place newspapers underneath to make for easier cleanup. For even faster drying, position a fan at one end of the screen and turn it on low speed.

METHOD #3: DRY THEM OUT IN YOUR OVEN. It's not the most energy-efficient way, but it works in a pinch, especially if your oven can be maintained at temperatures below 200°F. Preheat the oven to the lowest temperature it will go. Clean the mushrooms (see page xxvi). Cut the caps and stems into thin slices (¼ inch or less) or tear them into thin pieces. Lay them out on a cooling rack set over a large baking pan. You can put as many pans in the oven as will fit, on any rack. Every hour, change the positions of the pans. How long it takes to dry them depends on how wet they were initially and what type of mushroom you are working with. Don't consider them dry until they audibly snap in half. If they bend, back in they go. Start checking on them after an hour or two, but they may take longer.

Once dried, you can use your mushrooms to make mushroom powder (see page xxiii).

STORING DRIED MUSHROOMS

For short stays (a month or two), place your dried mushrooms in a glass jar with a tight-fitting lid and store in the pantry away from heat and light. If you are storing mushrooms for more than 2 months, and for the greatest protection from critter damage, they are best stored in the freezer, sealed in airtight, freezer-strength plastic bags (or vacuum sealed).

Rehydrating Mushrooms 101

You might think it would be as simple as dunking in hot water, but there is a technique for rehydrating mushrooms, especially those that tend to be dirty or gritty. Refer to the video on rehydrating shrooms at www.shroomthecookbook.com.

FOR DRIED WILD MUSHROOMS: These can be very gritty, sandy, or dirty, especially morels, porcini, and black trumpet mushrooms. I recommend a two-step rehydration method.

STEP 1: Put the dried mushrooms in a small bowl, pour a generous amount of warm tap water over the top, wait 5 minutes, and then aggressively agitate them in this water. (This important step ensures that any grit hiding in or on the mushrooms comes out.) Carefully lift them out, discarding the water left behind (unless you are working with porcini, then see Notes).

STEP 2: Now place the mushrooms in a new container, such as a quart-size heatproof pitcher or glass measuring cup, a quart-size canning jar, or a French coffee press. (A tip I learned from Connie Green's fabulous book *The Wild Table* is to rehydrate mushrooms in a tall container, as it allows plenty of room for the hot clean water to circulate around the mushrooms, while the dirt, sand, and grit can settle to the bottom, well below where the mushrooms are floating. I find that a French coffee press is perfect. Use the plunger to submerge the mushrooms just under the boiling water.) I find that you get the most consistent results when you boil the water first before pouring it over the mushrooms. Using hot tap water for this longer step may result in mushrooms that can be anywhere from soft to still brittle. Use at least 2 cups boiling water per

½ ounce of dried mushrooms. If you don't have a French press and the mushrooms are floating above the surface of the water, place a small cup or plate on them to keep them submerged. Different types of mushrooms take varying amounts of time to rehydrate, typically anywhere from 10 to 30 minutes, or in the case of chanterelles, seemingly never (which is why I don't recommend using or buying dehydrated chanterelles). When the mushrooms are soft, make sure to lift them up and out of the soaking liquid, squeezing any liquid out of the mushrooms back into the soaking vessel. Avoid getting any sediment back on the mushrooms.

NOTES: The thriftiest of us save and use the soaking liquid from all mushrooms, but it's the wild morels, porcini, and black trumpet mushrooms that kick off the most flavorful liquid, in my opinion. For porcini mushrooms (where the rehydration liquid is arguably more flavorful than the pieces of mushrooms themselves), you'll want to save each round of the soaking/cleaning water, and *carefully pour it through a coffee filter or fine-mesh strainer set over a bowl*. Use all of that flavorful liquid in stock or sauce making. For morels and black trumpets (that you didn't clean and dry yourself), I advise getting rid of the first round of soaking liquid, as it can be terribly gritty.

FOR DRIED CULTIVATED MUSHROOMS: Dried cultivated mushrooms, such as shiitakes or maitakes, rarely have much dirt or grit to speak of, so I recommend just one soak (follow Step 2). Nonetheless, it's always a good idea to strain the rehydration liquid before using, even with cultivated mushrooms.

Freezing Mushrooms 101

There are only three types of mushrooms covered in this book that I would freeze raw: morels, porcini, and matsutake. These three mushrooms hold up fairly well texturewise, whereas many others do not (chanterelles and hedgehogs, for example). Important: I highly recommend investing in a FoodSaver or vacuum sealer if you are going to freeze these types of mushrooms raw. It's not enough to just freeze them; best results are achieved when they are frozen and then protected from the damaging effects of oxygen (via the FoodSaver or vacuum-sealing process).

FREEZING WHOLE RAW MORELS, PORCINI, AND MATSUTAKE

Clean and trim according to the instructions for that type of mushroom, then lay them out on a baking pan with plenty of room between them.

Freeze them until they are rock solid and then vacuum-seal; this is known as individually quick freezing or IQF and it's the way to go when you are freezing fruit, too, or frankly most anything. IQF prevents moisture from creating big icy mushcicles or a whole block of raspberry, instead giving you lovely individual items that can be used one at a time.

FREEZING COOKED MUSHROOMS

If you'd like to freeze any of the other types of mushrooms in this book, I recommend cooking them first. Chop or tear them into bite-size pieces and make duxelles. Or as my friend Amy would do, panfry them dry (or with a small amount of oil or butter) until they've given up their water. Freeze them in 1-cup or ½-pint widemouthed containers, ready to use in any recipe.

WHAT Shroom

It's Saturday night. Are you . . .

1. Home trying to figure out how to use the rented steam cleaner;

→ 2. Drinking just one very small glass of wine and playing cards with your friends;

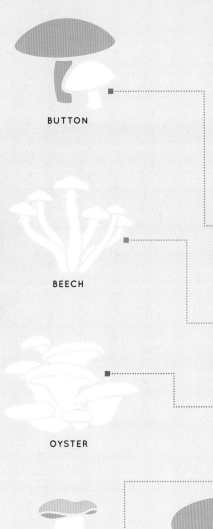

BUTTON

BEECH

OYSTER

IF YOU ANSWERED 1.
The steam cleaner isn't working, so do you:

1A. Take it back and rent a new one that same night;

1B. Say the hell with it and walk next door to play backgammon with your neighbor; or

1C. Decide that the steam cleaner is a piece of crap and you can do better on your hands and knees with a sponge and lots of elbow grease.

IF YOU ANSWERED 2.
Your friend is drunk (*again*) and cheating at cards (*again*), so do you:

2A. Take the blame for your friend, claiming that you were a little heavy-handed with the punch and the others should go easy on him;

2B. Tease your friend mercilessly and tell him you put laxatives in his drink (even if you didn't);

2C. Tie him up and take his drunk ass to AA.

IF YOU ANSWERED 1A:
You, my fair-weather friend, are a BUTTON mushroom. It's not that you don't have good taste, but you're a predictable, steady Eddie. If you don't pay a bill on time, creditors call the morgue.

IF YOU ANSWERED 1B:
You're a BEECH mushroom. You're pretty reliable, and not too adventurous, but when life throws you some lemons, you're willing to Google a recipe for limonata.

IF YOU ANSWERED 1C:
You're an OYSTER mushroom, kind of milquetoast, but hey, you're in the game and people see lots of potential in you, especially when you put some effort into it.

IF YOU ANSWERED 2A:
You're a KING TRUMPET mushroom. You're driven and passionate about things you care about, as long as it all occurs before 10 p.m., and you often stand up for others in your group. You have a motivational poster on your wall that says, "Go big or go home."

IF YOU ANSWERED 2B:
You're a SHIITAKE mushroom. You're well respected by a multicultural friendship group and you've been around the block a few times. Sometimes you can be tough.

IF YOU ANSWERED 2C:
You're a MAITAKE mushroom. You're driven, bold, and a little nutty. You don't mess around.

KING TRUMPET   SHIITAKE   MAITAKE   HEDGEHOG

CHANTERELLE

BLACK TRUMPET

TRUFFLE

MATSUTAKE

3. At a party having fun but sort of wishing you were home watching *The Colbert Report*;

4. At a dive bar singing karaoke off-key; or

5. Climbing a mountain with a sherpa named Tenzing.

IF YOU ANSWERED 3.
The party gets raided and the po-po are surrounding the house, so do you:

3A. Hide in the bedroom, hoping the cops don't find you;

3B. Watch while some douche outside is distracting the cops with some sad story, then wink at the cutie in the corner, steal a bottle of bourbon, and sneak out, undetected; or

3C. Walk outside and say loudly, "Hello Occifers, I didn't really want to be here tonight, but hey, here we are, care for a beverage?"

IF YOU ANSWERED 4.
The karaoke machine only has three songs on it, so do you sing:

4A. "That's Amore" by Dean Martin;

4B. "Don't Stop Believin'" by Journey;

4C. "Bohemian Rhapsody" by Queen.

IF YOU ANSWERED 5.
You're suddenly experiencing altitude sickness, so do you:

5A. Find some dead trees to make a temporary shelter, let your body acclimate while you write poetry on the back of some bark, and ascend the next morning;

5B. Ask Tenzing, your sherpa, to carry you on his back to the summit; or

5C. Shoot yourself in the finger to take your mind off your altitude sickness, and keep going.

IF YOU ANSWERED 3A:
You're a **HEDGEHOG** mushroom. Adorable by anyone's standards, you are worth knowing, a real catch, and deeply nuanced. Folks who get past your spiky exterior know how special you really are.

IF YOU ANSWERED 3B:
You're a **PORCINI** mushroom. You're confident, large, and in charge. You're so desirable that, come spring, everything is crawling on you.

IF YOU ANSWERED 3C:
You're a **LOBSTER** mushroom, prone to being a huge drama queen. You're capable of expressing many personalities and are never shy about being the center of attention.

IF YOU ANSWERED 4A:
You're a **LION'S MANE** mushroom. "Safety first" is your motto. You're mildly adventurous but know exactly when to lie low, blend in, and pretend you're a pillow. No one has ever told you, "Don't be a hero."

IF YOU ANSWERED 4B:
You're a **MOREL** mushroom. You're a little dark, maybe even goth, or perhaps a ninja. When you occasionally allow people to get close, they love you and can't get enough of you. Your exes claim you're hollow inside.

IF YOU ANSWERED 4C:
You're a **CHANTERELLE**. You're friendly, approachable, a little fruity, and gregarious. You wouldn't harm a fly and you stand out in a crowd.

IF YOU ANSWERED 5A:
You're a **BLACK TRUMPET** mushroom. You're lean and strung out, moody and mysterious, but full of flavor. You probably smoke too much, or used to.

IF YOU ANSWERED 5B:
You're a **TRUFFLE**. You will spare no expense to get what you want, often depending on the labor of others to get you there.

IF YOU ANSWERED 5C:
You're a **MATSUTAKE** mushroom. You're a person who lives life on the edge and typically gets hurt in the process. People think you're a badass and you've started to believe the hype. You have a tattoo that says "pain is weakness leaving the body."

PORCINI

LOBSTER

LION'S MANE

MOREL

I'M NOT A PARENT, but I'm convinced an essential part of good parenting consists of choking down some seriously questionable food. Come with me, if you will, back to the 1970s.

"Dad, I made you dinner!" I half screamed, standing at the door when he swung it open. My father was an engineer and commuted from the pretty part of New Jersey, an hour outside of New York City, to the not-so-pretty part of New Jersey.

"Yes, I see that," he said, clutching his briefcase and staring down at the plate I was presenting. He was smiling but his eyes looked funny.

"It's mushrooms on toast points!" I said excitedly, brushing the dark curls off my forehead. "I learned it on TV."

Let's forget for a moment that I'm eight and I've clearly used the stove without even a thought to ask an adult for permission. My older brothers, marginally in charge of my welfare, though more typically a threat to it, were upstairs playing Dungeons & Dragons with their dorky friends, oblivious to the crashing of pans one floor below.

No matter, I didn't need them and their nerdiness. I was supervised by real adults whose company I much preferred. Martin Yan and Julia Child took care of me. I hung out with them as often as I could, because they were my favorite babysitters. Ditto for the Galloping Gourmet, though he was more like a crazy, drunk uncle, so I limited his visits. From my perch on the yellow velour couch, I had my first taste of the culinary arts. My blind enthusiasm for cooking was not at all deterred by my total lack of common sense. I was a true blank slate, and Yan, Child, and Kerr quickly made their mark. I'm fairly certain I learned how to make mushrooms on toast points from Kerr.

The Galloping Gourmet and Julia Child were enamored with French food, so I figured it must be très glamorous. I didn't know much of anything about France or French food or culture, but I did know

the words derrière and bonbon, so I sprinkled them liberally into my chitchat when I wanted to sound sophisticated, which was often.

The day I saw mushrooms on toast points being demonstrated, I went into the kitchen and looked all around for mushrooms that seemed like the ones on TV. A strange kid, I loved mushrooms. Watching chefs put one of my favorite foods on something as cute as toast "points" was irresistible. The refrigerator was bare, so I moved on to the pantry. All I could find was a tiny can, a store-brand tin of sliced button mushrooms packed in water. What a genius move, I thought, to use this can and prove how flexible I could be when faced with a challenge. It's like I was on an episode of *Top Chef* three decades before anyone else.

I located a sauté pan and put it on the stove and, just like Graham Kerr, I grabbed some butter. Except our butter came in a yellow plastic tub, and I thought it was perplexing that it said something on the package about not believing it wasn't butter. Why was the butter paranoid? Cooking was confusing.

I added the "butter" to the pan and turned the heat to low. That seemed safer. I waited for it to melt but it was taking too long, so I opened the can of mushrooms, neglected to drain them, and then dumped the whole mess onto the butter. The dish wasn't really looking like Graham's, but I thought it would still taste fantastic. We didn't have any bread that looked like the hearty bread on TV, but that was OK, because we had something much more delicious: Wonder Bread. I was supposed to toast it, but I thought that seemed silly because the mushrooms were so wet that the crispness of toast wouldn't really matter. I poured the cold, watery canned mushrooms with the still-solid lump of what I now know was margarine onto triangles of Wonder Bread and set it on the dining-room table. Only four more hours until Dad comes home from work!

He ate (almost) every bite. I had never been more proud.

Chapter 1

Button
Cremini
Portobello

LATIN: *Agaricus bisporus*

Button | Cremini | Portobello

GENERALLY SPEAKING: This genus contains a diverse range of mushrooms, everything from the common supermarket button mushroom to the prince mushroom, a lovely and large wild *Agaricus*. While there are many wild types, I'm going to focus the recipes in this book on the three types of cultivated *Agaricus bisporus* you are most likely to find in your local market: button, cremini, and portobello. These three cultivated mushrooms are all essentially the same thing. White button mushrooms are selected as such for their color; cremini mushrooms are darker, but still the same species; and portobellos are simply bigger, older cremini.

AKA:

BUTTON MUSHROOMS: These simple white mushrooms are also known as *champignons de Paris*, common mushrooms, and table mushrooms.

- CREMINI: Cremini are also known as baby bella, Swiss brown, Roman brown, Italian brown, brown cap, and chestnut mushrooms.

- PORTOBELLO: I refer to this mushroom as pure marketing genius (see the Nerdy Factoids on page 4). Some alternate spellings worth noting are portobella, portabella, and portabello.

SEASON: As they are among the many cultivated mushrooms covered in this book, growers can bring them to market year-round.

FLAVOR, TEXTURE, AND AROMA NOTES: Button mushrooms are mild in flavor, just slightly earthy, with a more pronounced sweet and savory note when caramelized. They are creamy when raw (though I don't recommend eating mushrooms uncooked; see page xix for more information). Cremini are stronger in flavor and slightly nutty. Portobellos are the most meaty and savory of the three. All of these mushrooms are firm when raw, and succulent when cooked. While many mushroom lovers turn their noses up at these common supermarket mushrooms, they all add depth to any recipe. Their firm nature when stuffed is also welcome.

BUYING TIPS: For button and cremini mushrooms with the most delicate flavor, you are essentially looking for immature species. Pay attention to the caps—you are looking for closed caps with no visible gills. Once the mushrooms have aged a bit, the caps start to open and the gills darken in color. Also look at the stem where the mushroom was cut off from its growing medium. It should be slightly darker where the cut has caused some oxidation, but make sure it is just that, slightly darker, but neither dehydrated nor slimy. It should have the texture of a pencil eraser. For mushrooms you want to stuff or for a more pronounced flavor, look for larger cremini on which you can clearly see the gills. For all of these *Agaricus* mushrooms, look for firm and dry specimens. If the gills are exposed, especially in portobello mushrooms, make sure they are dry. Avoid any mushrooms with slimy gills or obviously wet or rotting caps.

CLEANING: A simple thin slice off the bottom of the stem is my only trimming requirement for button and cremini mushrooms. A damp cloth can be used to wipe off any obvious dirt, but honestly, I've never washed cultivated mushrooms. (See page xxvi for more information on cleaning mushrooms.) For portobello mushrooms, I scrape the gills off with a spoon and add them to my mushroom stock. They tend to darken a dish and get a little slimy when cooked. The stems are a bit tougher than the caps, so depending on what you are making, you can either trim the bottom off and proceed with the recipe (keeping in mind that the stems might retain more texture after cooking) or snap the entire stem off and dice it up or use it in stock.

STORAGE: These three types of cultivated *Agaricus* have a fairly long shelf life with the freshest species (at purchase) keeping for 1 to 2 weeks in your refrigerator. As with all mushrooms, store them in the refrigerator in a brown paper bag. Second choice would be to store them in a basket or box with a dry piece of paper towel or newsprint on top of them (replace this each day).

PRESERVATION:

DRYING: With nearly every large grocery store selling fresh button, cremini, and portobello mushrooms, there is really no need to dry them for future use.

FREEZING: See page xxxi for detailed tips on freezing mushrooms. My recommendation is to freeze these mushrooms only after cooking them. They make great duxelles (see page xxii).

LOVES: Button and cremini mushrooms work well in any dish where mushrooms are called for; they are extremely versatile and more flavorful than chefs give them credit for being, but next to wild mushrooms, they are admittedly sort of ho-hum. Portobellos adore the grill and when roasted in thick slices are fantastic tucked between bread in all kinds of sandwiches (try the Bahn Mi Sandwiches with Red Curry Roasted Portobellos and Pickled Vegetables on page 10).

COOKING NOTES: When cooking button, cremini, and portobello mushrooms, expect them to release a lot of water. The key to cooking them, therefore, as with all mushrooms, is high heat and plenty of room. It is always better to sauté in batches, roast in a single layer in the oven, or use multiple skillets on the stovetop for efficiency and space. Caramelization is also key to adding extra flavor, especially important with the milder white button mushrooms.

SUBSTITUTIONS: I doubt you'll ever be unable to find button mushrooms and only have porcini to act as a stand-in, but if that happens, imagine how excited you'll be! Cremini and button can be substituted for each other.

NERDY FACTOIDS:

- Button mushrooms have been cultivated in Paris, France, since as far back as the early eighteenth century. In 1893, the Pasteur Institute in Paris discovered and produced sterilized spawn for cultivation on composted horse manure.

- Half of the mushrooms grown in the United States are cultivated in southeastern Pennsylvania, near the town of Kennet Square. You could almost say that portobello mushrooms were invented there. Italian immigrant farmers allowed cremini mushrooms to grow to a bigger and more developed stage (mushrooms that had formerly been too big to sell). They called these large mushrooms portobello and charged more for them, in a brilliant marketing strategy to get Americans to eat an older, more expensive version of what they were already eating. What's even more interesting from a marketing perspective is that these days, cremini mushrooms are being rebranded as "baby bellas," thanks to the popularity of the overgrown version.

Button Mushroom, Walnut, and Pomegranate Spread with Serrano Chile

Muhammara is a traditional spread from Aleppo, Syria, though there are versions found all over the eastern Mediterranean. It's typically made with roasted red peppers, chiles, garlic, pomegranate molasses, walnuts, and bread crumbs. It's been one of my favorite dishes for years because it's simple to make and can easily be doubled to serve a crowd, yet it surprises the palate with its complex flavor. This is my version of a mushroom-based muhammara; I've left the bread crumbs out to make it gluten-free and added serrano and chipotle chiles for heat and smokiness. Use it on sandwiches with grilled halloumi cheese, as part of an appetizer platter with bowls of olives, extra roasted red pepper slices, and chunks of Israeli or French sheep's feta. If you happen to find a tart-sweet spice called sumac, grab it and sprinkle it liberally over the top of the spread.

SERVES: 4 as an appetizer | PAIRING: French Blanquette de Limoux (sparkling wine)

1 cup pure unsweetened pomegranate juice (see Note)

¼ cup extra-virgin olive oil, plus more for garnish

½ pound button mushrooms, cut into ¼-inch-thick slices

1 teaspoon fine sea salt

Freshly ground black pepper

¼ cup minced shallot

1 serrano chile, stemmed and halved (seeds/membranes removed if you prefer less spice)

¼ cup whole walnuts, toasted (page xxiv)

2 small jarred roasted red peppers

1 clove garlic, minced

⅛ teaspoon ground chipotle chili powder, plus more for garnish

¼ cup fresh mint leaves, cut into ribbons

4 pita bread rounds, warmed or grilled

Preheat the oven to 400°F.

In a small saucepan set over medium-high heat, boil the pomegranate juice until it is thick and syrupy and reduced to about 2 tablespoons, about 10 minutes.

Line a rimmed baking pan with aluminum foil. Add the olive oil and tilt the pan to spread the oil. Add the mushrooms and mix into the oil (your hands are the best tool here). Arrange the mushrooms in an even layer, sprinkle with the salt, and grind some black pepper over the top. Roast for 7 to 8 minutes, until the mushrooms have started to give off a lot of their water. Stir in the shallot and serrano chile, again distributing everything evenly in the pan. Roast until the mushrooms have fully released their liquid and started to brown, 10 to 12 more minutes.

Transfer the hot mushroom mixture to the work bowl of a food processor, and add the walnuts, reduced pomegranate juice, roasted red pepper, garlic, and chipotle chili powder. Process until the mixture is pureed. Taste and adjust the seasoning. Transfer to a serving bowl and drizzle more olive oil around the edges. Sprinkle a bit of ground chipotle over the top and garnish with the mint. Serve with the pita.

NOTE: If you can find pomegranate molasses, you can skip the step of reducing the pomegranate juice. Substitute 1 tablespoon of pomegranate molasses plus 1 tablespoon water for the reduced juice. Look for bottled pomegranate molasses in specialty markets or large grocery stores selling Middle Eastern foods.

Portobello Shakshuka
with Baked Eggs and Israeli Feta

Shakshuka, despite what it might sound like (some say it is derived from the Hebrew word leshakshek, meaning "to shake"), is not some awesome new dance, though it might inspire you to create one. Shakshuka has its roots in North Africa and is very popular in many Middle Eastern countries. Tunisian Jews supposedly brought this dish to Israel, where it became popular. It's the best kind of dish—simple, soulful, healthy, and satisfying. I added portobellos to make this dish "meatier" and mushroom stock to increase the savory quality (increasing the umami factor). Look for portobellos with deep cups to better hold the eggs. All you need is a big cast-iron skillet, some bread, maybe a side salad, and a glass (or bottle) of red wine. Feel free to improvise with this basic recipe. For instance, sometimes I like to add mint in addition to the parsley. Traditionally, you'd fry chiles along with the onions, and that is also wonderful. I'm sure I speak for Israel when I say: Thank you, Tunisian Jews. Thank you.

SERVES: 4 | PAIRING: Italian Chianti Classico

SPICE MIX
1 teaspoon ground cumin

½ teaspoon cayenne pepper

½ teaspoon smoked paprika (substitute sweet paprika)

½ teaspoon fine sea salt

¼ cup extra-virgin olive oil

4 portobello mushrooms, stems removed and gills scraped out (10 to 12 ounces total)

½ teaspoon fine sea salt

1 small yellow onion, small diced (about 1 cup)

½ cup Mushroom Stock (page xxiii)

4 cloves garlic, minced

1 tablespoon tomato paste

1 (28-ounce) can Muir Glen fire-roasted crushed tomatoes, with juices

1 teaspoon sugar (optional)

4 large eggs

Freshly ground black pepper

3½ ounces French or Israeli sheep's milk feta

⅓ cup chopped flat-leaf parsley

Pita or naan bread, warmed, for serving

To make the spice mix, in a small bowl, combine the cumin, cayenne, paprika, and salt. Set aside.

In a heavy 12-inch skillet, preferably cast iron, set over medium-high heat, add 1 tablespoon of the olive oil. Add the portobellos, stem side down, and cook until they start to wilt and brown a bit, 4 to 5 minutes. Turn the mushrooms over, sprinkle with ¼ teaspoon of the salt, and cook for an additional 1 to 2 minutes, until you get some browning on the cap side. Transfer from the skillet to a plate and set aside.

Add the remaining 3 tablespoons olive oil to the skillet. Warm the oil and then add the onion. Sauté for 5 minutes, until the onion begins to soften, and then add the mushroom stock. Bring the stock to a boil, lower the heat so the stock simmers, and continue to cook until all the liquid is absorbed, 5 to 7 minutes longer. Stir in the garlic, tomato paste, and spice mix and sauté until the garlic and spices smell fragrant and the tomato paste has darkened a bit in color, about 1 minute. Add the tomatoes and sugar, if using. Increase the heat and bring the sauce to a boil. Simmer for 10 minutes.

Tuck the mushrooms into the sauce, stem side up. Simmer for 5 minutes longer. Carefully crack an egg into each mushroom "saucer." Season the eggs with the remaining ¼ teaspoon salt and a generous sprinkling of black pepper. Sprinkle the feta carefully around the eggs but not right on top of them. Cover the pan and cook until the eggs reach your desired degree of doneness. (I like this dish with runny yolks, but some folks will want to cook it longer to set the whole egg.) Garnish with the parsley and serve with warm pita.

Roasted Portobello Tacos with Cacao-Chili Sauce and Cabbage and Lime Slaw

On a kayak trip on idyllic Lopez Island in the San Juan Islands of Washington State, I experienced a bite of the best quesadilla of my life. The secret was in the sauce. Made by local resident Randall Waugh, it's called Chicaoji (chipotle/cacao/goji), and it was a revelation. This cacao-chili sauce recipe is my attempt at re-creating his sauce. If you want to make the tacos but would rather skip the step of making the sauce, visit www.chicaoji.com to order Chicaoji sauce right from the man himself.

SERVES: 4 | PAIRING: Margaritas

CACAO-CHILI SAUCE

2 tablespoons cacao nibs

2 teaspoons ground chipotle chili powder

¼ cup dried goji berries (see Note)

½ cup warm water

¼ cup red wine vinegar

2 scant tablespoons honey

¼ teaspoon fine sea salt

CABBAGE AND LIME SLAW

10 ounces red cabbage (about ¼ of a large red cabbage), cored and shredded

1 tablespoon kosher salt

½ cup minced fresh cilantro, both stems and leaves

1 fresh Cherry Bomb, serrano, or jalapeño chile, seeded and minced

1 tablespoon freshly squeezed lime juice

1 tablespoon extra-virgin olive oil

MUSHROOMS

1 tablespoon coconut oil, melted, plus more for heating the tortillas

1½ pounds portobello mushrooms, gills scraped out and cut into ¼-inch-thick slices

¼ teaspoon fine sea salt

Small corn tortillas, for serving

GARNISH

1 avocado

6 ounces queso fresco (substitute French sheep's milk feta)

6 ounces full-fat sour cream

2 limes, cut into wedges

To make the sauce, combine the cacao nibs, chili powder, goji berries, water, vinegar, honey, and salt in a blender and let sit for 10 minutes to soften the goji berries, then blend to a smooth puree. Set aside.

To make the slaw, combine the cabbage and salt in a large bowl, and using your hands, massage the salt into the cabbage. Let soften for 15 to 20 minutes. Rinse the cabbage under cold running water and then drain it through a colander, using your hands to squeeze all of the water out of the cabbage (like you were getting every last drop out of a wet dishrag). Taste a piece, and if it's too salty, rinse and repeat. Put the cabbage in a bowl and add the cilantro, chile, lime juice, and olive oil. Mix well and set aside.

To prepare the mushrooms, preheat the oven to 400°F. Line a rimmed baking pan with aluminum foil and brush the foil with a little of the coconut oil. Mound the portobellos in the pan, and drizzle the rest of the oil over the top. Toss to coat the mushrooms and then spread them out in an even layer. Season with the salt. Roast until the mushrooms have kicked off most of their water and begun to shrink in size, about 15 minutes. Remove the pan from the oven, drizzle 2 tablespoons of the cacao-chili sauce over the mushrooms, toss and mix well, and then spread them back out and pop them back into the oven for 2 more minutes.

Meanwhile, warm the tortillas (see Notes) and pit, peel, and slice the avocado. When ready to serve, instruct your guests to fill their tacos with some portobello slices, cabbage slaw, extra cacao-chili sauce, and all the other garnishes.

NOTE: Goji berries are native to Asia and southeastern Europe. Vaguely cranberry-like, the dried berries are a bright red-orange color and have a tart flavor. You can find them in specialty markets, natural food stores, or online. Note: There are a number of ways to heat corn tortillas. Here are two methods I often use.

PANFRYING: Place a scant amount of melted coconut oil in a hot skillet or on a griddle and cook the tortillas until they start to get a few light brown spots on each side, about 2 minutes per side. Place them in a tortilla holder or in a foil pouch stacked one on top of the other to stay warm.

BAKING: Position a rack in the center of the oven and preheat the oven to 250°F. Line a baking sheet with parchment paper. Spread the tortillas on the parchment, one slightly overlapping the other, like a fanned-out deck of cards. Lightly dampen a kitchen towel and completely cover the tortillas with the towel, making sure the towel isn't hanging down below the baking sheet. Warm the tortillas in the oven until they are soft and hot, about 15 minutes. Stack them on top of each other in a tortilla holder or in a foil pouch.

Bahn Mi Sandwiches with Red Curry Roasted Portobellos and Pickled Vegetables

For at least two summers in a row I was completely addicted to these sandwiches. Often stuffed with pork or pâté, they cost a whopping $1.50 to $2 at little hole-in-the-wall Vietnamese sandwich shops in Seattle, where I live. This is my take on an umami-rich vegetarian version. If you happen to make the Black Trumpet Pâté (page 157), you can spread one side of the bread with that and the other side with the mayonnaise and then call your friends, 'cause that sandwich is going to be awesome.

SERVES: 4 | PAIRING: Jamaican lager (Red Stripe) or Vietnamese beer (333, pronounced ba ba ba)

PICKLED VEGETABLES
1 (3-inch) piece daikon radish, peeled and cut into fine julienne

1 large carrot, peeled and cut into fine julienne

½ of an English cucumber, seeded and cut into julienne

½ cup seasoned rice vinegar (or add sugar and salt to unseasoned rice vinegar)

RED CURRY ROASTED PORTOBELLOS
1 cup coconut milk

1 tablespoon freshly squeezed lime juice

2 teaspoons Thai red curry paste

3 large or 5 small portobello mushrooms, gills scraped out and cut into ¾-inch-thick slices

SPICY LIME MAYONNAISE
½ cup mayonnaise

Finely grated zest of 1 lime

1 serrano chile, minced

4 (6-inch long) Vietnamese baguettes (see Note)

1 bunch cilantro

1 jalapeño, cut into slices (optional)

Arrange an oven rack in the center of the oven and preheat the oven to 400°F. Line a baking sheet with aluminum foil.

To make the pickled vegetables, combine the daikon, carrot, and cucumber in a medium bowl and toss with the vinegar, mixing well. Let sit at room temperature, stirring occasionally, until the vegetables have softened somewhat, about 30 minutes. Squeeze the liquid out of the vegetables and set them aside (don't discard the vinegar—store it in the refrigerator and use it again for salad dressings or another round of pickling).

To make the red curry roasted portobellos, in a medium bowl, whisk together the coconut milk, lime juice, and curry paste until smooth. Lay out the portobello slices on the prepared baking sheet. Pour the sauce over the mushrooms and make sure they are well coated on all sides. Roast until the mushrooms have released all their liquid and shrunk down a bit, about 15 minutes. Flip the slices over and turn the heat to broil. Broil until the liquid is absorbed and the mushrooms are browning, about 10 minutes (but check after 5 minutes). The sauce around the edges will burn a little, but you don't need to worry about it. What you are looking for is really nice caramelization on the mushrooms.

To make the spicy lime mayonnaise, in a small bowl, mix together the mayonnaise, lime zest, and serrano.

Bahn Mi Sandwiches with Red Curry Roasted Portobellos and Pickled Vegetables

CONTINUED

To assemble the sandwiches, slice the baguettes lengthwise, leaving the two halves attached on one side. Pull out about one-quarter of the inside of the bread (in a channel down the middle of both sides) to make room for the sandwich ingredients. (This creates a more flavorful filling-to-bread ratio.) Spread the mayonnaise on both sides of the bread, and add a handful of the pickled vegetables, some sprigs of cilantro, and several slices of the mushrooms. Grab your beer, toast your friends, and pass around some jalapeño slices, if using, for the hotheads in the group.

NOTE: Purists insist that you must use a rice flour– and wheat flour–based Vietnamese-style baguette for these sandwiches. That would be most authentic, but if you don't happen to live in a place where there are Vietnamese bakeries, as a substitute, I'd advise buying a non-crunchy, non-artisanal French baguette. You want the crust to be flaky and barely crunchy and the inside to be soft and fluffy. If the baguette cuts up the roof of your mouth, it's not the right one for bahn mi.

Cremini and Beef Bourguignon
with Angel Biscuits and Bay Brown Butter

I've tried to distill all the best parts of different versions of this classic dish that I've made or tasted over the years. Some versions are simply too rich for my blood, so I've cut down the amount of beef and upped the amount of mushrooms. To give the sauce extra body without adding a roux, I reduce the liquids to concentrate the flavors and pull out some of the vegetables and liquid toward the end of braising to puree. Adding this puree back to the pot gives the stew a velvety and naturally rich texture without added fat. I wish Julia Child could try my version of this classic dish. I'd like to think she'd enjoy it, especially given the fact that I only use half the bottle of Burgundy in the dish, leaving two extra glasses of wine for the cook to slosh down while lazily, slowly sautéing onions on a rainy or snowy Sunday, enjoying the smell of caramelized mushrooms, beef, and cognac filling the house.

SERVES: 4 | PAIRING: French red Burgundy (Pinot Noir)

½ pound applewood-smoked bacon, cut crosswise into ¼-inch strips

1 pound cremini mushrooms, stems trimmed, caps quartered

2 teaspoons fine sea salt, plus more as needed

Freshly ground black pepper

1¾ pounds boneless beef chuck, cut into 1-inch cubes

2 large yellow onions, halved and cut crosswise into thick half-moons (about 4 cups)

¾ pound carrots, peeled and cut into 1½- to 2-inch chunks

2 tablespoons tomato paste

½ cup cognac (substitute other brandy)

1½ cups red Burgundy (save the rest for drinking, so make it one you like)

3 cups Mushroom Stock (page xxiii)

1 tablespoon chopped fresh thyme

2 dried bay leaves

1 teaspoon red wine vinegar, or more as desired

⅓ cup chopped fresh flat-leaf parsley

Angel Biscuits with Bay Brown Butter (recipe follows)

Preheat the oven to 250°F.

In a large ovenproof pot set over medium-low heat, cook the bacon, stirring occasionally, until it's lightly browned and the fat has rendered, about 10 minutes. Using a slotted spoon, transfer the bacon to a large paper towel–lined plate, leaving the fat in the pan.

Remove 1 tablespoon of the fat from the pot and place it in a small bowl. This will be used to sauté the vegetables. Place a large skillet over medium-high heat. Divide the remaining fat between the pot and the skillet. Evenly divide the mushrooms between the two vessels. Sprinkle ½ teaspoon of the salt over each batch of mushrooms and brown them, stirring occasionally, 6 to 8 minutes. Transfer to a bowl and set aside.

Sprinkle the remaining 1 teaspoon salt and a generous grinding of black pepper over the beef. Divide the beef between the pot and skillet. Spread the cubes out and cook over medium-high heat until browned, about 10 minutes. Stir them only occasionally, making sure that you get deep color on most of the sides. Once the beef is browned, transfer the beef in the skillet to the pot. Add the bacon to the beef and remove from the heat.

Cremini and Beef Bourguignon
with Angel Biscuits with Bay Brown Butter

CONTINUED

Now sauté the vegetables in the skillet. Add the reserved 1 tablespoon bacon fat to the skillet, along with the onions and carrots. Cook over medium-high heat until starting to soften and color, about 10 minutes. Scrape a clearing in the middle of the vegetables, add the tomato paste, and fry in the pan until it darkens in color a bit, 2 to 3 minutes. Slowly add the cognac, stepping back a bit in case the alcohol ignites. Use a wooden spoon to scrape up the bits sticking to the bottom of the pan and then dump all the contents into the pot, along with the wine, stock, thyme, and bay leaves. Place the pot back over high heat and bring to a boil. Cover the pot and transfer to the oven. Braise the stew for 2 to 3 hours until the beef is silky and tender.

Remove the pot from the oven. Use a slotted spoon to lift out the meat and vegetables and transfer to a large bowl. Place the pot over medium-high heat and boil the braising liquid until reduced by half.

While the liquid is reducing, pull out about 1 cup of carrot, onion, and bacon, leaving the beef behind, and place in a blender. Add 1 cup of the boiling liquid to the blender and puree. Add this mixture back to the pot. (This gives the stew a lovely body.) Once the braising liquid is reduced and at the thickness you like, add the mushrooms, beef, and the remaining vegetables back to the pot. Simmer gently for 10 minutes. Season to taste with the red wine vinegar and salt. Garnish with the parsley and serve with the biscuits.

Angel Biscuits and Bay Brown Butter

Southern cooks are damn serious about their biscuits—so serious that this New Jersey girl would not even remotely think about including a biscuit recipe without consulting a legitimate Southerner. Jenifer Ward (originally of Toad Suck, Arkansas) contributed the base recipe for these biscuits, and I bastardized them with the addition of the bay butter. They don't look like your typical biscuit, either. These get folded over prior to baking so they resemble small tacos or Chinese bao buns more than traditional biscuits.

SERVES: 8 to 16 (makes 16 biscuits)

2½ cups unbleached all-purpose flour, plus more for dusting

2 tablespoons sugar

1½ teaspoons baking powder

½ teaspoon baking soda

½ teaspoon fine sea salt, plus a pinch

½ cup (1 stick) cold unsalted butter, plus 3 tablespoons unsalted butter

½ package active dry yeast (1⅛ teaspoons)

2 tablespoons warm water (105°F to 110°F)

1 cup buttermilk

4 dried bay laurel leaves (or 2 fresh)

In a large bowl, sift together the flour, sugar, baking powder, baking soda, and salt. Cut the stick of butter into thin slices and scatter over the dry ingredients. Using a pastry blender or your hands, blend in the butter until the mixture looks like coarse cornmeal, with some pea-size clumps. (Alternatively, place the flour mixture in a food processor, scatter the cold butter over the top, and pulse.)

Dissolve the yeast in the warm water and confirm it is alive by looking for the show of activity (like a little mushroom cloud) after a few minutes. Add the yeast mixture and buttermilk to the flour mixture and stir into a stiff dough. Knead just a tiny bit. Form the dough into a fat disk and wrap tightly in plastic wrap. Refrigerate for 8 hours or overnight. (You can easily double this recipe and freeze one disk of dough for later use; when you are ready to make the biscuits, thaw in the fridge and proceed with the recipe.)

Preheat the oven to 400°F.

In a tiny saucepan, melt the remaining 3 tablespoons of butter along with the bay leaves, immersing the bay leaves in the butter. Keep cooking the butter until the milk solids separate and you see little brown dots at the bottom of the pot. Add a pinch of salt to the butter.

Remove the dough from the refrigerator. Lightly flour a work surface and, using a rolling pin, roll out the dough until it is ½ inch thick. Using a 2½-inch biscuit cutter, carefully cut straight down to form as many biscuits as you can. Gather up any extra dough, press together, and cut into squares (to distinguish them from the first ones). These second biscuits are for the cook—they will be a little tougher but still good. Brush the biscuits on the top and bottom with the flavored butter (leave the bay behind in the saucepan), fold in half (over onto themselves), and place on a large baking sheet about 1 inch apart. Bake until golden brown, about 15 minutes. Serve hot out of the oven.

Chapter 2

Beech

LATIN: *Hypsizygus tessulatus*

Beech

GENERALLY SPEAKING: Lesser known, but I predict soon to become quite common, are these cultivated little beauties. They come in both white and light brown and are only a few inches tall, and are sold in one large clump. Think enoki mushrooms, but with flavor.

AKA: The white type are also known as white clamshell, white beech, Bunapi, and Alba Clamshell. The brown type are also known as brown beech, Buna, and Brown Clamshell. Both types are sometimes referred to as *hon-shimeji* (though technically this refers to the true *shimeji*, which is in another family altogether— *Lyophyllum shimeji*—and is gathered in the wild).

SEASON: Because these are cultivated, growers can bring them to market year-round.

BUYING TIPS: You'll find beech mushrooms in Asian markets or high-end grocery stores. Make sure there is no sliminess or soft spots, examining them as best as you can through the packaging.

CLEANING: Simply slice a thin bit off the base end and you're good to go. You'll soon sense a theme here, but cultivated mushrooms in general (and these beauties, in particular) are pretty clean when you get them. If you choose not to brush, wipe, or wash them (like me), you might have people questioning you prior to dinner: "But aren't mushrooms grown in, um . . . crap?" This isn't actually accurate (the substrate is composted and sterilized), and I would point out that rinsing mushrooms wouldn't sanitize them anyway. Tell them that high heat, not cold water, kills microscopic critters. Oh, and stop inviting those people over for dinner.

FLAVOR, TEXTURE, AND AROMA NOTES:
Beech mushrooms are nutty, and slightly tart, with a subtle iodine-like minerality. The texture is firm and crunchy, with an aroma that follows the nutty flavor.

STORAGE: They are often sold in what looks like a plastic-bag death trap for mushrooms, but the bags have microscopic pores in them, allowing for a slightly longer shelf life. You can choose to leave them in the bags until you are ready to use them, though my expert-forager friend recommends against it. They are marketed as being packaged in "breathable" plastic, but funky molds and aromas can nonetheless develop inside those bags. I don't think it's much of a concern if you will use the mushrooms within a week or two, but if you plan on storing them any longer, I suggest transferring them to a brown paper bag or a basket with a dry piece of paper towel or newsprint on top of them (replace this each day).

PRESERVATION:

DRYING: I don't recommend drying cultivated mushrooms such as the beech; substitute with a different mushroom if necessary, or only buy what you need.

FREEZING: See page xxxi. Cook beech mushrooms prior to freezing.

LOVES: Beech mushrooms, being so cute, love to garnish dishes. Consider quickly sautéing and then floating them in soups. Use them to top crostini, or drape some over a piece of seared salmon.

COOKING NOTES: Beech mushrooms can be a little bitter when raw or undercooked, so make sure you cook them all the way through. Some chefs will give them a quick blanching before using them in recipes (to ease the astringency and slight bitterness); I haven't found that to be necessary.

SUBSTITUTE: Shiitake or oyster mushrooms would make a good substitute for beech mushrooms.

NERDY FACTOIDS:

- Beech mushrooms (similar to maitake mushrooms) contain immune-modulating beta-glucan polysaccharides, also known to possess anti-tumor properties.

- Takara Shuzo Company was the first to patent a cultivated brown beech mushroom breed, in 1972.

Sweet Potato Soup with Lime Leaves, Beech Mushrooms, Basil, and Peanuts

The beech mushrooms are less the star here and more of a textural element used as a garnish. Because of this, it's extra important to use homemade mushroom stock (page xxiii) to highlight the mushroom flavor. This soup started in my mind's eye somewhere in Thailand (lime leaves, basil) and then—somewhat inexplicably—migrated to West Africa (sweet potatoes, peanuts). This is the perfect kind of soup to serve when it's raining, you're snuggled up on the couch with a blanket, a fire is lit, Thai music is playing, and a zebra is running through your living room.

SERVES: 4 | PAIRING: French Riesling

3 tablespoons coconut oil

1 small yellow onion, small diced (about 1 cup)

¾ teaspoon fine sea salt

2 pounds orange-fleshed sweet potatoes, peeled and large diced

5 lime leaves (substitute 1 teaspoon finely grated lime zest)

¼ cup white wine

5 cups Mushroom Stock (page xxiii)

1 tablespoon seasoned rice vinegar, plus more as needed

1 tablespoon fish sauce

7 ounces beech mushrooms, base trimmed and broken apart into bite-size clumps

½ cup lightly packed fresh Thai basil

⅓ cup roasted, salted peanuts, chopped

Chili oil (page xxii) or store-bought Asian chili oil, for garnish

In a soup pot over medium-high heat, melt 1½ tablespoons of the coconut oil. After a moment, add the onion and ¼ teaspoon of the salt and sauté for 10 minutes, until starting to brown. Add the sweet potatoes and lime leaves. Sauté for 2 to 3 minutes, then turn the heat to high, add the wine, and deglaze the pan, scraping up any brown bits. Add the stock, bring to a boil, and then lower the heat to a gentle simmer. Cook until the sweet potato cubes are tender, 20 to 25 minutes.

Add the vinegar. Remove the lime leaves. Puree the soup in a blender until very smooth, or puree in the pan using an immersion blender. Season with the fish sauce, another ¼ teaspoon salt, and more rice vinegar. If you feel it needs more salt, add more fish sauce (a little at a time). Keep tasting until it's right for you.

Meanwhile, prepare the beech mushroom mixture. In a large sauté pan over high heat, melt the remaining 1½ tablespoons of coconut oil. After a moment, add the mushrooms and the remaining ¼ teaspoon salt. Toss the mushrooms around in the oil, and then spread them out. The idea is to get them to release their liquid and brown quickly. When they brown, stir in the basil and peanuts and transfer to a small bowl.

Serve the soup in wide bowls, garnished with the mushroom mixture and drizzled with some chili oil.

Pan-Seared Trout with Sautéed Beech Mushrooms, Sage, and White Wine

Despite how buttery and quick cooking they are, trout fillets are somewhat undervalued. I think people get stymied by the bones, so here's my suggestion: You'll need to find the best fish place near where you live and ask the man or woman behind the counter to kindly fillet your trout and remove the pinbones. If your request is refused, you'll want to invest in some needle-nose pliers or fish tweezers. And then you'll want to ditch that fish shop and find a better one that knows how to give good customer service. Once deboned, trout fillets are a cinch to pan sear for a quick weeknight dinner along with some steamed or sautéed green beans. Lean on the side of undercooking; high heat, quick browning, in and out of the pan is the way to go. Covered with a little foil off the heat, the carryover cooking will leave you with succulent, moist fillets.

SERVES: 4 | PAIRING: French white Burgundy (Chardonnay)

2 whole trout, filleted, skin on, pinbones removed

¾ teaspoon fine sea salt

Pinch of cayenne pepper

Freshly ground black pepper

4 tablespoons unsalted butter

3 tablespoons vegetable oil

7 ounces beech mushrooms, base trimmed and broken apart into bite-size clumps

¼ cup sliced shallot

2 cloves garlic, thinly sliced

¼ cup lightly packed fresh sage leaves (use ones on the small side)

¼ cup sliced almonds, toasted (page xxiv)

1 tablespoon dried currants

⅓ cup dry white wine

Sprinkle the fillets with ½ teaspoon salt, cayenne, and black pepper. Turn on your kitchen fan and open a window.

Heat a large skillet (not nonstick, but one that you know doesn't have a lot of sticking problems) over medium-high heat. Add 1 tablespoon of the butter and 1 tablespoon of the vegetable oil. After a moment, raise the heat to high and add 2 fillets to the pan, flesh side down. After a couple of minutes, peek under the fillets. You want to see a nice bit of browning on them before you flip them. Cook on the other side to crisp the skin. In total, these thin fillets shouldn't be cooked for longer than a few minutes on each side. Transfer the fillets to a serving platter and cover loosely with aluminum foil. Wipe the pan out with a paper towel (use a metal spatula to scrape up anything stuck on the pan). Add another 1 tablespoon butter and 1 tablespoon vegetable oil. Cook the remaining fillets, and add to the platter. Wipe out the pan again, and add the remaining 1 tablespoon vegetable oil.

Add the mushrooms and shallot to the pan, along with ¼ teaspoon salt, and quickly brown them over high heat. Add the garlic, sauté for a minute or so, and then add the sage leaves. Toss the leaves around until they darken. Add the almonds and currants, and then the wine. Scrape the bottom of the pan to release any stuck-on brown bits. Turn the heat down to low, and swirl in the remaining 2 tablespoons butter. Taste the sauce and add more salt, if you'd like, to your taste. Pour the sauce down the middle of the reserved fillets and serve.

NOTE: Go to www.goodfishbook.com and I will show you how to fillet a fish and pull the pinbones out of salmon (essentially the same technique as for trout).

Sesame-Miso Broth with Caramelized Beech Mushrooms and Wakame

I think some folks would be surprised to know that miso soup doesn't have to come from a soup mix or a restaurant. It's one of the simplest soups to make at home from scratch. So, yes, you could go buy a little packet of instant miso broth, but where is the self-satisfaction in that? Furthermore, once you realize that making your own mushroom or vegetable stock is easy and that you've been throwing away perfectly good food that could have gone toward a stock, you'll be busting out your own superior miso any time you feel a cold coming on. This recipe is infinitely adaptable—it's soothing just on its own without any of the add-ins, but with the extras it becomes a meal.

SERVES: 4 | PAIRING: Green tea or Junmai Daiginjō-shu (sake)

2 (2 by 4-inch) pieces kombu (dried kelp)

4 cups Mushroom Stock (page xxiii; see Note)

2 teaspoons vegetable oil

¼ pound beech mushrooms, base trimmed

⅛ teaspoon fine sea salt

3 tablespoons red miso paste

1 teaspoon toasted sesame oil

⅛ ounce (.125 ounce) dried wakame (1 scant teaspoon), rehydrated in cold water for 5 minutes and cut into bite-size pieces

ADD-INS (OPTIONAL)
Cubes of soft tofu

Cooked soba noodles

Soft-boiled eggs

Grated fresh ginger

Sliced scallions

Shichimi tōgarashi (jarred Japanese spice mixture) or ground chile of your choice

Wipe off the kombu with a damp paper towel. Add the kombu to a saucepan, along with the stock. Turn the heat to medium and slowly bring the soup to just below a boil, about 10 minutes. Remove the kombu (you may slice half of one of the sheets into very thin short ribbons and garnish the soup with it, if you like).

Meanwhile, add the vegetable oil to a medium skillet over high heat. After a moment, add the mushrooms and salt. Sauté for 5 to 7 minutes, until caramelized and nearly crispy at the edges. While the mushrooms are caramelizing, remove 1 cup of the stock and whisk the miso into it until all lumps are gone. Add the mixture back to the saucepan, along with the sesame oil. Set the mushrooms aside.

For each serving, put an equal portion of sautéed mushrooms, kombu, and wakame in a soup bowl. Pour the soup over the top and stir in any add-ins.

NOTE: If you purchase mushroom stock instead of making it, look for a low-salt option. If that is not possible, you'll need to use less miso paste to keep the soup from getting too salty.

Bread Pudding with Seared Beech Mushrooms and Thyme

This is a decadent dish that would make for a fabulous vegetarian comfort-food main course served with a salad, or it could easily be used in a supporting role to a roast chicken. Recently it bumped out my family's traditional Thanksgiving stuffing. After baking, cooling, and cutting it into large squares, you could also freeze this for a later date. This is the dish to make if you have a lot of mushrooms on hand and a hungry crowd. I'm clearly not one for an Atkins-Paleo no-carb lifestyle, because when I see the words BREAD + PUDDING, I get very, very excited. The beech mushrooms contribute nuttiness and earthiness to the dish, but you could very easily substitute whatever mushrooms you might have on hand. I've made this dish with chanterelles, buttons, and mixes of other types with great success.

SERVES: 4 to 8 | PAIRING: French white Burgundy (preferably a Meursault)

1 tablespoon unsalted butter, plus more for greasing the pan

¼ cup extra-virgin olive oil

½ cup minced shallot

1¾ teaspoons fine sea salt

6 large cloves garlic, minced

1 pound button mushrooms, medium diced

1 pound beech mushrooms, base trimmed, mushrooms separated but left intact

¼ cup minced fresh flat-leaf parsley

1 tablespoon minced fresh thyme

1 tablespoon minced fresh sage

1 tablespoon tomato paste

1 teaspoon Dijon mustard

¼ teaspoon cayenne pepper

½ cup dry (white) vermouth

5 large eggs

½ cup grated Parmigiano-Reggiano

2 cups half-and-half

1 cup heavy cream

6 cups day-old 1-inch rustic bread cubes (or bake at 350°F for 10 minutes)

Preheat the oven to 350°F. Grease a 9 by 12-inch baking dish with a little butter.

Heat 2 large skillets over medium heat and place 1½ teaspoons butter and 2 tablespoons olive oil in each skillet (if you don't have 2 large skillets, prepare the mushrooms in batches). After a moment, evenly divide the shallot and 1 teaspoon of the salt between the skillets and sauté for 2 to 3 minutes, until soft. Add half the garlic to each skillet and sauté for another minute. Add half of both kinds of mushrooms to each skillet. Increase the heat to medium-high and sauté for 4 to 6 minutes, until the mushrooms have wilted and have started to brown. At this point, combine everything into one skillet. Add the parsley, thyme, sage, tomato paste, mustard, and cayenne. Cook for 1 more minute. Turn the heat to high and add the vermouth. Reduce until the vermouth has evaporated, and then turn off the heat.

In a very large bowl, whisk the eggs. Add the cheese to the eggs and whisk together. Whisk in the half-and-half and cream. Add the bread cubes and mushroom mixture, along with the remaining ¾ teaspoon salt, and mix together. Pour the bread mixture into the greased baking dish and bake, covered, for 30 minutes. Raise the heat to 375°F, uncover, and bake until browned on top, another 15 to 20 minutes. Serve warm.

Beech Mushrooms in Phyllo with Georgian Walnut Sauce and Pomegranate

I can't remember when and how I first learned about Georgian walnut sauce (and to be clear, it is the nation of Georgia and not the fine state that I'm referring to here), but I've been making this unique sauce for years, typically with chicken—a traditional dish called satsivi. I had a feeling that this walnut sauce would go very well with mushrooms, and I was inspired to use phyllo dough in the preparation because when I looked up Georgia on a map, I realized it shared a border with Turkey, and, well, when I think of Turkey I can't help but think of baklava, one of my favorite desserts. These little mushroom roll-ups—varnished with a flaky brown, crispy exterior, served with a velvety walnut sauce, and garnished with pomegranate seeds—make a perfect New Year's Eve appetizer or first course for a winter holiday gathering. With the leftover phyllo dough, make baklava and then, be a dear—call me.

SERVES: 4 | PAIRING: Austrian Grüner Veltliner

2 tablespoons unsalted butter, melted, plus more for buttering baking sheet

2 tablespoons coconut oil

1 pound beech mushrooms, base trimmed and torn into pieces

1 pound button mushrooms, quartered

1 teaspoon grated fresh ginger

½ teaspoon fine sea salt

Freshly ground black pepper

1 (1-pound) box phyllo dough, thawed overnight in the refrigerator

Georgian Walnut Sauce (recipe follows)

¼ cup pomegranate seeds

Leaves of ½ bunch cilantro

Preheat the oven to 350°F. Lightly butter a baking sheet.

Heat 2 large skillets over medium-high heat (or cook in batches in 1 skillet). Add 1 tablespoon oil to each pan and then half of both kinds of mushrooms to each pan, along with half the ginger, half the salt, and a few grinds of black pepper, and sauté until browned and caramelized, about 10 minutes. Transfer the mushrooms to a bowl and let cool. Taste and season with more salt and pepper, if needed.

Cut 2 sheets of phyllo into 6-inch squares, and keep them covered with a slightly damp cloth. Brush 1 square with melted butter, top with another square of phyllo, brush with butter, and then add a scant portion (no more than ¼ cup) of the cooled mushroom mixture on top of the dough about 1 inch from the bottom, leaving a ½-inch border on each side. Fold both sides over the filling and then, starting with the edge closest to you, roll up tightly, as you would a spring roll. Place the mushroom rolls on the prepared baking sheet, seam side down. Brush the tops with butter and keep covered until ready to bake. Repeat until you have used up the filling and phyllo sheets.

Bake for 18 to 25 minutes, until brown and crisp. Serve with the walnut sauce. Garnish with the pomegranate seeds and cilantro leaves.

Georgian Walnut Sauce

½ teaspoon coriander seeds

½ teaspoon fenugreek seeds

½ teaspoon fine sea salt

¼ teaspoon cayenne pepper

¼ teaspoon ground turmeric

1 cup walnuts, toasted (page xxiv)

3 tablespoons chopped fresh cilantro

¼ cup pure unsweetened pomegranate juice

2 teaspoons red wine vinegar

Freshly ground black pepper

In a small skillet over medium-high heat, toast the coriander and fenugreek seeds until they darken slightly and become quite aromatic. Transfer to a spice grinder, and add the salt, cayenne, and turmeric. Grind to a powder. Add the spice mixture to a food processor along with the walnuts, cilantro, juice, vinegar, and black pepper and blend to a smooth sauce. Taste and adjust the seasonings as needed.

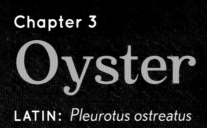

Chapter 3

Oyster

LATIN: *Pleurotus ostreatus*

Fact Sheet:
Oyster

FLAVOR, TEXTURE, AND AROMA NOTES: Some say oyster mushrooms have an abalone-like flavor. The caps are tender and the stems are firm. The aroma carries with it whiffs of almond, anise, cucumber, and white pepper.

GENERALLY SPEAKING: Oyster mushrooms can be found in the wild, but they are much better known in their cultivated version on supermarket shelves. In fact, oyster mushrooms are one of the easiest mushrooms to grow. As I write this, I'm staring at my own homegrown oyster mushrooms, spilling out of a box. Oyster mushroom spawn was inoculated in a sawdust-compost blend. I misted it twice daily, and after eight days, oyster mushrooms exploded (growing nearly before my eyes) out of the side of the box. Oyster mushrooms are quite the opportunists, growing on a wide variety of substrates: straw, paper, wood, seeds. In the wild, you will find them growing on the sides of trees.

AKA: Oyster mushrooms are also known as straw mushrooms, tree oyster, oyster shelf, *hiratake* or *tamogitake* (Japanese), and *pleurotte*. *Pleurotus*, from the Greek, means "side ear," and if you stare at an oyster mushroom and tilt your head to the side, it will become very clear where it got its name.

SEASON: Cultivated oyster mushrooms are available year-round; in the wild they are found in the fall through the winter.

LOVES: Oyster mushrooms pair beautifully with cream-based dishes, nuts, stir-fries, steak, and fish dishes.

BUYING TIPS: Make sure there are no dried-out edges. The mushrooms should smell fresh and feel moist.

CLEANING: Cultivated oyster mushrooms are typically extremely clean; just trim the base a bit, and keep in mind that the stems will be just slightly tougher than the caps, though I enjoy the slightly chewy texture.

STORAGE: Cultivated oyster mushrooms, provided you purchase great specimens to begin with (not dried out), can keep for up to 2 weeks. Wild oyster mushrooms have a shorter shelf life and should be used within a few days. As with all mushrooms, store them in the refrigerator in a brown paper bag. Second choice would be to store them in a basket or box with a dry piece of paper towel or newsprint on top of them (replace this each day).

PRESERVATION:

DRYING: See page xxix. Dried oyster mushrooms are not really worth purchasing; they're relatively ho-hum in flavor when rehydrated.

FREEZING: See page xxxi. Freezing is not really recommended for oyster mushrooms unless you cook them first as duxelles (see page xxii) or simply sauté them in butter or oil and freeze for use at a later date.

COOKING NOTES: You can certainly dice oyster mushrooms for cooking, but keep in mind that they easily tear into smaller pieces by grasping the cap and pulling apart through the stem. You can do the same thing with chanterelle mushrooms, and this technique makes for a more natural presentation of the mushroom in your cooking. If the texture of the oyster stems, small though they are, isn't pleasing to you, consider separating stem from cap and giving the stems a head start in the cooking for a few minutes.

SUBSTITUTE: King trumpet mushrooms (in the same family; see Chapter 4) would make the best substitute.

NERDY FACTOIDS:

- According to Paul Stamets in his book *Mycelium Running*, "oyster mushroom mycelium can digest 5 pounds of wood, reducing it to less (than) 50 percent of its mass, in a few months." Just my suggestion, but you might not want to grow oyster mushrooms on any good pieces of furniture in your house.

- Oyster mushrooms can break down petroleum-based pollutants in the soil and have been proven to assist in habit restoration after an industrial contamination.

Oyster Mushroom Ragout with Cognac and Herbs

One of the great joys of writing cookbooks is that I get to hit up a few of my so-called "chef crushes" for recipes, both for inspiration and to introduce my readers to the chefs and authors that I have long admired. Virginia Willis, acclaimed author of *Bon Appétit, Y'all* and *Basic to Brilliant, Y'all*, is the French-influenced, Southern U.S. chef-author who graciously offered me her mushroom ragout recipe. We bonded several years ago over our mutual admiration of Isabella Rossellini (in other words: star crush). I've adapted Virginia's core recipe here, adding cognac (Virginia adds: "Tell them bourbon would be great, too"), thyme, and cayenne to warm and further deepen the flavor of the mushrooms. If you live in the North, this is the perfect winter-insulating weeknight pasta dish. After all, it will be months until you're in a swimsuit again. If you live in the South and you're eating big bowls of this— you may want to turn down the air-conditioning.

SERVES: 4 | PAIRING: French Bordeaux (blend of Cabernet Sauvignon and Merlot)

1 heaping tablespoon kosher salt

2 tablespoons extra-virgin olive oil

2 tablespoons unsalted butter

1 pound oyster mushrooms, base trimmed and torn into bite-size pieces

1 pound button mushrooms, quartered

1 teaspoon fine sea salt

1 pound dried egg noodles

¼ cup minced shallot

2 cloves garlic, minced and mashed into a paste

⅛ teaspoon cayenne pepper

1 teaspoon minced fresh thyme

1 teaspoon minced fresh rosemary

¼ cup cognac (substitute other brandy or bourbon)

½ cup Mushroom Stock (page xxiii)

¼ cup dry red wine

¼ cup heavy cream

¼ cup chopped fresh flat-leaf parsley

Freshly ground black pepper

¼ cup grated Parmigiano-Reggiano

Bring a large pot of water to a boil. Add the kosher salt.

Divide the oil and butter between 2 large skillets. Set them over medium-high heat. Add the mushrooms in equal amounts to the skillets and sprinkle ½ teaspoon fine sea salt over each pan. Sauté the mushrooms until brown and just tender, about 10 minutes. Start cooking the pasta, stirring a few times in the first minute of cooking, while you finish the sauce.

When the mushrooms are tender and reduced significantly in volume, combine them into one pan. Add the shallot and sauté for a few minutes, then add the garlic and cook until fragrant, 45 to 60 seconds. Add the cayenne, thyme, and rosemary and, after a moment, the cognac. Once the cognac has cooked down, add the mushroom stock, wine, and cream. Bring to a boil, then lower to a simmer and cook, uncovered, until the mushrooms are fully tender and the sauce coats the mushrooms, about 5 minutes. Add the parsley and toss to coat.

Drain the pasta once it is al dente (save ¼ cup of the pasta cooking liquid), put it back in the pasta pot, and pour the ragout over the pasta. Over low heat, gently stir the sauce into the pasta. Taste and adjust for seasoning, adding pasta cooking water if it needs more salt. Add pepper to taste. Sprinkle grated Parmigiano-Reggiano over the top of each dish.

Crispy Striped Bass with Oyster Mushrooms, Delicata Squash, and Green Beans

This is a simple weeknight dish that can be adapted to whatever vegetables and fish you have at home or at your market. The vinaigrette can be doubled and kept in the refrigerator for a week. If you are concerned about the house smelling like pan-seared fish, you can broil or bake the fish instead, but keep in mind that the skin won't get crispy.

SERVES: 4 | PAIRING: Austrian Grüner Veltliner

1 tablespoon extra-virgin olive oil, plus more for brushing the pan

½ pound oyster mushrooms, base trimmed and torn into bite-size pieces

½ pound green beans, ends trimmed and cut crosswise on the bias

½ pound Delicata squash, seeded, and cut into ⅛-inch half-moons

2 teaspoons fine sea salt

Freshly ground black pepper

1 pound striped bass fillets, bones removed, skin on, cut into 4 (4-ounce) pieces

1 tablespoon vegetable oil, plus more as needed

Toasted Shallot and Balsamic Vinaigrette (page 132)

Preheat the oven to 400°F.

Line a baking pan with aluminum foil and generously brush it with olive oil. Pile the mushrooms, green beans, and squash into the pan, drizzle the 1 tablespoon olive oil over the top, and mix well. Sprinkle 1 teaspoon of the salt and as much black pepper as you like over the top. Pop the pan into the oven and roast for 15 minutes. Stir everything up and then roast for another 10 to 15 minutes, until the squash and mushrooms are tender and a little crispy at the edges.

Bring the fish to room temperature prior to cooking (at least 10 to 15 minutes). Dry the skin side of the fish with paper towels (it makes for easier crisping of the skin). Sprinkle the remaining 1 teaspoon salt on both sides of all 4 pieces of bass. Heat a large skillet over high heat. Turn over a slightly smaller skillet and wipe the bottom with vegetable oil. Add the 1 tablespoon vegetable oil to the larger pan. Slide in the fillets, skin side down. Place the smaller skillet down on the fillets. This helps press the fish down so that the skin can get nice and crisp. Turn the heat down to medium-high. Cook for 5 to 6 minutes on the skin side, and then lift the smaller pan off. Use a fish spatula or a metal spatula, but flip it upside down and gently but firmly scrape along the bottom of the pan, releasing the skin without going up and into the fish with the tool. Flip the fillets and cook on the other side for a few more minutes (about 8 minutes total cooking time per inch of thickness).

Serve the fish skin side up on top of the vegetables. Drizzle the vinaigrette over the fish and the vegetables.

Spicy Black Bean, Poblano, and Oyster Mushroom Burgers with Red Onion Jam

I eat beef, so when I decided to create a mushroom-based vegetarian burger, I wanted it to be as satisfying as a beef burger without it being beef-like (most vegetarians will tell you that's not really the point). The few times I've tried veggie burgers, I've been amazed that people could regularly eat them; it would take a lot of mustard and ketchup for me to get past how dry most of them are. This is one of several recipes in this book that you can make for vegetarians (or really, anyone) who is an avowed mushroom hater. The mushrooms take a background role in these burgers, providing texture (from a shorter cooking time on the stems) and umami. The feta just starts to melt when the burgers are done browning, forming little pools of awesome. This is a perfect dish to make if you have leftover beans and rice in the house. Keep in mind that it is really important to squeeze your hands together when forming the burgers. This helps to bind the mixture and keep them from crumbling in the pan. That being said, this is a messy burger affair, so tuck a napkin into your shirt when eating. There is a fair amount of prep involved in making these, so feel free to double the recipe. Freeze any uncooked burgers on a baking pan and then pack them away in a container or freezer bag for another day.

SERVES: 4 | PAIRING: Ice-cold lager or California Zinfandel

SPICY LIME AND CHIPOTLE MAYO

½ cup mayonnaise (I love Best Foods/Hellmann's)

Finely grated zest of 1 lime

1 teaspoon freshly squeezed lime juice

½ teaspoon ground chipotle chili powder (substitute spicy pure chili powder of your choice)

⅛ teaspoon fine sea salt

RED ONION JAM AND BURGERS

2 poblano chiles

¼ cup plus 1 tablespoon coconut oil

2 small red onions, small diced (about 3 cups)

1 teaspoon fine sea salt

1¼ cups Mushroom Stock (page xxiii)

2 tablespoons sugar

2 tablespoons red wine vinegar

1 portobello mushroom, gills and stem removed, cap small diced

½ pound fresh oyster mushrooms, stems separated from caps and both small diced

1 bunch cilantro, stems chopped to make ¼ cup, leaves reserved for garnish

1 tablespoon tomato paste

2 teaspoons soy sauce

1 teaspoon ground cumin

Freshly ground black pepper

1 cup cooked brown rice

¾ cup cooked and drained black beans, squished with a potato masher (leave some texture)

3 ounces French or Israeli feta

1½ cups panko bread crumbs

4 hamburger buns, toasted if you like

FOR SERVING

1 avocado

Lettuce leaves

Tomato slices

Spicy Black Bean, Poblano, and Oyster Mushroom Burgers with Red Onion Jam

CONTINUED

To make the mayo, in a medium bowl, whisk together the mayonnaise, lime zest and juice, chili powder, and salt. Taste and add more salt if you'd like. Store in the fridge until you are ready to use.

To make the burgers, over a gas flame or under the broiler, blacken the poblano chiles (you want all parts to be blackened). Transfer the chiles to a bowl and cover with plastic wrap to trap the steam, about 15 minutes.

Meanwhile, in a large skillet over medium heat, add 2 tablespoons of the coconut oil. After a moment, add the onions and salt. Sauté for 5 minutes. Add 1 cup of the stock and simmer until all the liquid is evaporated; continue to cook until the onions are caramelized, 15 to 20 minutes (add a little water if necessary if it gets too dry). Once the onions are browned and very soft, pull half of the onions out of the pan and reserve. Add the sugar to the pan and cook for a minute, then add the vinegar and the remaining ¼ cup stock. Cook over medium heat until the liquid evaporates. Scrape the red onion jam into a small bowl and set aside to serve with the rest of the toppings. No need to clean the pan—you'll be using it again.

Remove and discard the skin and seeds from the roasted chiles and cut them into small dice. Add 1 tablespoon of coconut oil to the pan, along with the chiles and the reserved sautéed onions. Set the pan over medium-high heat. Add the chopped portobello, oyster mushroom caps, and cilantro stems and sauté until lightly browned and tender, 5 to 6 minutes. Add the tomato paste, soy sauce, cumin, and black pepper and sauté for another minute or two. Add the chopped oyster mushroom stems and sauté for another minute or two, adding a little water if necessary. Add the contents of the pan to a big bowl, along with the rice, black beans, feta, 1 cup of the panko, and 1 tablespoon of the chipotle mayo. Mix well, and form into 4 large burgers (see headnote). Spread the remaining ½ cup panko onto a plate and coat each side of the burgers.

Heat a large skillet over medium-high heat. Add the remaining 2 tablespoons coconut oil. When the skillet heats up, carefully place the burgers in the skillet and cook until you get a nice deep dark brown sear on each side, 4 to 5 minutes per side.

Spread the chipotle mayo all over the insides of the toasted buns. Pit, peel, and slice the avocado. Add the burgers to the buns and top with lettuce, tomato, avocado, and cilantro leaves.

Oysters Rockefeller[2]

There is something linguistically satisfying about serving oyster mushrooms with oysters (so much so, in fact, that I also have a recipe in this book for lobster mushrooms with lobster on page 150). But it's not just about word play. Oyster mushrooms are a great foil for oysters of the sea. The mushrooms are light enough to complement the bivalves without taking anything away from their ocean brininess; they ground and balance the dish, bringing it one step closer to land. The oysters can be shucked earlier in the day. Even the topping and the sauce can be done ahead and reheated. Assemble and quickly bake when your guests arrive.

SERVES: 4 as an appetizer | PAIRING: French Sancerre (Sauvignon Blanc)

3 to 4 cups rock salt or kosher salt

24 oysters in the shell, shucked, liquor reserved (top shell discarded, bottom shell cleaned; see Note)

4 tablespoons unsalted butter

1/3 cup panko bread crumbs

1/4 cup grated Parmigiano-Reggiano

1/4 cup minced shallot

1/2 pound oyster mushrooms, small diced

1/4 pound chopped fresh spinach (about 2 cups)

1/4 cup white wine

1/4 cup heavy cream

1/2 teaspoon Tabasco sauce (or hot sauce of your choice)

1 scant teaspoon minced fresh tarragon

Fine sea salt (optional)

1 lemon, cut into wedges

Position a rack in the top third of the oven and preheat to 450°F.

Pour the rock salt onto a baking pan or a shallow baking dish. Place the oyster meat (making sure there are no bits of shell on them) in a bowl. Tip the oyster shells with their liquid, aka oyster liquor, through a fine-mesh strainer into another bowl. Keep the oysters in the refrigerator or on ice until you are ready to use them. Tuck the bottom shells into the salt so that they are steadied.

In a large skillet over medium heat, melt the butter. Transfer half of it to a small bowl along with the panko and Parmesan. Mix and reserve. Add the shallot to the pan with the remaining melted butter and sauté for 2 to 3 minutes, until the shallot is soft. Add the mushrooms. Sauté for 5 to 6 minutes, until the mushrooms start to brown a little. Add the spinach and sauté for 1 minute, just long enough for the spinach to wilt and release its moisture. Add the wine and cook until there is no liquid left. Add the cream, Tabasco, tarragon, and reserved oyster liquor. Cook for 1 minute more. Taste this mixture for salt, keeping in mind that the Parmesan is salty. Add salt if you feel it really needs some (a lot of this depends on how salty the oyster liquor is). Turn off the heat.

Place an oyster in each bottom shell and then top with a heaping tablespoon of the mushroom-spinach mixture. Sprinkle a small amount of the panko-cheese mixture over the top. Bake for 8 to 10 minutes, until the oysters are cooked through and the panko-cheese mixture has browned. Serve with lemon wedges.

NOTE: Go to www.goodfishbook.com and I will show you how to shuck an oyster.

Oyster Mushroom and Corn Empanadas with Charred Poblano and Pumpkin Seed Sauce

A tortilla press makes quicker work of this dish, but if you don't have one you can press out the masa balls using a skillet or a glass dish. Get creative, because even if the empanadas are ugly, you won't care once you taste them. See the photo of me forming the empanada, because it takes some practice and the visual cues might help; notice how I'm using the plastic to keep everything from getting sticky. The sauce will keep for up to a week in your fridge, and you can bake and freeze the empanadas and reheat them right from the freezer in a 350°F oven until they are warmed through and crispy. If you have leftovers, you can make a form of "ghetto enchiladas" by layering the empanadas in a large dish and pouring tomato, chile, or tomatillo sauce over the top, plus a sprinkling of cheese and a drizzle of the poblano sauce.

SERVES: 2 to 4
(makes 10 empanadas)

PAIRING: Margheritas or a lager

DOUGH
2 cups masa harina (I like Bob's Red Mill)

1¼ cups warm water (100°F to 115°F)

¼ teaspoon fine sea salt

FILLING
¼ cup extra-virgin olive oil

1 pound fresh oyster mushrooms, base trimmed and torn into small bite-size pieces

2 teaspoons fine sea salt

½ small yellow onion, small diced (generous ½ cup)

1 tablespoon minced garlic

1 tomato, medium diced (about 1 cup)

½ teaspoon ground chipotle chili powder (or more if you like it spicy)

1 bunch cilantro, leaves chopped to make ⅓ cup, stems reserved for sauce, rest of leaves reserved for garnish

1 ear corn, kernels cut off, corn "milk" scraped off cob with a spoon (substitute 1 cup thawed frozen corn)

¼ pound cotija cheese, crumbled

1 large egg, beaten with 1 tablespoon water

CHARRED POBLANO AND PUMPKIN SEED SAUCE
1 poblano chile

¼ cup pumpkin seeds, toasted

Stems from cilantro bunch (see left)

½ cup neutral oil, such as grapeseed

⅓ cup red wine vinegar

1 teaspoon honey

2 dashes Tabasco sauce (or hot sauce of your choice)

1 teaspoon fine sea salt

3 cups vegetable oil (if you are frying them)

Preheat the oven to 400°F.

To make the dough, mix the masa, water, and salt together in a medium bowl. It should come together fairly easily, be slightly sticky, and not fall apart at all. If it seems dry, add a little more water. Divide it into 10 equal pieces. Roll the pieces into balls. Put them on a plate and cover with a damp cotton towel to prevent them from drying out. Place a ball between 2 pieces of plastic wrap or waxed paper. Place under a tortilla press or squish the balls into flat rounds by pressing down on them with a skillet or flat dish. Whether by tortilla press or other means, once the ball has been squished into a 5- to 6-inch round, pull the top piece of plastic off and reuse for the next ball. Lay the pressed dough (on its piece

of plastic wrap) to the side. Place the already used piece of plastic down on the press, sandwich a new ball between it, and a new piece of plastic. Press out another round. Place the next round on top of the first, so that there is plastic or waxed paper between each round. Repeat to form all the rounds. Cover with a lightly damp towel.

To make the filling, line a baking pan with aluminum foil and pour 2 tablespoons of the olive oil onto the foil. Toss the mushrooms in the oil, spread out in a single layer, and season with 1 teaspoon of the salt. Roast in the oven until brown in parts and slightly crispy on the edges, 15 to 20 minutes, stirring once during the cooking process. Let cool, and chop the mushrooms into medium dice.

Oyster Mushroom and Corn Empanadas with Charred Poblano and Pumpkin Seed Sauce

CONTINUED

In a large skillet over medium-high heat, sauté the onion with the remaining 2 tablespoons olive oil and the remaining 1 teaspoon salt for about 10 minutes, until lightly browned and soft. Add the garlic, tomato, and chipotle chili powder to the pan and continue cooking over medium-high heat until all of the moisture is gone, 6 to 8 more minutes. Stir in the cilantro leaves, roasted mushrooms, corn kernels, and corn "milk," and sauté for 1 more minute. Cool slightly before stirring in the cheese. Store in the fridge until you are ready to form the empanadas.

To form the empanadas, you'll need 2 tablespoons of filling for each. Picking up a masa round on its piece of plastic, lay it in your hand like a taco. Place the filling on one side of the round, leaving a little room to brush a small amount of egg wash on the edges of just the side the filling is on. Using the plastic to help you, fold the empanada over on itself. Through the plastic, pinch the sides to seal. Set aside, still in its plastic cover, on a tray covered with a lightly damp towel. Repeat until all the empanadas are formed. You might have some extra filling left over, which you can use in an omelette the next day or for impromptu nachos.

To make the sauce, char the poblano over a gas flame or under the broiler until blackened. Transfer the chile to a bowl and cover with plastic wrap to trap the steam, about 15 minutes. Peel, knock the seeds out, and stem the chile; place into a blender or food processor along with the pumpkin seeds, cilantro stems, neutral oil, red wine vinegar, honey, Tabasco, and salt. Blend until smooth. Season to taste.

To bake the empanadas, arrange them on a baking pan ½ inch apart and bake until lightly brown, 20 to 25 minutes.

To fry the empanadas, heat the vegetable oil in a medium skillet over medium-high heat until it reaches 350°F to 360°F on an instant-read thermometer. Slip 2 empanadas into the oil at a time (or as many will comfortably fit in your skillet). Fry on both sides until brown, 4 to 5 minutes per batch. Drain on paper towels.

To serve, lay the empanadas on a platter, and garnish with the cilantro leaves. Serve with the poblano and pumpkin seed sauce.

Chapter 4

King Trumpet

LATIN: *Pleurotus eryngii*

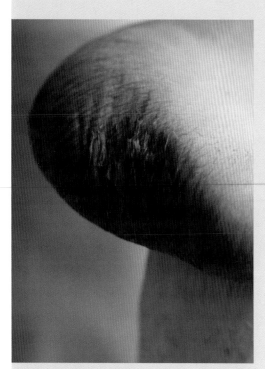

King Trumpet

FLAVOR, TEXTURE, AND AROMA NOTES: Reminiscent of abalone or oyster, king trumpet mushrooms are mild, seafood-like, and nutty. The texture is firm and juicy, not so unlike that of an eggplant. They are quite noisy in the pan, being one of the squeakiest of the mushrooms when you move them around. The aroma is sweet and mildly earthy.

GENERALLY SPEAKING: King trumpet mushrooms are the largest species in the oyster mushroom genus (*Pleurotus*). I've elected to separate them out as their own chapter even though I cover common oyster mushrooms in chapter 3 because this type of oyster mushroom looks and cooks very differently, and in my opinion they are well deserving of the alternate name of king oyster. While they do occur in the wild, what you are most likely to find in the marketplace is cultivated. When cultivated, they are typically grown on a mixture of grain, straw, and other organic waste materials. King trumpets are popular in Europe and Asia and are increasingly found in American supermarkets.

AKA: King trumpet mushrooms are also known as king oyster, trumpet royale, boletus of the steppes, scallop mushrooms, French horn mushrooms, shellfish mushrooms, *cardoncello* in Italian and Spanish, *xìng bào gū* in Chinese, *saesongi peoseot* in Korean, and *eringi* in Japanese.

SEASON: Cultivated king trumpet mushrooms are available year-round, especially in Asian markets.

BUYING TIPS: Look for firm stems, no drying out on the edges of the stems, and a mild, barely earthy, pleasant smell.

CLEANING: Typically, these are very clean, so just trim a sliver off the bottom of the stem and then they are good to go, with no cleaning necessary. Stem and cap are totally edible.

STORAGE: King trumpets have a fairly long shelf life, sometimes staying fresh and firm for over a week. As with all mushrooms, store them in the refrigerator in a brown paper bag. Second choice would be to store them in a basket or box with a dry piece of paper towel or newsprint on top of them (replace this each day).

PRESERVATION:

DRYING: As of this writing I've never seen dehydrated king trumpets in the marketplace, though they have a small presence online. Honestly, I wouldn't bother with buying them dried or drying them on your own. They are widely cultivated, so either buy them fresh or use one of the listed substitutes if you can't find them at your market.

FREEZING: See page xxxi.

LOVES: If you think of king trumpet mushrooms as you might think of scallops, you are on your way to wonderful pairings. Think brown butter, capers, lemon and other citrus, fresh herbs, and soy sauce and you're on the right track.

COOKING NOTES: What can you not do with this mushroom would be a better question. It grills and broils up beautifully, and sears like a steak or scallop in a cast-iron skillet. Sprinkled with smoked salt, sliced thin, and roasted or fried, it's like vegetarian crack. But my favorite way to cook king trumpets would have to be a hot sear followed by basting them with a flavorful oil or butter (see King Trumpet "Scallops" with Carrot Puree, Leek, and Parsley Vinaigrette on page 48 for an example of this technique).

SUBSTITUTE: The obvious substitution would be oyster mushrooms (*Pleurotus ostreatus*), which are in the same family. As a deep second choice, try substituting with button or cremini mushrooms.

NERDY FACTOIDS:

- King trumpet mushrooms may contain natural immune system–stimulating chemicals.

- Most mushrooms in the *Pleurotus* genus are straightforward wood-decaying mushrooms (saprotrophic), though the wild version of the king trumpet mushroom is also parasitic, living off of the roots of herbaceous plants.

King Trumpet and Tomato Sandwiches with Spicy Mayo

Come August, tomato sandwiches with mayo on white bread are a staple lunch in my household. I will, with no exaggeration, eat them every day for a week or two, but only when tomatoes are at their very best; here in Seattle we're looking at two weeks, tops. Adding smoky mushroom slices just gilds the lily here. Feel free to interpret this recipe as you like; use any kind of bread you prefer or substitute arugula, basil leaves, or watercress for the lettuce.

SERVES: 4 | PAIRING: French rosé

2 tablespoons extra-virgin olive oil

½ pound king trumpet mushrooms, sliced lengthwise into ¼-inch slices

¼ teaspoon smoked salt

⅛ teaspoon fine sea salt

1 large red heirloom tomato, cut into 4 thick slices

Freshly ground black pepper

8 slices potato bread, toasted

¼ cup Spicy Lime and Chipotle Mayonnaise (page 33)

4 butter lettuce leaves

In a large skillet over medium-high heat, heat 1 tablespoon of the olive oil. Add half of the mushroom slices to the pan and sprinkle with half of the smoked salt. Cook until the mushrooms release their water, crisp up, and brown; flip and repeat on the other side. Transfer to a paper towel–lined plate, add the remaining 1 tablespoon oil to the pan, and repeat with the rest of the mushrooms and smoked salt.

Sprinkle the sea salt over the 4 tomato slices. Grind some pepper on the tomatoes.

Lay out 4 pieces of the toasted bread. Spread 1 tablespoon of the mayonnaise on each slice, lay down a piece of lettuce, a slice of tomato, and one-quarter of the mushroom slices. Top with the remaining bread.

King Trumpet Toasts with Gouda, Apricot Jam, and Arugula

A few years back my friend Heather came over to our house for a dinner party, and she whipped up an appetizer that, while simple, had a surprisingly complex flavor with some unexpected ingredient combinations. Mushrooms with apricot jam? It didn't automatically sound like a winner to me, but I'm glad I didn't let the sound of it in my ear shut my mouth from hoovering down most of the toasts before she even had time to start the next round. This is my take on that simple appetizer.

SERVES: 6 (makes 12 toasts) | PAIRING: French Pinot Gris

12 baguette slices, cut on an angle ¼ inch thick

2 tablespoons extra-virgin olive oil, plus more for brushing the bread

½ pound king trumpet mushrooms, cut in half crosswise, then sliced ¼ inch thick

¼ teaspoon fine sea salt

¼ cup apricot jam

¼ cup small arugula leaves

½ cup grated Gruyère

Position a rack in the middle of the oven and preheat the broiler.

Lay the baguette slices on a baking sheet. Brush the slices with olive oil on the top side only. Broil until they are brown and crisp on top, checking every minute. Don't walk away because, man, they love to burn when your back is turned.

In a large skillet over medium-high heat, heat 1 tablespoon of the olive oil. Add half of the mushroom slices to the pan and sprinkle with half of the salt. Cook until the mushrooms release their water, crisp up, and brown; flip and repeat on the other side. Transfer to a paper towel–lined plate. Add the remaining 1 tablespoon oil and repeat with the remaining mushrooms and salt.

Spread a scant amount of jam on each toast. Top with an arugula leaf, a few pieces of mushroom, and a scant teaspoon of cheese. Put back in the oven just until the cheese melts, about 1 minute. Remove from the oven, and garnish with another slice of mushroom and a tiny dollop more of apricot jam.

Grilled King Trumpet Mushrooms with Orange and Black Pepper

My chef friend Jet was with me in the kitchen one day, and I asked her to help me come up with a simple recipe that required no more than five ingredients (oil, salt, and pepper didn't count). It was part culinary game, part pragmatic need, because I knew I wanted to grill the mushrooms and already I had enough more difficult recipes slated for this chapter. As soon as I told her that king trumpet mushrooms are scallop-like, she said "orange," and I knew she was right on. We added soy sauce to increase the umami factor and arugula for its peppery contribution and its color. The ironic thing here is that smoke is not considered an ingredient, but it should be, because it's key. You can serve this as a salad or as a side dish to a grilled ribeye. Take a peek at the photo to get an idea of what those crosswise scoring marks look like.

SERVES: 4 | PAIRING: Italian Pinot Grigio or Spanish Albariño

8 king trumpet mushrooms, halved and scored crosswise ⅛ inch deep

Zest and juice of 1 orange

¼ cup extra-virgin olive oil

2 teaspoons soy sauce

¼ teaspoon fine sea salt

Freshly ground black pepper

2 tablespoons unsalted butter

1 cup arugula

Flaky sea salt (such as Maldon), for garnish

Place the mushrooms in a wide dish. In a small bowl, mix together the orange zest (save a little for garnishing), juice, olive oil, soy sauce, and salt. Pour the marinade over the mushrooms and, with your hands, make sure it gets worked into the scored lines of the mushrooms. Grind a generous amount of black pepper over the mushrooms. Let them marinate for 20 minutes while you preheat a grill to medium-high heat.

If you have a gas grill, use a smoker box (or a foil package with holes poked into it) with soaked wood chips. The wood smoke flavor is key with this simple recipe. Remove the mushrooms from the marinade and reserve it. Grill the mushrooms on both sides until tender and caramelized with nice sear marks from the grill. Put the grilled mushrooms on a plate and tent loosely with aluminum foil.

Place the reserved marinade in a small pan, bring to a boil, and reduce by one-third. Add the butter and swirl the pan until the butter is fully melted. Arrange ¼ cup arugula leaves on each plate. Top with 4 mushroom halves. Drizzle the marinade over the mushrooms and arugula, garnish with the reserved orange zest and flaky salt, and serve right away.

Caponata with King Trumpet Mushrooms, Pine Nuts, and Currants

Don't be intimidated by the number of ingredients in this recipe—it's easier than it seems. The oven does all of the work on the mushrooms and eggplant while you sauté the aromatics on the stovetop. Then you mix everything together, essentially, in one pan to finish. The secret to the depth of flavor in this dish? Anchovies. Full of natural glutamate, anchovies (as well as mushrooms, tomatoes, Parmesan, and seaweed, among other items) contribute a meaty savoriness (umami) that adds mystery to foods. You won't taste the anchovy, but you'll notice the extra oomph it gives the dish. This is one of the recipes in the book where the mushrooms supply a background note, helping to build layers of flavors within the dish without it tasting like a mushroom dish (so, try this out on any friends who don't like mushrooms). This freezes beautifully and with more tomato puree turns itself into a quick pasta sauce. Stuff the caponata into a sandwich with thin slices of provolone or just eat it as I do, spooned on toast with a nice glass of Italian red wine.

SERVES: 4 to 6 | PAIRING: Italian Nero d'Avola or Italian Tuscan blend

¼ cup plus 3 tablespoons extra-virgin olive oil

1 small globe eggplant, medium diced (about 4 cups)

½ pound king trumpet mushrooms, medium diced

½ teaspoon fine sea salt

Freshly ground black pepper

1 red onion, small diced

2 stalks celery, small diced

1 red pepper, seeded and medium diced

1½ teaspoons tomato paste

½ cup red wine

1 pint cherry tomatoes, halved

1 large tomato, medium diced

6 cloves garlic, minced

¼ cup pine nuts, toasted (page xxiv)

¼ cup pitted kalamata olives, minced

¼ cup golden raisins

2 anchovy fillets

1 tablespoon capers, rinsed and minced

1 teaspoon honey

1 teaspoon red pepper flakes (1½ teaspoons for spice lovers)

2 tablespoons red wine vinegar

½ cup lightly packed fresh basil, torn or chopped into large pieces

1 loaf crusty bread, sliced and grilled or toasted

Preheat the oven to 400°F. Line a baking pan with aluminum foil. Spread 3 tablespoons of the olive oil on the foil and then top with the eggplant and mushrooms. Toss to coat with the oil. Season lightly with ¼ teaspoon of the salt and some grindings of black pepper. Roast until lightly browned around the edges, 18 to 22 minutes.

Meanwhile, heat a braising pot or wide, high-sided sauté pan over medium-high heat. Add 2 more tablespoons of the olive oil to the pan and, after a moment, the onion and celery. Season with the remaining ¼ teaspoon salt and some black pepper. Sauté for 2 to 3 minutes, until the onion becomes translucent. Increase the heat to high, then add the red pepper and sauté for another 2 to 3 minutes, until the peppers brown a little. Stir in the tomato paste and cook for another 2 to 3 minutes, until the tomato paste darkens in color. Deglaze the pan with the red wine, scraping the bottom of the pan to release any stuck-on bits. Turn the heat to medium. Add the tomatoes, garlic, pine nuts, olives, raisins, anchovies, capers, honey, red pepper flakes, red wine vinegar, and roasted eggplant and mushrooms. Add a few tablespoons of water if it appears dry at any point. Cook for 15 to 20 minutes, stirring occasionally.

Stir in the fresh basil, pull off the heat, swirl in the remaining 2 tablespoons olive oil, and season to taste with more salt and black pepper, if desired. Serve with toasts.

King Trumpet "Scallops" with
Carrot Puree, Leek, and Parsley Vinaigrette

When I was doing research on king trumpet mushrooms, I came across several recipes using the stems as faux scallops. An intriguing idea, for sure, but as a scallop lover I couldn't imagine for the life of me that anyone would be fooled into thinking a mushroom was anything like an unctuous, perfectly cooked scallop. Certainly it was different, but honestly, it was different in an equally satisfying way. As a huge seafood lover, I was surprised to note that I did not miss the scallops in this recipe. It's most important to get a good sear on the stems and baste, baste, baste!

SERVES: 4 as a first course or
2 as a main course

PAIRING: Austrian Grüner Veltliner or French Chablis (Chardonnay)

6 large king trumpet mushrooms (about ¾ pound)

1 tablespoon extra-virgin olive oil

Scant ¼ teaspoon fine sea salt

Freshly ground black pepper

CARROT PUREE

4 medium carrots (about 7 ounces), large diced

1 teaspoon fine sea salt

2 cups water

1 tablespoon unsalted butter, melted

Freshly ground black pepper

PARSLEY VINAIGRETTE

1 cup loosely packed fresh flat-leaf parsley (including stems)

¼ cup plus 2 tablespoons extra-virgin olive oil (choose a fruity mild one, not a peppery young one)

2 tablespoons apple cider vinegar

Scant ¼ teaspoon fine sea salt

1 tablespoon unsalted butter

1 tablespoon extra-virgin olive oil

4 (½-inch) sections leek (white and light green parts)

⅛ teaspoon fine sea salt

¼ cup water or Mushroom Stock (page xxiii)

Splash of white wine or dry (white) vermouth

GARNISH

Flaky sea salt (such as Maldon)

2 tablespoons tender celery leaves

2 tablespoons fresh flat-leaf parsley leaves

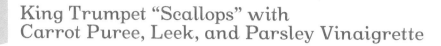

King Trumpet "Scallops" with
Carrot Puree, Leek, and Parsley Vinaigrette

CONTINUED

Preheat the oven to 400°F.

To prep and roast the mushrooms, starting at the bottom, cut two 1-inch rounds off the stem. Score the top of each mushroom with a grid pattern (see the photo on page 49). You should be left with the cap and some amount of stem left; slice this part into ¼-inch slices.

Pour the olive oil onto an aluminum foil–lined baking pan. Top with the sliced mushroom tops, and toss with the oil. Lay out the tops evenly in the pan and season with the sea salt and some black pepper. Bake for 10 minutes, then flip the mushrooms over, and bake for another 5 minutes. You're looking for a nicely caramelized, lightly crispy mushroom that ends up tasting a little bit like mushroom bacon.

To make the carrot puree, place the carrots and salt in a medium saucepan and cover with the water. Bring to a boil, then lower to a simmer and cook for 8 to 10 minutes, until the carrots are tender. Reserve ½ cup of the cooking liquid and then drain the carrots. Add the carrots, melted butter, and enough of the cooking liquid to a food processor or blender to get a very smooth puree. Season with pepper and keep warm.

To make the parsley vinaigrette, in a blender, combine the parsley, olive oil, vinegar, and salt and blend until bright green and emulsified.

To sauté the mushroom scallops, in a large skillet over medium-high heat, add the butter and olive oil. Place the stem pieces scored side down in the skillet, along with the leek sections. Sprinkle the salt over the stems and leeks. Cook, undisturbed, until the stem and leek pieces have started to brown (see the photo on page 49). Press down on the mushroom pieces to get even browning. Once browned, flip over the mushroom stems and leeks, add the water and wine, decrease the heat to medium-low, and cook until the liquid is almost gone. While the liquid slowly evaporates, occasionally tilt the pan and, using a spoon, baste the mushrooms and leeks to help keep them moist and give them a nice glaze.

To assemble, spoon a portion of carrot puree onto each dish, along with a drizzle of the parsley vinaigrette. Add 3 mushroom scallops and some crispy cap pieces, and garnish with flaky sea salt and celery and parsley leaves.

Chapter 5
Shiitake

LATIN: *Lentinula edodes*

Fact Sheet:
Shiitake

FLAVOR, TEXTURE, AND AROMA NOTES: Shiitake mushrooms are among my favorites. They are lightly smoky, assertive, and earthy, with a chewy, meaty, buttery texture. The aroma reminds me faintly of adhesive bandages (but in a good way), black pepper, and wet wood.

GENERALLY SPEAKING: Shiitake mushrooms get their name from the Japanese word for the decaying tree on which the shiitake grows (the *shii* tree). *Take* translates to "mushroom." Shiitakes are native to Korea, China, and Japan. They are not found wild in North America, but luckily for us, they are widely cultivated. You can find fresh shiitake mushrooms in almost every supermarket.

AKA: Shiitake mushrooms are also known as Chinese black mushrooms, black mushrooms, oakwood mushrooms, golden oak mushrooms, oak tree mushrooms, and black forest mushrooms.

SEASON: Because they are cultivated, growers can bring them to market year-round.

BUYING TIPS: When buying fresh shiitake, pick plump, firm, and clean ones, and pass by any that are slimy, wrinkled, or clearly dried out. The cap should be curled under; if it starts to flop outward, it's past its prime. Shiitakes with attractive white markings on the cap are especially prized; in China they are known as *huāgū*, which translates to "flower mushroom." When purchasing dried shiitake, look for intact mushrooms, though the stems need not be on the mushrooms.

CLEANING: Shiitakes are pretty straightforward to clean. First, pop off the stems (I find that a gentle rocking of the stem back and forth while holding the cap in the other hand will pull it off cleanly, without ripping the cap). A damp cloth can be used to wipe off any obvious dirt. Shiitakes are rarely very dirty at all, so there's no need to wash them in a bowl of water.

STORAGE: Shiitakes have a fairly good shelf life, staying fresh for up to a week. As with all mushrooms, store them in the refrigerator in a brown paper bag. Second choice would be to store them in a basket or box with a dry piece of paper towel or newsprint on top of them (replace this each day).

PRESERVATION:

DRYING: Shiitakes are arguably better dried. See page xxix for more information on how to dry mushrooms; see page xxx for a description of rehydrating mushrooms.

FREEZING: See page xxxi. I recommend cooking shiitakes prior to freezing them.

LOVES: Though they are often associated with Asian cuisine and ingredients such as soy sauce, sesame oil, rice, and miso, there is no reason why shiitakes can't be used in other cuisines.

COOKING NOTES: Shiitakes are quite dense, especially when rehydrated. Make sure you cook them until they are soft enough for your liking. Whether you slice them thin or thick or leave them whole, they retain their shape very well. Shiitakes really shine when you simmer them in a flavorful liquid.

SUBSTITUTE: The best substitute for a fresh shiitake mushroom is a dried shiitake mushroom, and vice-versa. And truly, you shouldn't ever be without them (not only because of their widespread availability, but also because of how great they are). But if you don't have either and you are stranded in a cabin on a high peak in Tibet, button or cremini mushrooms will do in a pinch. Hold the yak butter.

NERDY FACTOIDS:

• Shiitake mushrooms have been cultivated for over 1,000 years.

• Studies on animals have shown that shiitakes contain compounds that lower cholesterol, inhibit viruses, and have antitumor properties. Clinical trials on humans need to confirm that the compounds in shiitakes are effective in preventing or treating disease.

• Shiitake mushrooms were banned in the United States until after 1972 because the USDA confused shiitake's Latin name (*Lentinula edodes*) with that of a fungus, *Lentinus lepideus*, which attacks railroad ties.

Spiced Basmati Rice with Shiitake Mushrooms and Garbanzo Beans (Biryani)

Celebrated cookbook author Raghavan Iyer is one of my favorite people whom I have never met in person. I got the chance to do the food styling on one of his many cookbooks and have since struck up a virtual friendship with him. We share a mutual love of earthy spices, fresh herbs, and twisted humor. He agreed to contribute a recipe to this book, which I've adapted and to which I've added a version of my raita (spiced yogurt) as a garnish. From Raghavan: "Biryanis (from the Persian term biriyan, meaning "to fry before cooking"), of which there are more than thirty-five varieties across India, were introduced and made popular by several invaders—the Moghuls being of prime influence, having gathered the knowledge from the Persians. The Nawabs of Lucknow and the Nizams of Hyderabad popularized these layered meat-rice-nut dishes all across India. This particular biryani is a simplified version of the layered creations that grace our tables. For simple dinners, on many an occasion, I have sat down in the peaceful cushioned comfort of my favorite rocking chair (yes, I am old, get over it!) with a large plateful of mushroom biryani and plain yogurt. Heaven could not be better than this!"

SERVES: 4 | PAIRING: French Gewurtztraminer

1 cup white Indian or Pakistani basmati rice

2 tablespoons ghee (substitute 1 tablespoon unsalted butter and 1 tablespoon coconut oil)

6 whole cloves

6 green or white cardamom pods

1 teaspoon cumin seeds

½ teaspoon fennel seeds (optional)

2 (3-inch) cinnamon sticks

1 fresh or dried bay leaf

½ pound fresh shiitake mushrooms, stems removed (saved for stock) and thinly sliced

2 large cloves garlic, minced

2 to 3 green serrano chiles, stems removed and finely chopped

1 tomato, cored and finely chopped (about ¾ cup)

¼ cup finely chopped fresh cilantro (leaves and stems)

2 teaspoons fine sea salt

1 (15.5-ounce) can garbanzo beans, rinsed and drained

2 cups cold water

¼ cup chopped fresh mint

Raita (recipe follows), for serving

Place the rice in a medium bowl. Fill the bowl halfway with water to cover the rice. Gently rub the slender grains between the fingers of one hand, without breaking them, to wash off any dust or light foreign objects (like loose husks), which will float to the surface. The water will become cloudy. Drain this water (you don't need a colander for this; just carefully tip the bowl over the sink to pour off the water, making sure the rice stays in the bowl). Repeat 3 or 4 times until the water, after you rinse the grains, remains relatively clear; drain. Now fill the bowl halfway with cold water and let the rice sit at room temperature until the kernels soften, 20 to 30 minutes; drain.

Heat the ghee in a medium saucepan over medium-high heat. Once it appears to shimmer, sprinkle in the cloves, cardamom, cumin seeds, fennel seeds, if using, cinnamon, and bay leaf. Allow them to sizzle and perfume the oil, 20 to 30 seconds. Add the mushrooms, garlic, and chiles; stir-fry to soften and lightly brown the mushrooms and garlic, 2 to 3 minutes.

Add the drained rice, tomato, cilantro, salt, and garbanzo beans. Toss everything together gently. Pour in the 2 cups cold water. Stir the mixture once or twice to incorporate the ingredients. Allow the water to boil, uncovered, still over medium-high heat, until it has evaporated from the surface and craters start to appear in the rice, 5 to 8 minutes. Then (and not until then) stir once or twice to bring the partially cooked layer from the bottom of the pan to the surface. Cover the pan with a tight-fitting lid and decrease the heat to the lowest possible setting. Let steep for 8 to 10 minutes (8 for an electric burner, 10 for a gas burner). Then turn off the heat and let the pan stand on that burner, undisturbed, for an additional 10 minutes.

Uncover the pan, fluff the rice with a fork, and serve sprinkled with the fresh mint. You may choose to remove the cloves, bay leaf, cardamom, and cinnamon before you serve. I usually leave them in since they continue to perfume the rice and just instruct the folks eating the rice to watch for those whole spices and eat around them. Serve with the raita.

Raita

1 teaspoon ghee or coconut oil

½ teaspoon cumin seeds

1 cup plain whole-milk yogurt

¼ cup seeded and small diced cucumber

¼ teaspoon fine sea salt

Heat the ghee in a small sauté pan over medium-low heat. Add the cumin seeds and cook until they darken in color and you can smell their distinct earthy aroma. Pour into a bowl along with the yogurt, cucumber, and salt, and stir to combine. Chill until you are ready to serve the biryani.

Shiitake-Noodle Salad with Nuoc Cham and Herbs

This recipe is based on one of my favorite summertime dishes: Vietnamese bun or noodle salad. Traditionally room-temperature rice noodles are served with both hot and cold garnishes and sauced with what I consider the "salsa" of Vietnamese cuisine: *nuoc cham* or spicy lime and fish sauce. Shiitakes are my favorite cultivated mushroom, and they really take a starring role in this dish. They are bursting with flavor, especially when you add ingredients that support their savory nature—ingredients with natural glutamates such as soy sauce and tomato. This healthful and light dish is an excellent example of the whole being greater than the sum of its parts. The mushrooms can be made the day before and reheated. The dressing can be made several days ahead. If you end up frying the shallots for the bonus garnish (and I highly recommend it), they can be fried earlier in the day and left at room temperature.

SERVES: 4 | **PAIRING:** French Riesling

1 heaping tablespoon kosher salt

1½ pounds wide rice noodles (it may say "stir-fry rice noodles" on the packaging; I use thin pad thai noodles for this dish)

SHIITAKE SEASONING
1 tablespoon tomato paste

2 teaspoons soy sauce

2 teaspoons seasoned rice vinegar

2 teaspoons toasted sesame oil

2 tablespoons coconut oil, melted, plus more for brushing the pan

Freshly ground black pepper (optional)

1 teaspoon Porcini Powder (page xxiii; optional, though awesome)

1 pound shiitake mushrooms, stems removed (saved for stock)

BONUS GARNISH
1 cup vegetable oil

½ cup thinly sliced shallots, separated into rings

⅛ teaspoon fine sea salt

FIXINGS
1 head red leaf or green leaf lettuce, cut into bite-size pieces

1 medium carrot, peeled and julienned

1 medium cucumber, seeded and julienned

1 cup thinly shredded red cabbage

½ cup roasted, salted peanuts

1 cup packed fresh basil leaves

½ cup fresh mint leaves

Nuoc Cham Sauce (recipe follows)

Place a rack in the middle of the oven and preheat the broiler to high.

Bring a medium pot of water to a full rolling boil. Add the salt and then the noodles, turn off the heat, stir well, and let sit in the water for 8 to 12 minutes. Stir from time to time. Check for doneness at about 8 minutes. You want the noodles to be al dente (soft but just slightly firm in the middle). As soon as they are done, drain them through a colander and run cold water over them to stop the cooking. Set aside at room temperature.

In a small bowl, whisk together all of the ingredients for the shiitake seasoning. Add the mushrooms and, with your hands, mix the seasoning onto the shiitakes. Brush a little melted coconut oil onto a parchment paper–lined baking pan and add the shiitakes, gills down. Broil for 5 to 6 minutes on one side, until browned, then flip over and broil on the other side for 3 to 4 minutes. Alternatively, grill over a medium-hot fire until caramelized on both sides.

To make the garnish, heat the oil in a small saucepan to 350°F. Add the shallots and fry until lightly browned. Remove with a slotted spoon and drain on paper towels. Sprinkle the salt over the top of the shallots and reserve at room temperature until ready to serve.

To serve, rewarm the mushrooms either in a hot oven or in a skillet, if necessary. Place an equal amount of lettuce at the bottom of 4 bowls. Top with the noodles, carrot, cucumber, cabbage, peanuts, basil, mint, fried shallots, and warm mushrooms. Serve the *nuoc cham* sauce at the table. Instruct your guests to apply liberally.

Nuoc Cham Sauce

⅔ cup water

½ cup freshly squeezed lime juice (about 4 limes)

2 tablespoons fish sauce

¼ cup sugar

6 Thai chiles, minced (substitute 1 serrano chile with seeds and 1 Cherry Bomb chile, seeded)

2 cloves garlic, minced and mashed to a paste

2 tablespoons finely shredded carrot (optional)

Whisk the water, lime juice, fish sauce, sugar, chiles, garlic, and carrot, if using, together in a bowl. Make sure the sugar gets dissolved. This sauce will keep in your fridge for 1 week.

Ma Po Tofu with Shiitakes and Broad Bean and Chili Paste

If sitting cold and blobby on a forlorn salad bar is skid row for a cube of tofu, then swimming in this spicy, tingly sauce is nirvana. I almost want to drop tofu from the recipe title because people get so judgmental when they see that word. They imagine that depressed salad bar from their college days or recipes with names like TofuLoaf. Good tofu, when prepared correctly, can be silky or crispy, absorbing all the neighboring flavors while still maintaining its subtle, slightly nutty character. The shiitakes in this recipe take the place of the traditional beef, making this Sichuan classic vegetarian. The chili paste (*doubanjiang*) is crucial to the success of this recipe, so see the Note for more information on how to source it.

SERVES: 4 | PAIRING: Off-dry German Riesling

1 tablespoon kosher salt

¾ pound firm tofu, cut into ½-inch cubes

2 tablespoons coconut oil

¾ pound fresh or rehydrated dried shiitakes, medium diced

1 teaspoon fine sea salt

1 tablespoon sugar

1½ tablespoons soy sauce

¼ cup Shaoxing rice wine

2 cups shredded red cabbage, plus ¼ cup very finely shredded

2 tablespoons doubanjiang (see Note), very finely minced

2¼ cups Mushroom Stock (page xxiii)

1½ teaspoons Sichuan chili oil

1 teaspoon toasted sesame oil

1 bunch scallions, green parts cut into 1-inch sections, white parts cut thinly on the bias

2 teaspoons cornstarch

Steamed rice, for serving

Fill a wok or saucepan with water. Add the kosher salt and bring to a boil. Turn the heat down to a low simmer and carefully drop the tofu cubes into the water. Cook for 1 to 2 minutes and then gently transfer to a colander to let the tofu drain for a minute. This process helps firm up the tofu so it doesn't crumble as easily when stirring later. Discard the water.

Reheat the wok over medium high heat. Add 1 tablespoon of the coconut oil and then the shiitake mushroom pieces, along with a rounded ¼ teaspoon of the fine sea salt. Cook, stirring occasionally, until they start to brown, about 5 minutes. Add 1 teaspoon of the sugar, the soy sauce, and rice wine and sauté until all of the liquid evaporates.

Add the 2 cups shredded cabbage to the wok, along with the remaining ¾ teaspoon sea salt, and cook for 2 to 3 minutes, until the cabbage begins to soften. Scoop out a clean space in the middle of the wok and add the remaining 1 tablespoon coconut oil. Right on top of the oil, add the *doubanjiang* and fry the paste, stirring it around on the bottom of the wok (don't inhale too deeply or the chiles will git ya), about 2 minutes. Add 2 cups of the stock, the remaining 2 teaspoons sugar, the tofu, Sichuan chili oil, and sesame oil. Carefully stir the tofu around in the sauce (I find a lift-and-turn method with a flat wooden spatula or wok tool works well here). Reduce the sauce by one-third, 5 to 7 minutes. Stir in the scallion greens.

In a small bowl, mix the cornstarch with the remaining ¼ cup stock. Clear out some space in the middle of the wok. Add the slurry and gently stir. The slurry will lightly thicken the sauce in about a minute, making everything glossy. Don't boil the liquid for more than a minute, as the cornstarch will break down and the sauce can thin out. Garnish with the scallion whites and finely shredded red cabbage. Serve with steamed rice.

NOTE: *Doubanjiang* is a salty, spicy paste made from fermented soybeans, broad beans, salt, rice (or wheat), and chiles. The best *doubanjiang* is from the town of Pixian, in Sichuan Province, China. You can order it online through Amazon (look for the one from Pixian), though if you live in a city with good Asian markets, you might find it locally.

Shiitake Temaki
with Shiso and Avocado

The hand roll is Japan's answer to the sandwich. It's at its best when eaten right away after being made so that the nori stays crisp. *Shiso* or perilla, also known as Japanese mint, is for some an acquired taste but for others an instant addiction. Shiso has the perfume of cilantro and the spark of mint, but it's really its very own thing, nearly impossible to describe. I find it to be the perfect bright note to accent the depth of the braised shiitake mushrooms.

SERVES: 4 (makes 8 hand rolls) | PAIRING: Green tea or Daigingō-shu (sake)

RICE
1 cup sushi rice

1 cup plus 1 tablespoon water

Dash of sake (optional)

BRAISED SHIITAKE MUSHROOMS
1½ teaspoons coconut oil

16 medium fresh or dried shiitake mushrooms, stems removed (saved for stock)

1½ teaspoons soy sauce

1 tablespoon sake

1 teaspoon mirin

¼ cup Mushroom Stock (page xxiii)

3 to 4 tablespoons seasoned rice vinegar

OTHER FILLINGS
4 sheets nori (the standard sheets used for sushi), halved (following the direction of the lines)

Wasabi

½ avocado, cut into ¼ by 3-inch strips

3 ounces cucumber, seeded and julienned

8 shiso leaves, torn in half

FOR SERVING
Soy sauce

Pickled ginger

To make the rice, first wash it by placing it in a large bowl. Fill the bowl with cold water. Using your hands, agitate the rice in the bowl as if you were "hand-washing socks" (as my Japanese chef instructor from culinary school, Chef KG, told us). Scrub the rice well and then drain the water off the rice. Fill the bowl of rice with more cold running water and this time let the water run over the rice freely. Run the water until it's clear. Fill the bowl with cold water to cover and let the rice sit for 30 minutes (this step is crucial for the rice to come out right, because during the 30-minute soak, the rice kernels soften).

Now you are ready to cook the rice. Drain thoroughly in a colander, then add to a medium saucepan or rice cooker along with the measured water. Add the sake, if using. Cook on the stovetop by boiling the rice over high heat. Turn the rice down to a gentle simmer, cover, and cook for exactly 20 minutes (you can start braising the shiitakes while you wait). Remove from the heat and leave the lid on to finish steaming the rice for 10 more minutes. If you have a rice cooker, follow the manufacturer's directions, keeping in mind you should let it steam in its "warm" or off mode for the same 10 minutes without opening the lid.

To braise the shiitakes, in a medium skillet over medium-high heat, melt the coconut oil. Add the shiitakes, cap side down. Cook until browned, then flip over and brown the other side, about 6 minutes total. Mix the soy, sake, mirin, and stock in a cup. Pour over the mushrooms. Bring to a boil, then decrease to the lowest heat setting and cover. Cook for 5 minutes, remove the cover, flip the mushrooms, raise the heat to medium-high, and cook until all the liquid evaporates and the mushrooms are glazed. Remove and slice the mushrooms in half.

When the rice is done and has rested for the 10 minutes, gently (you don't want to smash the rice) transfer to a wide bowl. Have a friend help you fan the rice with a fanning tool of your choice while you gently incorporate the rice vinegar. The fanning will give your rice a nice shine. Try to use the sushi rice as soon as possible. Keep a warm, damp towel over the rice in between making rolls. Don't keep out at room temperature for longer than 2 hours.

To form the rolls, have all the components ready, including a bowl of cold water spiked with some seasoned rice vinegar to dip your hands into. Put a half sheet of nori down in front of you with the long side closest to you, shiny side down. Wet your hands lightly. Grab a large golf ball–size round of rice. Spread the rice on the left side of the nori, leaving a little room in the lower left corner. With your finger, channel out a little space in the rice at an angle from the upper left of the nori down toward the bottom. Spread a little bit of wasabi along the channel. Add a slice of avocado, a few slices of cucumber, 4 shiitake halves, and 2 shiso halves. Start rolling the nori around the fillings by picking up the lower left corner and folding it up and over the filling at an angle toward the right upper corner; keep rolling it up (ideally you start to form a point at the bottom, like an ice-cream cone). Use a few kernels of sushi rice to seal the corner (Japanese spackle). Repeat to form all the rolls. Serve right away before the nori gets soft, with soy sauce, more wasabi, and pickled ginger.

Dan Dan Noodles with Shiitakes, Pork, Pickled Mustard Greens, and Spicy Chili Oil

This recipe is named after the shoulder pole (dan) that vendors in Sichuan Province, China, used to hoist their baskets of secret mouth-numbing sauces and noodles. I'll be perfectly honest: I don't know much about Sichuan cuisine. Or I didn't, until quite recently. As a Jew from the East Coast, my knowledge of Chinese cuisine began and ended with Christmas Day bowls of crispy fried wonton strips dipped in duck sauce and hot mustard, egg drop soup, and chicken with cashews. One of my very close friends is obsessed with Sichuan cuisine. He went to Sichuan Province to study culinary arts for two weeks and came back slinging noodles, Pixian broad bean chili paste, and tingly Sichuan peppercorns. It was like Christmas, but every day and much, much spicier. Five stars, blow-your-mouth-up spicy. I've put my twist on dan dan noodles (aka Sichuan Bolognese) by relying on the natural umami-giving flavor of mushrooms and making my own quick-pickled mustard greens and chili-peanut oil. This is what I like to call White Girl Safe™, though certainly not so dumbed down as to be unrecognizable as the real thing. Trust me: I was sweating while eating my test batches. To reach maximum Sichuan fire in the hole, use a generous ⅓ cup chili oil rather than ¼ cup, though be warned that next-day side effects are unpredictable.

SERVES: 4 | PAIRING: Off-dry German Riesling

PICKLED MUSTARD GREENS
2 tablespoons kosher salt

8 ounces mustard greens

½ cup seasoned rice vinegar

PORK-SHIITAKE MIXTURE
3 tablespoons coconut oil

½ pound shiitake mushrooms, halved

½ teaspoon fine sea salt

2 tablespoons soy sauce

1 teaspoon sugar

¼ cup Shaoxing rice wine

½ pound ground pork

2 tablespoons julienned fresh ginger

1 tablespoon minced garlic

1 bunch scallions, greens cut into 1-inch pieces and then julienned, whites sliced into thin rounds

2 teaspoons fermented flour paste (tianmianjiang, or substitute hoisin)

1 cup Mushroom Stock (page xxiii)

1 tablespoon Chinese black vinegar

¼ cup homemade chili-peanut oil (page xxii; or substitute purchased chili oil, but make sure it has chunks of chile in it), plus more for garnish

1 pound fresh wheat noodles (Korean, Chinese, or dried spaghetti)

Dan Dan Noodles with Shiitakes, Pork, Pickled Mustard Greens, and Spicy Chili Oil

CONTINUED

To make the pickled mustard greens, bring a large pot of water to a boil (you can use it for the pasta afterward). Add the kosher salt. Blanch the mustard greens in the water for 2 minutes. Get a bowl of cold water ready. Plunge the mustard greens into the cold water to stop the cooking. Once cool, drain the greens, squeezing out all the water with your hands. Bunch up the greens and chop into bite-size strips. Put back in the empty bowl, pour the rice vinegar over the top, mix well, and let it sit for 30 minutes while you work on the rest of the dish.

To make the pork-shiitake mixture, heat a large skillet or wok over medium-high heat. Add 1 tablespoon of the coconut oil. Add the shiitakes and salt. Panfry the shiitakes until they kick off their moisture and start to brown, about 5 minutes. Add 1 tablespoon of the soy sauce, sugar, and rice wine and simmer until all the liquid evaporates. Transfer the shiitakes to a bowl.

Add another 2 tablespoons coconut oil to the pan and then the pork, breaking it up as you fry it. Once all the pink is gone, add the ginger, garlic, the sliced white part of the scallions, and the fermented flour paste. Fry for 1 to 2 minutes. Add the remaining 1 tablespoon soy sauce, mushroom stock, black vinegar, and chili oil. Simmer for 5 minutes, and then keep warm.

Squeeze all of the rice vinegar out of the mustard greens and set aside (you can reuse the rice vinegar for salad dressings; just refrigerate it for up to 3 weeks).

Cook the noodles according to the package directions. Drain the water from the noodles when they are al dente. Pour the pork-shiitake sauce over the noodles and mix well. Serve each person a portion of noodles, and top with the shiitakes, some pickled mustard greens, and julienned scallions. Drizzle some more chili oil on and around the noodles and serve more at the table.

Chapter 6

Maitake

LATIN: *Grifola frondosa*

Fact Sheet:
Maitake

FLAVOR, TEXTURE, AND AROMA NOTES: Maitake mushrooms are pretty powerful—they are strongly nutty and earthy, with a crunchy, resilient, firm texture. Sometimes they smell like blue cheese or beer-like to me, musty (in a good way), and woodsy.

GENERALLY SPEAKING: Maitake mushrooms grow wild in deciduous, temperate northern forests. They can be found in eastern Canada, northeastern and Mid-Atlantic states in the United States, northeastern Japan, and temperate hardwood forests of China and Europe (where it was first discovered). They are also known as bracket fungi and are mostly found living on tree trunks or branches (oak and elm are typical), but some can inhabit the soil. Maitakes are one of the few mushrooms that taste arguably as good cultivated as they do wild.

AKA: Maitake means "dancing mushroom" in Japanese, and this mushroom is also known as hen-of-the-woods, dancing butterfly, *kumotake* ("cloud mushroom"), ram's head, sheep's head, and signorina (Italian American).

SEASON: The U.S. East Coast season for wild maitake is in the fall. Most maitake mushrooms you'll find in the marketplace, however, are cultivated and available year-round.

BUYING TIPS: Make sure there is no drying or shredding at the edges. The aroma should be a good musty and not a fermented, off-putting, stinky musty. I bet you never knew there were different forms of musty.

CLEANING: Cultivated maitake will be extraordinarily clean. Simply slice the woodier/tougher parts off the stem where the cap clusters converge. If you happen to get your hands on a wild maitake, you might need to carve out some cleaning time—and rinsing it in a big bowl of water might be a good start. It's easier if you cut the large maitake into manageable sections to expose more of the crevices where the dirt hides.

STORAGE: Maitake, like beech mushrooms, are often sold in what looks like a plastic-bagged death trap for mushrooms, but the bags have microscopic pores in them, allowing for a slightly longer shelf life. You can choose to leave them in the bags until you are ready to use them, though my expert-forager friend recommends against it. They are marketed as being packaged in "breathable" plastic, but funky molds and aromas can nonetheless develop inside those bags. I don't think it's much of a concern if you will use the mushrooms within a week or two, but if you plan on storing them for any longer, I suggest transferring them to a brown paper bag or basket with a dry piece of paper towel or newsprint on top of them (replace this each day).

PRESERVATION:

DRYING: See page xxix; see page xxx for a description of rehydrating mushrooms.

FREEZING: See page xxxi. For maitakes, I'd recommend cooking them prior to freezing.

LOVES: Maitakes are bold and as such can hold up to big ingredients and assertive cooking techniques. Think grilling and smoking, spice and butter.

COOKING NOTES: Maitakes really show off their deep woodsy flavor when caramelized by either grilling or roasting.

SUBSTITUTE: If you can't find maitake, a good substitute would be morels or oyster mushrooms plus some dried porcini.

NERDY FACTOIDS:

- Many studies point to the antitumor properties of the maitake mushroom.

- In Japan, the maitake can grow to more than 50 pounds.

- There are no poisonous lookalikes.

- They are one of the few excellent edible wild mushrooms that do not grow in the bountiful mushroom-growing nirvana that is the West Coast of the United States.

Maitake with Roasted Red Pepper Sauce and Smoked Paprika

Squishing the maitake "steaks" between two pans—faux panini-style—is a great way to speed up the cooking process. The water is forced out as the mushrooms are pressed into a very hot skillet (cast iron highly recommended here). You'll be left with some extra sauce, so if the mood strikes you, feel free to turn this appetizer recipe into a main course by cooking up some pasta, tossing the red pepper sauce (thin it a bit with some pasta cooking water or mushroom stock) with the pasta, and sprinkling the maitake over the top. Alternatively, serve this appetizer with a nice crusty bread so that people can dip it liberally into the sauce.

SERVES: 4 as an appetizer | **PAIRING:** Spanish rosado

1 tablespoon coconut oil

½ pound maitake mushrooms, broken or sliced into 4 sections or "steaks," tough parts of the stems removed (saved for stock)

½ teaspoon fine sea salt

Freshly ground black pepper

RED PEPPER SAUCE
12 ounces bottled roasted red peppers, drained

2 small cloves garlic

½ cup walnuts, toasted (page xxiv)

¼ cup extra-virgin olive oil

1 tablespoon freshly squeezed lemon juice

1 teaspoon Spanish smoked paprika

1 teaspoon fine sea salt

½ teaspoon honey

¼ teaspoon cayenne pepper

1 tablespoon fresh flat-leaf parsley leaves, cut into chiffonade

In a large skillet over medium-high heat, melt the coconut oil. Add the maitake mushroom pieces. Rub a little coconut oil on the bottom of a smaller heavy skillet (cast iron is perfect, or if you don't have one, use a lightweight skillet and put a can or two in the skillet to add heft) and use it to weigh down the mushrooms to create a nice sear on the bottom of the sections. After a few minutes, check the mushrooms; once the liquid has evaporated and the bottom has started to brown, flip the mushroom sections over and weigh down with the small skillet again. The mushrooms are done when they are crispy at the edges, brown in sections, and tender. Break off a little piece and taste to check for proper doneness. Season with the salt and pepper.

To make the red pepper sauce, combine all of the ingredients in a food processor and blend to a creamy consistency. Taste for salt and pepper.

Place a generous spoonful of sauce on each plate. Top with a portion of mushrooms. Garnish with the parsley.

Clay Pot Maitake and Bok Choy with Sake and Ginger Sauce

You can find unglazed clay pots at Asian markets or online. The first time you use them you'll need to soak them overnight in a bucket of water or in the sink (weighing them down if necessary). The next day they will be oven-safe. They make fun individual serving vessels; just make sure you have trivets to set them on at the table, and warn your guests not to touch them. It's fun to come around the table with an oven mitt, lifting everyone's lid off (*Downton Abbey* style). There is no better way to enjoy the aromas. Foil pouches are less sexy but no less flavorful, so I've included information on how to prepare the dish that way, too. Serve with a pot of steamed rice, and if you've made the chili-peanut oil on page xxii, the heat seekers in your family will love you more.

SERVES: 4 | PAIRING: French Riesling

2 tablespoons coconut oil

1 pound fresh maitake mushrooms, broken into large pieces

¼ teaspoon fine sea salt

4 cups chopped baby bok choy (about 3 heads)

2 cups thinly sliced red cabbage

½ pint cherry tomatoes, halved, or 1 tomato, medium diced

4 scallions, sliced in half crosswise and then lengthwise

¼ cup soy sauce

¼ cup sake

¼ cup mirin

1 teaspoon brown sugar

1 tablespoon grated fresh ginger

4 cloves garlic, thinly sliced

1 or 2 jalapeños, halved, seeded, membranes removed, and sliced

4 tablespoons unsalted butter

GARNISH

Toasted sesame seeds

Chopped fresh cilantro

Homemade Chili-Peanut Oil (page xxii)

Soak 4 clay pots in water overnight; or substitute by using foil packages, no advance prep needed. Preheat the oven to 400°F if you are using foil packages.

Heat 2 large skillets over high heat. (If you don't have 2 large skillets, cook the mushrooms in 2 batches.) Add 1 tablespoon coconut oil to each pan. Add half of the maitake mushrooms and ⅛ teaspoon sea salt to each pan. Mix the mushrooms once, then spread them out, and then don't flip over until there is some color on the bottom of them. Don't cook for longer than 5 minutes. Remove from the pans.

In the bottom of the 4 clay pots or on one side of 4 (17-inch) sheets of aluminum foil, lay down the bok choy, cabbage, tomatoes, and scallions. Top with the browned maitake mushrooms.

Mix the soy sauce, sake, mirin, brown sugar, ginger, garlic, and jalapeño in a small bowl and distribute equally over the 4 bowls or foil packages. Top each with 1 tablespoon of the butter. Cover the pots or tightly fold the edges of the foil packages so no liquid leaks out. If you are using clay pots, place them on a large baking pan and place in a cold oven that you set to 400°F (clay needs to gradually be heated up or you risk cracking it). Bake the clay pots for 25 minutes. Bake the foil packets for 15 minutes in the preheated oven. Season to taste and garnish with sesame seeds, cilantro, and chili oil.

Maitake, Pancetta, and Port-Soaked Dried Cherry Stuffing

I'm sure it comes as no surprise that Thanksgiving is the favorite holiday of most chefs and foodies. Sure, food plays an important role in other holidays. The candy binging of Halloween and Christmas, for example, or the absence of it for Yom Kippur, or the delaying of it at Passover or during Ramadan. But Thanksgiving exists purely for the celebration of food. Growing up, it was sort of a game to see who could be first to commandeer our grandparents' cushy "couch of perpetual sleep" in a tryptophan-induced turkey haze. The stuffing of my childhood was very simple: celery, onions, packaged who-knows-how-old bread cubes, and dried thyme. My grandmother would probably turn her nose up at my gourmet version. Cherries? Mai-what mushrooms? "Isn't Pepperidge Farm artisan bread?" she'd probably ask. Gummy (as she was known) lived to be 101 years old, making her more than entitled to think so.

SERVES: 6 to 8 | PAIRING: Oregon Pinot Noir

9 cups crunchy artisan bread, cut into 1-inch cubes (from a 22-ounce loaf)

½ cup ruby port

½ cup unsweetened dried Bing cherries

1 tablespoon minced fresh sage, plus 3 whole leaves

1 tablespoon fine sea salt, plus a pinch

¼ pound pancetta (substitute bacon)

4 tablespoons unsalted butter, plus more for greasing the baking dish

2 large yellow onions, small diced

6 stalks celery, small diced

⅓ cup dry (white) vermouth

½ pound button mushrooms

½ pound maitake mushrooms

½ cup coarsely chopped fresh flat-leaf parsley

¼ cup pine nuts, toasted (page xxiv)

2 teaspoons minced fresh thyme

½ teaspoon cayenne pepper

3 large eggs, lightly beaten

3 to 4 cups Mushroom Stock (page xxiii)

Freshly ground black pepper

Preheat the oven to 300°F. Butter a 9 by 12-inch casserole dish.

Lay the bread cubes on a large baking pan. Bake for 30 minutes to dry the bread out.

Heat the port, cherries, the 3 sage leaves, and a pinch of salt over medium-high heat until it starts to boil. Lower to a simmer and cook until the liquid is almost all gone. Remove the sage leaves.

In a large skillet over medium heat, add the pancetta and lower the heat slightly. Render the fat from the pancetta, occasionally stirring it to prevent sticking. When it is nicely browned and crisp, transfer it with a slotted spoon to a paper towel–lined plate, leaving the fat behind in the pan. Add 1 tablespoon of the butter to the pancetta fat and then add the onions, celery, and 2 teaspoons salt and, stirring occasionally, cook until the vegetables are soft and beginning to brown, about 15 minutes. Deglaze the pan with the vermouth, scraping the bottom of the pan for any delicious brown bits. Transfer the vegetables to a large bowl. Meanwhile, preheat the oven to 400°F.

Add 2 tablespoons of the butter to the skillet and, when the bubbles have died down, add the mushrooms, along with ½ teaspoon salt and black pepper, tossing them frequently until the water has evaporated and the mushrooms have shrunk in size. Then spread them out in the pan and let them cook undisturbed for a couple of minutes so they can start to brown. Give them a final toss and one more opportunity to brown. Place the mushrooms in the bowl with the vegetables. Then add the bread, cherries, parsley, pine nuts, thyme, minced sage, and cayenne. In a separate bowl, beat the eggs, and add 3 cups of the stock and ½ teaspoon salt. Mix well. Pour over the bread and vegetables and mix everything up really well. If it seems dry, go ahead and add up to 1 more cup of stock. The stuffing should be fairly wet going into the oven.

Place the stuffing in the prepared casserole dish, dot the top with the remaining 1 tablespoon butter broken up into small pieces, and cover with aluminum foil. Bake for 25 minutes. Uncover and bake until golden, another 15 to 20 minutes.

Báhn Xèo: Vietnamese Crepes with Caramelized Maitake Mushrooms and Oregon Pink Shrimp

The beauty of this dish lies in the contrasts: crispy crepe edge meets soft middle; warm ingredients rolled in cool lettuce and herbs; and a savory, earthy filling with a sweet, spicy, bright sauce. *Bánh xèo* (pronounced bun SAY ow) translates to "sizzling bread"; you'll know exactly how it got its name when you pour the batter into the pan. I won't lie to you. This dish takes experience to master. You will definitely want to use a nonstick pan. I rank this dish in my top 10 "Death Bed Dinners." I surely hope that when my time comes, my wife, April, will know how to make it.

SERVES: 4 to 8
(makes 4 large crepes)

PAIRING: French Gewurtztraminer or Thai or Vietnamese beer, such as Singha or 333 (pronounced ba ba ba)

CREPES

2 cups white rice flour

1 teaspoon fine sea salt

1 teaspoon sugar

1 teaspoon ground turmeric

1 teaspoon curry powder (Vietnamese or Indian Madras-style)

4 scallions, sliced

½ cup coconut milk

4 cups water, plus more if needed

FILLING

1 tablespoon peanut or coconut oil, plus more for cooking the crepes

½ medium yellow onion, halved and sliced into thin half-moons

½ pound maitake mushrooms, torn into bite-size pieces

¼ teaspoon fine sea salt

½ pound Oregon pink shrimp (cooked and peeled tiny salad shrimp)

FIXINGS

1 head green leaf lettuce, leaves separated

½ bunch cilantro

½ bunch basil

1 cucumber, thin decorative strips peeled off with a vegetable peeler or citrus stripper, then cut into ¼-inch slices

Nuoc Cham Sauce (page 59)

To make the crepes, whisk all of the ingredients together in a bowl. Set aside.

To prepare the filling, heat the oil in a large sauté pan over medium-high heat. Add the onion, mushrooms, and salt and sauté until browned and tender, 10 to 15 minutes. Add a splash of water if it starts to stick. Add the shrimp and cook until the shrimp are heated through, 2 more minutes. Taste and adjust the seasonings if necessary. Set aside and keep warm.

To cook the crepes, heat a medium nonstick sauté pan over medium-high heat. Add a film of oil. Wait 30 seconds to heat the oil, whisk the batter to ensure it's well mixed, and then ladle out enough crepe batter to cover the bottom of the pan, tilting the pan to spread it over the bottom. (If it has thickened while you were cooking the filling, thin out with a few tablespoons of water. It should be the consistency of thin pancake batter.) Do not disturb the crepe. Let it cook for 5 to 7 minutes on one side (it takes longer than you think). Check it carefully by lifting up one edge with a rubber spatula. It should be crisp around the outside, lacy, and brown. At that point, carefully flip the crepe over onto the other side (using 2 spatulas might be helpful here). Cook the other side of the crepe for a minute or two and then flip back over. Cook until the original side has become nice and crisp, especially around the edges. Slide the crepe out of the pan. You can lay them out on a parchment–lined tray and hold them at room temperature until you are ready to fill them. Repeat with the remaining batter.

To fill the crepes, layer one-quarter of the filling over one side of the crepe (like an omelette) and flip half of the crepe over on itself. It may crack—that's fine.

Serve with the fixings. It's traditionally eaten by putting a slice of the crepe inside a piece of leaf lettuce along with some herbs and cucumber. Dip it in the *nuoc cham* sauce and try not to drip the sauce all over your shirt.

Maitake Tikka Masala

Caramelized, smoky maitake mushrooms meet spiced, velvety tomato cream and an Indian love child is born, right in your own kitchen. When it comes to my heritage, I firmly believe there was a switch-up in the hospital. When the aroma of toasting cumin, coriander, cinnamon, and turmeric reaches my nose, I'm reminded of where my soul was actually born, and it wasn't New Jersey. The dried fenugreek leaves that are called for (menthi) are unusual but an absolutely addictive addition to the sauce. You can find them at Indian grocers or online. Serve this dish with fragrant basmati rice, perhaps even with the shiitake dish on page 54, as well as various Indian pickles and chutneys.

SERVES: 4 | PAIRING: French Pinot Blanc

1½ teaspoons coriander seeds

1 teaspoon cumin seeds

½ teaspoon red pepper flakes

Seeds of 3 cardamom pods (about ¼ teaspoon)

1 (1-inch) piece cinnamon stick

½ teaspoon ground turmeric

1½ tablespoons menthi (fenugreek leaves)

1 charcoal briquette (I recommend using a natural hardwood charcoal)

3 tablespoons ghee

½ cup small-diced shallot

1½ teaspoons fine sea salt

1 tablespoon minced garlic

1 tablespoon grated fresh ginger

14 ounces maitake mushrooms, main stem trimmed, caps torn into bite-size pieces

2 medium red tomatoes, cored

½ cup Mushroom Stock (page xxiii)

2 teaspoons honey

½ cup Greek yogurt

½ cup heavy cream

1 medium Yukon Gold potato, medium diced (about 1½ cups)

In a medium skillet over medium-high heat, toast the coriander seeds, cumin seeds, red pepper flakes, cardamom seeds, and cinnamon stick until they darken lightly and start to smell, 1 to 2 minutes (no oil necessary). When toasted, add the ground turmeric and stir into the spices for 10 to 15 seconds. Transfer to a spice grinder, add the menthi, and grind into a fine powder.

Light the charcoal briquette outside (in your grill or other suitable place).

In a large sauté pan over medium-high heat, place 2 tablespoons of the ghee. After a moment, add the shallot and salt and sauté for 2 to 3 minutes, until translucent. Add the garlic and ginger and sauté for 1 minute, until aromatic, and then add the maitake. Increase the heat to high and sauté, allowing the mushrooms to brown around the edges, 4 to 5 minutes.

Meanwhile, in a blender, puree the tomatoes, stock, honey, yogurt, cream, and spices. Add to the sauté pan along with the potato. Simmer for 15 minutes, or until the potato is tender. Turn the heat off. Now here's the really fun part. Open a window, turn on your kitchen fan, and place a small heatproof dish in the middle of the curry. Once the charcoal briquette is covered with white ash, carefully bring it into the kitchen, and place it in the little dish sitting in the curry. Pour the remaining 1 tablespoon of ghee over the briquette. It will smoke up, so slap the lid on the curry and let the ghee smoke infuse the curry with its magic; let it sit, undisturbed, for at least 10 minutes. Remove the bowl with the briquette before serving.

Chapter 7

Lion's Mane

LATIN: *Hericium erinaceus*

Fact Sheet:
Lion's Mane

GENERALLY SPEAKING: Both wild and cultivated, lion's mane mushrooms are not your typical-looking cap and stem mushroom. They have hanging teeth-like protrusions that would make Cousin Itt from *The Addams Family* jealous. I think they would look at home next to my loofah in the shower. In the wild they can be found in North America, Asia, and Europe. They are saprotrophic and feed on dead and dying trees such as walnut, maple, beech, and oak, among others. They can be cultivated on sawdust or outdoors on logs. Lion's mane are used in Chinese vegetarian dishes as faux meat, often to replace pork or lamb.

AKA: Lion's mane mushroom is also known as bearded tooth, *yamabushitake* (Japanese), pom pom, pom pom blanc, bearded tooth fungus, sheep's head, old man's beard, and monkey head.

SEASON: The season for wild lion's mane is late summer through fall; cultivated mushrooms are available year-round.

BUYING TIPS: Look for mostly white specimens; if they are yellow or light brown, they are older (and sometimes bitter).

CLEANING: Lion's mane mushrooms are like sponges. You literally need to squeeze them out before using them to get rid of excess water.

STORAGE: Squeeze any water out of the mushrooms when you get them home (or ideally before buying them). Store them in the refrigerator in a brown paper bag. Second choice would be to store them in a basket or box with a dry piece of paper towel or newsprint on top of them (replace this each day).

FLAVOR, TEXTURE, AND AROMA NOTES: Lion's mane mushrooms are as close to a lobster or crab as a mushroom can get. They are seafood-like and chewy, with a slightly sweet aroma.

PRESERVATION:

DRYING: I don't recommend drying lion's mane mushrooms; it's more work than it's worth, and it doesn't improve the flavor or texture. It's better to cook and freeze them.

FREEZING: See page xxxi. Cook prior to freezing.

LOVES: Pair lion's mane mushrooms with butter, ginger, apples, sake, and mirin.

COOKING NOTES: They can be bitter unless they are cooked through.

SUBSTITUTE: Because of their seafood-like qualities, if you can't find lion's mane mushrooms, look for oyster or king trumpet mushrooms as a possible substitution.

NERDY FACTOIDS:

- They are considered a medicinal mushroom in Chinese medicine. Western medicine is finally catching up and finding that this mushroom has compounds that may have antioxidant and lipid-regulating effects (as shown in rat studies). Studies have also showed that the compounds might reduce blood glucose levels in humans.

- Clinical trials in humans have shown that lion's mane mushrooms have anti-dementia effects.

Lion's Mane with Lemon, Garlic Butter, and Vermouth

With a simple preparation such as this, you get a good sense of the mushroom itself. It's also an effective way to focus on your technique. These mushrooms can be spongy and are best if you get them crispy and brown all over. If the thought of juggling two pans of mushrooms seems too much, no problem: Simply cook them in two batches, combining them at the end of the browning process before you add the garlic and vermouth.

SERVES: 4 | PAIRING: French white Bordeaux (blend of Sauvignon Blanc and Semillon)

4 tablespoons unsalted butter

1 pound lion's mane mushrooms, moisture squeezed out and cut or torn into bite-size pieces

½ teaspoon fine sea salt

Freshly ground black pepper

3 cloves garlic, minced

½ cup dry (white) vermouth

Finely grated zest of 1 lemon

½ cup Mushroom Stock (page xxiii)

¼ cup chopped fresh flat-leaf parsley

Crusty bread, for serving

In 2 large skillets over medium heat, melt the butter. Once the bubbles subside, add the mushrooms, spreading them out (divide them between the pans). Season each pan of mushrooms with ¼ teaspoon of the salt. Grind a generous amount of black pepper over the top. Cook the mushrooms until most of the sides are brown and the edges are crispy, 8 to 10 minutes. Dump the contents of one pan into the other. Add the garlic and toss with the mushrooms until it becomes very fragrant. Add the vermouth and lemon zest, scraping up any brown bits stuck to the bottom of the pan, and cook for another minute. Add the stock and simmer for 3 to 4 minutes more, reducing the sauce by half. Season to taste. Stir in the parsley and serve with bread to sop up the juices.

Roasted Lion's Mane and Cauliflower with Zante Currants and Red Onion

This is a simple and unusual side dish that could easily be turned into a main-course vegetarian meal by roasting some cooked chickpeas (add them halfway through the cooking time) and serving with naan, raita (page 55), and chutney. Or, keep it as a side dish and serve with lamb chops and a bit of pesto.

SERVES: 4 | PAIRING: French Syrah (with lamb) or Washington Riesling (vegetarian)

1 head cauliflower, cut into very small florets, stem thinly sliced

½ pound lion's mane mushrooms, moisture squeezed out and cut or torn into bite-size pieces

½ red onion, cut into thin half-moons

2 tablespoons extra-virgin olive oil, plus more for drizzling

½ teaspoon fine sea salt

⅛ teaspoon cayenne pepper, or more if you like things hot

Freshly ground black pepper

¼ cup Zante currants

1 tablespoon red wine vinegar

¼ cup coarsely chopped fresh flat-leaf parsley

Preheat the oven to 425°F.

Line 2 baking pans with parchment paper or aluminum foil. Toss the cauliflower, lion's mane, and onion with the olive oil and then season with the salt, cayenne, and black pepper. Roast in the oven until light brown and tender, 15 to 20 minutes.

While the cauliflower and mushrooms roast, soak the currants in the red wine vinegar. As soon as the cauliflower is tender, remove from the oven and toss with the currants and parsley. Drizzle more olive oil over the top. This dish is best served at room temperature.

Seared Scallops with Lion's Mane and Truffle-Honey Pan Sauce

There are certain key words that are considered "menu gold." Put them on a menu or, in this case, in a recipe title, and—snap—your attention is captured. Truffle? Honey? I bet you stopped at this page for those two words. And for good reason. Truffles (chapter 14) are musky and mysterious, and add sultry sexiness to any food they touch. Combined with honey (most of us have a sweet tooth) and we're deep into menu magic mode and we haven't even gotten to the scallops: sweet and succulent with crispy, nutty, briny lion's mane gilding the lily and bridging the gap between ocean and earth.

SERVES: 4 | PAIRING: Italian Roero Arneis or French Chablis (Chardonnay)

1 tablespoon unsalted butter

6 ounces lion's mane mushrooms, water squeezed out and cut into thin slices

½ teaspoon plus ⅛ teaspoon truffle salt, plus more to taste

Freshly ground black pepper

1 pound sea scallops

1 tablespoon vegetable oil

2 cups mâche (substitute watercress)

1 cup halved cherry tomatoes

1 teaspoon extra-virgin olive oil

½ lemon, for squeezing on salad, plus 2 teaspoons freshly squeezed juice

1 teaspoon honey

¼ cup Mushroom Stock (page xxiii)

Heat a large skillet over medium heat. Add the butter and then add the lion's mane, making sure they are not overlapping in the pan. Sprinkle with ¼ teaspoon of the truffle salt. Grind a generous amount of black pepper over the top. Cook until most of the sides are brown and the edges are crispy, 8 to 10 minutes. Transfer to a plate and keep warm.

To prepare the scallops, dry them with paper towels. Place them on a plate and season on one side only with ¼ teaspoon of the truffle salt and black pepper. Heat a heavy skillet over high heat. Add the vegetable oil and, when it is really hot, carefully add the scallops to the pan (seasoned side down), being careful not to splatter oil on yourself or crowd the pan with too many scallops. Cook the scallops for 2 to 4 minutes on one side without disturbing them, or until they are caramelized, then flip, cooking the other side for only a minute for small scallops and up to 2 to 3 minutes more for larger scallops. The scallops should be firm but still a little bouncy in the middle (that's medium-rare). Transfer the scallops to a plate and cover lightly with aluminum foil.

Add the mâche and cherry tomatoes to a medium bowl. Drizzle the olive oil over the top along with a squeeze of lemon juice and the remaining ⅛ teaspoon truffle salt. Toss gently with your fingers. Taste for salt and lemon and adjust to your liking. Divide the salad into the middle of 4 plates.

To make the pan sauce, add any accumulated scallop juices back to the pan. Over low heat, add the honey, the 2 teaspoons lemon juice, and the stock. Scrape the pan to deglaze any good brown bits. When the sauce has thickened and reduced down enough to coat the back of a spoon (only a couple of minutes), pour it through a small sieve. Add truffle salt to taste. Arrange the scallops around or on the salad. Top the scallops with pieces of lion's mane mushrooms. Drizzle a scant amount of the truffle pan sauce around the plates.

Wok-Seared Lion's Mane with Bok Choy, Squid, and Roasted Red Chili Paste

Once you get past the silly look of the lion's mane mushrooms, straight out of the Star Trek costume closet for Tribbles, you can turn your focus to the impressive sponge-like abilities of this bizarre gill-free mushroom. (Do an image search for "Tribble" on Google if you're not a nerd and didn't automatically know what I was referring to. I'll wait.)

Right? A lion's mane mushroom totally looks like a Tribble. Anyway, squeeze all the water out of them, brown them, and then throw them back into this flavorful Thai-leaning stir-fry at the end and you'll see how versatile they become, sucking up all the good flavors they come near. It's a powerful ability and at the end of the day, impressive but no less silly looking.

SERVES: 4 | PAIRING: French Riesling

3 tablespoons coconut oil

½ pound lion's mane mushrooms, moisture squeezed out and torn or cut into small bite-size pieces

⅛ teaspoon fine sea salt, plus more as needed

⅓ cup thinly sliced shallot

5 kaffir lime leaves

2 tablespoons minced lemongrass (see Note)

1 tablespoon Thai Kitchen roasted red chili paste

1 pound baby bok choy, cut crosswise into 1-inch pieces

2 red serrano chiles, seeds and membranes removed (unless you really like heat) and cut into long thin strips (substitute other hot red chile)

1 pound squid tubes and tentacles, cleaned (see Note), tubes sliced ⅛ inch thick

1 tablespoon freshly squeezed lime juice, plus more as needed

1 tablespoon fish sauce, plus more as needed

⅓ cup chopped roasted salted peanuts (substitute toasted cashews)

1 teaspoon palm sugar (substitute brown sugar)

½ cup fresh Thai basil leaves, torn or left whole, your preference

Heat a wok over medium-high heat. Add 1 tablespoon of the coconut oil and then the mushroom pieces. Sprinkle with the salt. Cook until crispy around the edges and light brown, about 10 minutes. Transfer to a plate. Increase the heat to high. Add the remaining 2 tablespoons coconut oil and the shallot. Sauté for 2 to 3 minutes, then add the lime leaves, lemongrass, and roasted red chili paste. Sauté for 2 to 3 more minutes, then add the bok choy and cook until it starts to soften, about 5 more minutes. Add the serranos and squid and cook, stirring quickly, just until the squid tubes turn white and firm up. Add the lime juice, fish sauce, peanuts, and palm sugar. Sauté for just another minute. Pull off the heat and stir in the basil leaves. Add the mushrooms back to the stir-fry and taste, adding more fish sauce, lime juice, or salt if needed. Remove the lime leaves, or tell your guests to eat around them.

NOTE: I find the easiest way to mince lemongrass is to first cut it into small chunks, then pulse in a spice grinder (occasionally clearing out any stuck fibers around the blade) until it looks like a ball of powder and fiber. Transfer this ball to the cutting board and work your knife through the whole thing until you can't see any long fibers. If this all seems way too tedious, take the bottom third off of 2 lemongrass stalks (compost the rest) and cut into 2-inch pieces. Whack these pieces with the side of a knife to release the oils, sauté these with the stir-fry, and instruct your guests to eat around them.

NOTE: If you can't find already cleaned and cut tubes and tentacles, buy whole squid. You can refer to my how-to video online for assistance on cleaning and cutting squid at www.goodfishbook.com.

Sautéed Lion's Mane with Apples, Delicata Squash, and Ginger

I have always liked the combination of crabmeat with apple, and it was this mushroom's knack for imitating the look and texture of crab that inspired this recipe. I think this dish would stand up well on a Thanksgiving table or be an unusual base for a seared fillet of striped bass with extra-crispy skin or as a side for poached or seared halibut. It would also make a fine first course followed by a roast chicken.

SERVES: 4 | **PAIRING:** French Savennières (Chenin Blanc)

2 tablespoons unsalted butter

2 tablespoons extra-virgin olive oil

½ pound lion's mane mushrooms, moisture squeezed out and cut or torn into bite-size pieces

1 teaspoon fine sea salt

Freshly ground black pepper

⅓ cup minced shallot

1 teaspoon grated fresh ginger

6 ounces Delicata squash, seeded and medium diced

½ Honeycrisp apple, small diced

1 stalk celery, cut into thin slices on the bias (save some celery leaves)

¼ cup white wine or dry (white) vermouth

1 teaspoon apple cider vinegar

2 tablespoons almonds, toasted (page xxiv)

Fresh chervil leaves (substitute flat-leaf parsley), for garnish

In a large skillet over medium heat, melt 1 tablespoon of the butter along with 1 tablespoon of the olive oil. Add the mushrooms, spreading them out, and sprinkle with ¼ teaspoon of the salt. Grind a generous amount of black pepper over the top. Cook until most of the sides are brown and the edges are crispy, 8 to 10 minutes. Transfer to a plate.

Add the remaining 1 tablespoon each of the butter and olive oil to the pan. Sauté the shallot for 1 to 2 minutes, then add the ginger and squash, along with the remaining ¾ teaspoon salt, and cook until the squash cubes are starting to brown, 6 to 8 minutes. Add the apple, celery, wine, and vinegar and sauté for just a moment longer (you want the apple and celery to maintain their texture). Add the mushrooms back in and heat through. Season to taste with salt and black pepper. Garnish with the almonds, celery leaves, and chervil leaves. Serve right away.

Chapter 8
Morel

LATIN: *Morchella spp.*

Fact Sheet:
Morel

**FLAVOR, TEXTURE,
AND AROMA NOTES:**
One of my personal favorites,
morels have an earthy, almost
beefy flavor. Sometimes I get
hints of caraway. Their texture is
spongy and satisfyingly chewy. If
you are lucky enough to stick your
head into a basket of morels, you
might detect the aromas of old
books, soil, forest, and smoke.

GENERALLY SPEAKING: *Morchella elata* (natural black morel)
is the species that most of us think of when we think of the morel
mushroom. Once you get your "morel eyes" focused, they are easy
to spot in the woods, but until that happens, you are probably
walking right past them. With their closer proximity to the
ground, children make excellent foragers in general, but especially
with the darker morels (train 'em young). *Morchella conica* is the
fire morel, most likely to show up at burn sites or even in mulched
areas of your garden. There is also *Morchella esculenta*, or the blond
morel, and the obscure but much lauded *Morchella tomentosa* or gray
morel. Morels have the distinction of being found in almost every
state in the union. They can also be found in the Mediterranean,
Canada, Mexico, and Peru, among other places. They have a
mutually beneficial relationship with trees: *Morchella elata* (black
morels) hang around true firs and pines in general. *Morchella
esculenta* are river-bottom dwellers and are associated with poplar
trees. The only mushrooms that are remotely similar looking
to morels are those from the genera *Verpa* and *Gyromitra* (aka
the "false morels"). While some of these are considered edible,
occasionally people can get stomach upset when eating them.

AKA: Morels are also known as corncob mushrooms, honeycomb
mushrooms, hickory chickens (in parts of Kentucky), fuzzy foot
(referring to the tiny hairs on the gray morel), sponge mushrooms,
dryland fish (due to their shape when sliced in half), and my
favorite, "merkels" (say it with a Southern accent); in other words,
"miracles," based on lore that a mountain family in Kentucky was
saved from starvation by finding and eating morels.

SEASON: Impatiently waited for all winter, morels are a
harbinger of spring and can be found through late summer.

BUYING TIPS: Look for morels that have a greater cap-to-stem ratio. If they are slightly dry around the edges, they will still cook up well and in some ways are preferable to morels that might be overly wet, with soft spots (you'll have to trim those soft bits off). Make sure there is no weakness between the stem and cap (this suggests rot)—in simpler terms, it shouldn't be floppy. Look for insect damage, such as little holes where the stem attaches to the cap, or a sawdust-like crumbliness; pass those by.

CLEANING: Many times fresh morels will be a bit sandy but otherwise free of dirt, debris, or extra, um, "protein." All morels, whether sandy or not, need a little trim at the stem line. If you are lucky enough to get a batch that don't seem sandy or dirty at all, trim the very end, slice one into rings, sauté it up for a few minutes, and taste it: no sand? no grit? You most likely have a batch of ready-to-go morels, so save yourself some time: Peek into the middles to confirm they are empty and clean looking and then proceed with the recipe.

Not so lucky? You'll need a more aggressive cleaning strategy. Keep in mind: Bugs love to hide in the hollow center and seem to take extreme pleasure in crawling out when you least expect it. Of all the mushrooms I include in this book, morels seem to recover the best from a good healthy (and assertive) plunge in a bowl of water. If you spy some wildlife peeking out of the honeycombs or out of the core, or if your sauté test yielded a gritty or sandy specimen, get thee to a bowl of water. Plunge the morels into the water and swish them around quickly; give them a fast but gentle massage with your fingers and then pull them up and out of the water. Repeat with another bowl of clean water. Pull them out again, give them a gentle squeeze, and lay them out on a clean, absorbent towel. Pat dry (or alternatively, gently spin them in a salad spinner). See the video on cleaning mushrooms at www.shroomthecookbook.com

For dried morel cleaning, refer to the general rehydration information on page xxx.

STORAGE: It's best to use morels within a few days after you get them, though really fresh specimens can keep for up to 1 week. As with all mushrooms, store them in the refrigerator in a brown paper bag. Second choice would be to store them in a basket or box with a dry piece of paper towel or newsprint on top of them (replace this each day).

PRESERVATION:

DRYING: See page xxix on drying mushrooms. Morels can be dried extremely well—they are one of the best for this, in fact—and lose very little of their original flavor or texture. The soaking liquid captures a good dose of the flavor of the fresh morel; make sure you use it in soups and sauces. Also see page xxx for a description of rehydrating mushrooms.

FREEZING: See page xxxi on freezing whole mushrooms. Morels can be frozen whole with some success, but they may get a little mushy when thawed. Best to cook them first, prior to freezing.

LOVES: Morels first pop up in the spring, and they naturally pair well with other harbingers of the season. They love green things, like peas, asparagus, or artichokes; or for a more adventurous dish, pair them with forest greens such as spring nettles, miner's lettuce, or dandelion. Certainly a no-brainer pairing would be morels with cream sauces, pasta, or eggs.

COOKING NOTES: Raw morels are mildly poisonous. Make sure to cook them until they are tender and cooked through. Morels are usually less waterlogged than other mushrooms due to their honeycomb structure and hollow middles. For this reason, you may need to add a splash of wine, stock, or even water to keep the mushrooms from drying out if you are sautéing them. While I've never experienced this myself, nor is this true for anyone I know, some people have gotten sick when drinking alcohol and eating morels. As with all wild mushrooms, try a little bit the first time; with morels, if you've never tried them with alcohol, tread carefully and conservatively the first time, just to make sure you don't have a reaction. All good? Head straight to the last recipe in the chapter and make the Seared Douglas Fir–Scented Squab with Pinot Noir–Morel Sauce and Braised Cabbage (page 100).

SUBSTITUTE: Black trumpet mushrooms, with their dark color, rich smokiness, and intense, almost chocolaty nature, are a great substitute for morels.

NERDY FACTOIDS:

- False morel mushrooms in the *Gyromitra* and *Verpa* genera contain a minute amount of a substance, monomethylhydrazine, that is used in rocket fuel.

- The official state mushroom of Minnesota is the morel.

Pasta with Morels, Leeks, and Oven-Roasted Tomatoes

This is the kind of dish I wish I had known how to make in college, back when haute cuisine was Top Ramen and Kraft mac and cheese. My senior year, I lived in a house where we could opt out of the school meal program and fend for ourselves. One of the guys who lived there was a pretty inspired cook. Sometimes late at night, the smell of garlic and tomatoes would waft into my room and pull me into the kitchen on the fumes alone. He'd be smashing clove after clove of garlic and mincing them, peel and all. I didn't know much about cooking, but I knew that he probably should have pulled the peels off. He saw me staring and said, "Yeah, man, if you chop it all up, it saves time and you don't even notice the skins." Turns out he was higher than a kite that night (and most nights), but I did learn from him the benefits of expediting dinner when you're really hungry. This dish, aromatic with lightly warmed garlic, charred tomatoes, and morels, will set you back 30 minutes, tops. Pitch the garlic peels, despite what that stoner said.

SERVES: 4 │ PAIRING: Italian Chianti Classico

1 tablespoon kosher salt

½ pound fresh morels or 1 ounce dried

¼ cup plus 2 tablespoons extra-virgin olive oil

1 pint cherry tomatoes, halved

1 large leek, thinly sliced (about 1½ cups; dark green parts removed and saved for stock)

1 medium zucchini, cut into large pieces (roughly 1-inch chunks)

1 tablespoon minced fresh oregano or 1 teaspoon dried

½ teaspoon red pepper flakes

1 scant teaspoon fine sea salt

1 pound small penne

1 to 2 cloves garlic, minced

Pecorino Romano, grated or shaved, for serving

Preheat the oven to 450°F. Bring a large pot full of water to a boil over high heat. Add the kosher salt.

Clean fresh morel mushrooms as directed on page 91. Rehydrate dried morel mushrooms as directed on page xxx (add the soaking liquid to the pasta cooking water to infuse some mushroom flavor into the pasta, or reserve for another use). Cut the fresh or rehydrated morels into ¼-inch rings.

Line a baking pan with aluminum foil. Pour ¼ cup of the olive oil on the prepared pan and then top with the morels, tomatoes, leek, zucchini, oregano, and red pepper flakes. With your hands, toss all the ingredients together with the olive oil, coating everything evenly. Sprinkle with the sea salt and spread all the ingredients out on the baking pan. Roast in the oven until parts of the vegetables are caramelized, about 15 minutes.

Add the pasta to the boiling water and cook until al dente. When the vegetables are done, remove them from the oven, mix the minced garlic into the hot vegetables, and cover loosely with aluminum foil while you wait for the pasta to finish cooking.

When the pasta is ready, reserve ¼ cup of the pasta cooking water, drain the pasta, and put it back in the pot. Using a rubber spatula, scrape all the roasted veggies, along with the remaining 2 tablespoons olive oil, into the pasta. Over medium-low heat, gently stir everything together so that the pasta can absorb the juices from the vegetables. Taste, and if the pasta needs more salt, stir in some of the reserved pasta cooking liquid. Serve with plenty of Pecorino Romano to sprinkle over the top at the table.

Morels on Brioche Toast Points with Brandy and Thyme

This is the dish that I thought I was making at age eight when, in reality, I had made something entirely different (see page xxxiv). Morels on toast points is a classic French recipe that features the sublime, earthy flavor of this highly prized mushroom, gilding the lily with booze, butter, and fresh herbs. In simple dishes like this, you come as close as possible to the essence of the woods on a plate.

SERVES: 4 as an appetizer | PAIRING: French Châteauneuf-du-Pape

½ pound fresh morels or 1 ounce dried

4 (½-inch) slices of brioche (or bread of your choice)

3 tablespoons unsalted butter

¼ cup minced shallot

½ teaspoon fine sea salt or (optional) truffle salt

Freshly ground black pepper

1 teaspoon chopped fresh thyme leaves

1 cup Mushroom Stock (page xxiii) or mushroom rehydration liquid

1 teaspoon sherry vinegar

2 tablespoons brandy

¼ cup plus 2 tablespoons heavy cream

2 tablespoons chopped fresh flat-leaf parsley

Place an oven rack in the middle position and preheat the broiler to high.

Clean fresh morel mushrooms as directed on page 91. Rehydrate dried morel mushrooms as directed on page xxx, saving the rehydration liquid if using it. Cut the morels into ¼-inch rings. Trim the crust from the brioche slices and cut them diagonally into 2 triangles. In a large frying pan or cast-iron skillet over medium-low heat, melt the butter. Remove 1 tablespoon of the melted butter and reserve for the brioche.

Add the shallot to the skillet, along with the salt and black pepper, and cook for 1 minute, or until they start to soften. Add the morels and thyme to the pan and increase the heat to high. Once the mushrooms have started to brown, after about 5 minutes, deglaze the pan with the stock (or mushroom rehydration liquid), sherry vinegar, and brandy, making sure to scrape up any bits stuck to the pan.

Simmer until the liquid reduces by two-thirds, about 5 minutes. While the liquid is reducing, place the brioche on a baking pan and brush both sides with the reserved melted butter. Broil on the middle rack until the top side is toasted, then flip and toast the bottom (watch it carefully!). Once the liquid has reduced, add the cream. Continue to simmer until the sauce has thickened, 3 to 5 minutes more. Add the parsley. Season to taste with more salt and black pepper.

Serve the toast points topped with the mushroom mixture.

NOTE: To be extra-fancy, you can make a mini herb salad to place on top of the mushrooms. Combine the leaves of various soft fresh herbs, such as flat-leaf parsley and thyme, with nasturtium and/or other edible flowers, and dab them lightly with a little extra-virgin olive oil and lemon juice.

Fried Duck Eggs with Artichoke and Morel Salad

It may seem indulgent to pair morel mushrooms with artichokes and duck eggs—deep-fried, crunchy, oozy duck eggs. Consider it my nod to decadence, in the spirit of Hangtown fry—that famous dish from Gold Rush California where the goal was to combine the three most expensive ingredients at that time: cormorant eggs, oysters, and bacon. You can certainly substitute chicken eggs for duck eggs, canned artichokes for fresh, and button mushrooms for morels, but why on earth would you ever want to do that? You may not be panning for gold and striking it rich, but you are worth the occasional extravagance.

SERVES: 4 | PAIRING: French Sancerre (Sauvignon Blanc)

¼ pound fresh morels or ½ ounce dried

4 duck eggs (use older eggs, as they are easier to peel)

Unbleached all-purpose flour, as needed

1 large egg, beaten

1 cup panko bread crumbs

1 lemon

1 globe artichoke

3 tablespoons extra-virgin olive oil

¼ teaspoon fine sea salt

Freshly ground black pepper

¼ cup dry (white) vermouth

3 cups vegetable oil (see Note)

4 slices rustic bread, toasted

1 clove garlic, halved

Flaky sea salt

¼ cup sliced fresh chives

Clean fresh morel mushrooms as directed on page 91. Rehydrate dried morel mushrooms as directed on page xxx, saving the rehydration liquid to use as stock in another recipe.

Bring a medium pot of water to a boil. Carefully lower the whole duck eggs into the water and cook them for 6 minutes exactly. Transfer the duck eggs to a bowl and pour cold water over them, replacing the water frequently, until they are cool. Remove the eggs from the water and gently tap all around them with the back of a spoon to break the shells. Then place them back in a bowl of cold water. Let sit for 10 minutes, and then peel carefully (easiest under cold running water). Pat the eggs dry with a paper towel.

Place the flour, egg, and bread crumbs in separate small bowls. First, dust the peeled eggs with flour, shaking off any excess, and then dip into the beaten egg, also shaking off any excess, and finally dip into the bowl of panko. Transfer the coated eggs to a plate.

Cut the lemon in half and squeeze one half into a bowl of cold water. Reserve the other half. Chop about 1 inch off the flower end of the artichoke. Peel off all the dark green, tough outer leaves. You want to get rid of all dark green parts of the artichoke (including on the stem). You will only be using the tender yellow parts. As you are cutting and peeling, use the reserved half of the lemon, rubbing it liberally over the artichoke to prevent browning. Once you have gotten to the tender yellow heart, use a spoon to dig out the hairy, tough choke. (There are many good videos on YouTube showing this technique.) Rub the lemon all over the artichoke, inside and out. Using a very sharp knife, carefully slice the artichoke into very thin slices (as thin as you can manage). Transfer the slices to the lemon water right away so the artichoke doesn't brown.

Fried Duck Eggs with Artichoke and Morel Salad

CONTINUED

Slice the morels crosswise into ½-inch rings. Heat a medium sauté pan over medium-high heat. Add the olive oil and, after a moment, add the morels, along with the fine sea salt and some black pepper. Sauté gently until the morels are tender and lightly caramelized, 6 to 8 minutes. Add the vermouth to deglaze the pan, making sure to scrape up any bits stuck to the pan. When the vermouth has evaporated, turn the heat to very low and keep warm. Drain the artichoke pieces from the lemon water (making sure there are no errant lemon seeds in there). Pat them dry with a paper towel and then stir them into the warm morels in the pan. Season to taste with salt and pepper.

Lay out a few pieces of paper towel on a plate. Heat the vegetable oil in a small deep saucepan over high heat until it reaches 350°F. Carefully add the eggs and fry until golden brown on both sides, no more than 1 to 2 minutes. You may need to flip them over if the eggs aren't submerged all the way. When the eggs are done, transfer to the prepared plate to drain. Rub one side of the toasted bread with the garlic halves.

For each plate, pile some of the warm artichoke-morel salad in the middle. Carefully cut the duck eggs in half (the yolk will ooze out) and serve 2 halves per person. Sprinkle the eggs with a little flaky sea salt and chives. Serve with the garlic toast.

NOTE: Strain the oil when cool through a fine-mesh strainer. Kept free of sediment and away from light and heat (in the refrigerator), this oil can be used over and over again for frying. Pitch it when it darkens a lot or starts to smell like the inside of a McDonald's.

Grilled Asiago and Fig Stuffed Morels with Vin Cotto

Vin cotto is a sweet but balanced reduction of wine. The name literally means "cooked wine," yet the Italian-to-English translation takes some of the romance out of it, so we'll just go back to calling it vin cotto. You can find vin cotto in high-end food stores or online. This recipe is best using fresh morels—and not just any fresh morel. Pick out sizable ones with a large cavity, preferably without holes on both ends.

SERVES: 4 as an appetizer | PAIRING: Italian Primitivo

SAGE GARNISH
¼ cup vegetable oil

12 fresh sage leaves

Smoked salt (substitute flaky sea salt)

¼ pound fresh morels (1 or 2 large morels per person)

3 tablespoons extra-virgin olive oil

⅓ cup small-diced shallot

¼ teaspoon fine sea salt

¾ pound fresh figs (1 pint), stemmed, small diced, plus 2 figs, halved

Freshly ground black pepper

1½ teaspoons minced fresh sage leaves

1 tablespoon minced fresh oregano

2 tablespoons dry white wine

2 ounces Asiago fresco, small diced (DOP Mitica or any soft, mild, cow's cheese)

Vin cotto, for drizzling (substitute balsamic syrup)

1 cup small arugula leaves

To make the sage garnish, first line a plate with a few paper towels. Pour the oil into a small saucepan and bring to 350°F over medium-high heat. Carefully lower the sage leaves into the oil and fry until the leaves darken and firm up, 20 to 30 seconds. Using a slotted spoon, gently pull the leaves out and place on the paper towels. Sprinkle lightly with smoked salt and set aside.

Clean the fresh morels as instructed on page 91. Prepare a medium-hot fire in a grill (you'll be grilling them for no longer than 10 to 15 minutes).

In a medium skillet over medium-high heat, add 2 tablespoons of the olive oil and then add the shallot and fine sea salt. Sauté until caramelized, a minimum of 8 minutes. Carefully add a splash of water if it sticks or threatens to burn. Add the diced figs, along with a couple of grinds of black pepper, and sauté for another 5 to 7 minutes. Stir in the sage and oregano and deglaze the pan with the white wine, making sure to scrape up any bits stuck to the pan. Lower the heat slightly, add the cheese, and mix just until it has melted into the filling. Transfer the filling to a bowl. Taste for seasoning and add more salt if necessary. Chill in the refrigerator. To prevent runaway melted cheese on the grill, it's important that the filling is cold prior to grilling the morels.

Trim back the morel stems, leaving about a ¼-inch stem remaining. Fill the morel cavities with the cheese-fig mixture (it's easiest using a very small spoon). Don't overfill. Drizzle the stuffed mushrooms and the halved figs with the remaining 1 tablespoon olive oil and a sprinkling of fine sea salt. Grill the stuffed morels over the medium-hot fire for about 8 minutes, or until the cheese is melted and you have some browned and lightly crispy edges on the mushrooms. Also grill the halved figs, halved side down, until you get nice grill marks. Flip and cook for a minute on the other side.

To serve, brush or drizzle the *vin cotto* on each plate, and make a small nest on each plate with the arugula. Top with 1 or 2 grilled stuffed morels, the grilled figs, and a scattering of the fried sage leaves.

Seared Douglas Fir–Scented Squab with Pinot Noir–Morel Sauce and Braised Cabbage

If you ever get the chance to meet a Pacific Northwest woodland nymph and she happens to be into cooking, I'm fairly certain this is the dish she'd bust out for you. Douglas fir is a very popular "new" ingredient that has been around for thousands of years but is newly discovered by foraging-crazy chefs from Seattle like, apparently, me. It can be used much like rosemary. Look for the new chartreuse growth in the spring and twist or cut off the tips. It has a lemony, piney flavor that nine out of ten nymphs approve of.

SERVES: 4 | PAIRING: Oregon Pinot Noir

MOREL SPICE RUB
⅛ ounce dried morels

½ teaspoon caraway seeds

¼ teaspoon chopped Douglas fir tips (or fresh rosemary)

½ teaspoon fine sea salt

¼ teaspoon black peppercorns

4 whole semi-boneless squab (wing tips trimmed and reserved for stock)

PINOT NOIR–MOREL SAUCE
¼ pound fresh morels or ½ ounce dried

¼ cup small-diced shallot

1 teaspoon honey

½ (750-milliliter) bottle Pinot Noir (see cooking with wine on page xxiv)

2 cups chicken stock or Mushroom Stock (page xxiii)

Up to 1 cup trim from fennel, including stems

1 tablespoon extra-virgin olive oil

⅛ teaspoon fine sea salt

BRAISED RED CABBAGE
1 tablespoon extra-virgin olive oil

3 cups shredded red cabbage

1 cup thinly sliced fennel bulb (save fronds for garnish)

¼ teaspoon fine sea salt

2 teaspoons honey

1 teaspoon finely ground Douglas fir tips (or fresh rosemary)

¼ cup red wine vinegar

1 tablespoon bacon or duck fat (or ghee or clarified butter)

½ cup (1 stick) unsalted butter

Flaky sea salt

To make the spice rub (see Note), combine all of the ingredients in a spice grinder and grind together to a very fine powder. Set aside.

To prep the squab, cut each one in half vertically. Lay the 8 halves out on a baking pan. Sprinkle half of the spice rub over the top, flip the squab over, and season with the remaining rub. Cover and let sit in your refrigerator for up to 3 hours while you prepare the rest of the meal.

To make the sauce, clean fresh morel mushrooms as directed on page 91. Rehydrate dried morel mushrooms as directed on page xxx, saving the rehydration liquid to use as part of the stock amount. Cut the morels into ¼-inch rings. In a wide, high-sided pan (10 to 12 inches), combine the shallot, honey, wine, stock/rehydration liquid, and any fennel trim. Bring to a boil and then lower the heat to a simmer. Cook the sauce, letting it reduce in volume until you have about ¾ cup left, about 30 minutes. Strain it prior to measuring, discarding the solids but pressing on them to get all the goodness from them (it's important that you measure the reduction after you've strained it for best results).

Heat the olive oil in a medium sauté pan over medium heat. After a moment, add the morels and the salt. Cook until caramelized around the edges, 5 to 7 minutes. Add a tablespoon or two of red wine or water to deglaze the bottom of the pan, making sure to scrape up any bits stuck to the pan. Then transfer the morels and any juices to the reduced, strained sauce. Let sit off the heat while you continue with the rest of the recipe.

To make the braised red cabbage, heat the olive oil in a medium pot over medium-high heat. Add the cabbage, fennel, salt, honey, ground Douglas fir tips, and vinegar. Cook, stirring from time to time, covered, over medium-low heat for about 30 minutes. Check on it occasionally, giving it a stir and making sure all the liquid hasn't dried up. When the cabbage is tender, season to taste with salt and keep warm.

To cook the squab, heat 2 cast-iron or heavy pans (or preheat a grill) over medium-high heat. Add half the bacon fat to each pan and then add the squab halves, skin side down, leaving plenty of room between each squab half (4 squab halves per pan). Cook on the skin side until it starts to brown and crisp up, 5 to 6 minutes. Flip over, and cook for another minute or so. Squab are best served medium-rare to rare in the breast. Pull them from the pan when the breast registers 125°F to 135°F, depending on your preference. Let rest, covered loosely with aluminum foil, until you are ready to serve.

To finish the sauce, turn the heat to medium-low. Whisk the butter into the sauce 1 tablespoon at a time, and keep warm over very low heat. Pour any juices from the resting squab back into the sauce. Taste and add salt as needed.

To serve, slice the leg off each squab half and slice the breast into 3 pieces. Fan the pieces on top of some braised cabbage. Sprinkle flaky sea salt on the squab and spoon the morel sauce on the side, with just a little sauce draped over the squab. Garnish with the fennel fronds. Tell your guests to use their fingers to get all the meat off the squab bones—the flavor is best closest to the bone.

NOTE: Keep in mind that you can't really remove the gritty sediment from dried morels when you are making a morel spice powder (as you would when rehydrating). Make sure you choose high-quality dried morels (or better yet, clean ones that you've dehydrated yourself) and grind them to a very fine powder. Do that, and you shouldn't have any grit problems.

A Branch in the Eye
Is Worth Two in the Basket

FALL: It's overcast and threatening to rain, not to mention that the light is fading, so we don't have much time to check out the spot. I'm fast on my friend Amy's heels, and we're chitchatting, chanterelle-scanning, and bushwhacking all at the same time, a multitasking three-way not for the inexperienced. Not even five feet into the woods I get poked in the eye with a Douglas fir branch. This slows my friend down just long enough to make sure my cornea is still intact. She's on a mission, and a branch in the eye isn't going to come between us and a full basket of first-of-the-season chanterelles.

Foraging for mushrooms is like an adult Easter egg hunt minus the pastels and sugar high; otherwise staid folks romp and shout out into the forest canopy, "I found one! I found one!" The chanterelle peeking out of the pine needles and duff becomes an orange-colored egg filled with chocolates, just like when you were six.

When I ask Amy where we are that day (it's always hard to remember a location when you are spun around and blindfolded), she responds "in the woods," knowing full well that her answer is not even remotely helpful. Foragers are a secretive and paranoid lot, and I'm a cooking teacher with an open cookbook and no patience for secrets. "Fine," I say, "at least there are plenty of chanterelles at the market." I pause for dramatic effect. *"I don't need you,"* I yell, because she's already gone, bounding over a wooded slope of hemlock and fir, locked on the scent of the next chanterelle like a drug dog on a 10-pound bag of cocaine.

This fall I'm planning on heading back into the woods with Amy. I called her up and told her I was writing a story about chanterelles and asked her if she'd like to offer just a little more information to my readers about where we were that day. "Tell them we were on the Olympic Peninsula," she says, "and that should narrow it down a bit."

Chapter 9

Chanterelle

LATIN: *Cantharellus spp.*

Fact Sheet:
Chanterelle

GENERALLY SPEAKING: The word chanterelle comes from eighteenth-century France, but originally it's from the Neo-Latin *cantharella* or Latin *canthar*, meaning "tankard" or drinking vessel, which prompts the question of what exactly they were drinking out of chanterelles. The atypical gills run from mid-stem to stern, like lined stockings drawing your eye up and under its pretty, ruffled hemline. There are many varieties: whites (meaty and typically pretty dirty), *C. cibarius*, found on the East Coast with a more delicate stalk than the Pacific Northwest *C. formosus*, which is larger stemmed and meaty, among others.

AKA: Chanterelles are also known as "chanties," *Pfifferling* (German for "small pepper"), girolle (France), or egg mushrooms. I refer to them as Gateway Shrooms, as it was the first mushroom I ever picked in the woods.

SEASON: They can be found from June through December.

BUYING TIPS: Picking out a good fresh chanterelle is easy: Avoid ones that have dried-out edges and any that are moldy, have dark brown patches or edges, or are completely saturated with water. Look for chanterelles to appear in the marketplace in late July, and expect the season to rapidly slow down as November approaches. In the Pacific Northwest, you will occasionally find chanterelles (the big ones called "flowers") in markets through December. There are many types of chanterelles, but you may only see a few at farmers' market stalls or in supermarkets (the most common being yellow/golden or deep orange; less commonly seen in the marketplace is the white variety). Bonus: There are almost zero worm problems with chanterelles. Silly worms are missing out.

CLEANING: If they were harvested on a dry day and the pickers "picked clean," not letting pine needles and dirt into the basket, then you might not have to do any cleaning other than, perhaps, a trim off the stem or any parts that are slimy or worse for wear.

FLAVOR, TEXTURE, AND AROMA NOTES: Lightly nutty and buttery in flavor, chanterelles are especially praised for their firm texture. When raw they smell slightly sweet, nearly fruity; some say like apricots, though I think they may be swayed by the color. When sautéing them recently, I had the hardest time putting my finger on the earthy-nutty-sweet aroma until my friend Amy Grondin declared "popcorn and maple sugar candies!" I knew it to be true, especially the maple candy part; it smelled almost like you had stumbled upon someone cooking pancakes in a pine forest.

Sometimes chanterelles come to market filthy and sodden with the fall rains. For these, it's best just to rip the Band-Aid and go for the plunge-and-soak (see page xxvi). I prefer to tear chanterelles into pieces (from cap through the stem). It preserves their pretty form.

STORAGE: Chanterelles have a good shelf life; if stored properly they can keep for a few weeks. As with all mushrooms, store them in the refrigerator in a brown paper bag. Second choice would be to store them in a basket or box with a dry piece of paper towel or newsprint on top of them (replace this each day).

DRYING: I don't recommend drying chanterelle mushrooms or even buying dried chanterelles. They don't seem to hold up flavorwise, and there always seems to be a hard little nugget that, no matter how long you soak them, never softens. If you insist on buying them, look for very thin pieces of dried chanterelle, as they are more likely to rehydrate evenly.

FREEZING: See page xxxi. Cook chanterelles in either a dry pan or in a little butter or olive oil. My friend Amy likes to pack them into half-pint containers and top them with olive oil to protect against freezer burn. You can also cook them and then vacuum-pack them with or without the olive oil, your choice. Both methods work well, and deep into the winter it is a true luxury to pull the already cooked mushrooms out of the freezer to reheat, top toast with, add to a stew, stuff an omelette with, and so on.

LOVES: With their faint sweetness, chanterelles love being paired with late summer corn, tomatoes, bacon, onions, eggs, sour cream or crème fraîche, apples, pears, huckleberries, and basil. Probably not all at once.

COOKING NOTES: When it comes to cooking up chanterelles, simple is best. Due to their more subtle character, they are best paired with ingredients that won't overtake their flavor. That being said, one would be foolish to kick a steak with chanterelle butter out of bed. Do save your tannic and lush red wines for another dish, however: Chanterelles are great with Pinot Noir and lightly oaked Chardonnay.

SUBSTITUTE: Hedgehog mushrooms make a respectable stand-in for chanterelles during the winter months.

- Research is being done into insecticidal properties of chanterelle mushrooms (harmless to humans)—this characteristic may be why chanterelles, unlike so many other mushrooms, seem devoid of bug damage.

- Chanterelles are rich in beta-carotene and notably high in vitamin D, A, and some B-complex vitamins.

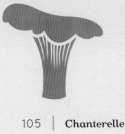

Acquacotta Soup with Chanterelles and Garlic on Toast

While many of the ingredients in this recipe might seem—at first blush—to be gourmet and expensive, if you were a thrifty Italian who knew the woods near where you lived, grew some humble vegetables in your garden, had some stale bread lying around, and kept chickens, this soup would cost you hardly anything. Acquacotta literally means "cooked water," and it's the veritable stone soup of Italian cuisine. Parmesan rinds are never thrown away but rather used to flavor stews and soups. The porcini add a rich mushroom back note to the fruitier delicacy of the chanterelles. If you don't have any mushroom stock, use water and feel totally authentic while doing so.

SERVES: 4 | PAIRING: Italian Barbera

½ ounce dried porcini mushrooms

3 tablespoons extra-virgin olive oil

½ pound fresh chanterelle mushrooms, torn into bite-size pieces

1 teaspoon fine sea salt

1 medium yellow onion, small diced

3 stalks celery, small diced

1 cup thinly sliced red cabbage

1 bunch Lacinato kale, leaves cut into bite-size pieces, stems discarded

½ to 1 teaspoon red pepper flakes

5 cups homemade Mushroom Stock (page xxiii)

½ cup white wine or dry (white) vermouth

1 piece Parmigiano-Reggiano rind (optional)

1 (28-ounce) can Muir Glen fire-roasted diced tomatoes, with juices

1 dried bay leaf

FOR SERVING

4 slices crusty bread, toasted

1 clove garlic, halved lengthwise

¼ cup fresh flat-leaf parsley leaves

Shaved Parmigiano-Reggiano (use a vegetable peeler)

Drizzle of your favorite extra-virgin olive oil

Freshly cracked black pepper

4 poached or fried eggs (optional)

Rehydrate the porcini in 1½ cups boiling water (see page xxx) and set aside for 20 minutes.

Heat 1 tablespoon of the olive oil over medium heat in a soup pot. Add the chanterelles, along with ¼ teaspoon of the salt. Sauté until lightly browned, 5 to 6 minutes. Transfer to a plate.

Add the remaining 2 tablespoons olive oil to the pot and then the onion, celery, cabbage, kale, red pepper flakes, and the remaining ¾ teaspoon salt. Sauté until the vegetables get nice and soft, about 15 minutes (add a little stock if it starts to get dry). Pull the porcini out of its soaking liquid, reserving the liquid. Chop the porcini and add to the sautéing vegetables. Deglaze the pot with the wine, making sure to scrape up any bits stuck to the pan. Add the cheese rind, if using, stock, tomatoes with their juices, bay leaf, and the strained porcini liquid to the soup pot (be careful to hold some back in the container, as sediment may have settled to the bottom). Bring to a boil, then lower to a simmer and let the soup cook for about 15 minutes. Add the chanterelles back in and cook for another 5 minutes. Remove the cheese rind before serving.

Meanwhile, toast the bread in a toaster or under the broiler and then scrape the garlic clove on one side of each slice. Serve the soup in wide bowls along with a piece of the garlic toast. Garnish with the parsley leaves, shaved cheese curls, and a drizzle of good olive oil. Add cracked black pepper over the top. If you end up poaching or frying the eggs, lay the toast in the middle of the soup and serve the egg on it (sprinkle the cheese shavings over the egg).

Chanterelle Risotto with Lemon Thyme

For both the purist and the comfort-food seekers, it seems mandatory to have a wild mushroom risotto on the stovetop at least at one point during the fall. This is a simple recipe that lives and dies on the quality of the ingredients. The reason why risotto can either be insipid or stunning is because with so few ingredients, it's hard to hide. I'm sure many Italians would find it disagreeable to make risotto ahead, but at the fine-dining restaurant I cooked at we would par-cook the risotto, stopping three-quarters of the way into the cooking process, and then spread it out on a baking pan and pop it in the walk-in. When it was time to finish it, we'd add it back to the pot and stir in hot stock and complete the dish. Trust me when I say there was absolutely no detectable loss in quality. Try this for your next dinner party: from the refrigerator to finished risotto in 10 minutes.

SERVES: 4 | PAIRING: Italian Vernaccia or French white Burgundy (Chardonnay)

4 cups Mushroom Stock (page xxiii)

2 tablespoons extra-virgin olive oil

5 tablespoons unsalted butter

6 ounces fresh chanterelle mushrooms, torn into small bite-size pieces

¼ teaspoon fine sea salt

1 small yellow onion, small diced

1 cup Arborio or Carnaroli rice

½ cup dry white wine or dry (white) vermouth

1 tablespoon fresh lemon thyme, chopped (substitute regular thyme plus 1 teaspoon finely grated lemon zest)

½ cup grated Parmigiano-Reggiano

Freshly ground black pepper

In a medium saucepan, bring the stock to a boil, then decrease the heat to low to keep warm. In a large sauté pan set over medium-high heat, add 1 tablespoon each of the olive oil and butter. Add the chanterelles and salt and cook until tender and just lightly caramelized, 3 to 5 minutes. Transfer to a bowl and reserve. In a large, heavy saucepan, melt 1 tablespoon each of the olive oil and butter over medium-low heat. Add the onion and a pinch of salt and cook until softened, about 5 minutes. Add the rice and cook, stirring constantly, until the rice is translucent at the edges, about 3 minutes.

Add the wine, stirring until the wine is almost completely absorbed. Add a ladle of warm stock (½ to ¾ cup) and stir until almost completely absorbed. Continue adding stock a ladleful at a time and cooking, stirring constantly, until it is absorbed, before adding another ladle of stock. After about 15 minutes, begin tasting the risotto before adding each new ladle of stock (now is when you could stop the cooking process to finish later). When the rice is nearly done, firm but not crunchy, add another ladleful of stock, along with the chanterelles and thyme. Continue stirring, and when the stock has been absorbed, the rice should be al dente. Stir in a little more stock, along with the cheese and the remaining 3 tablespoons butter. Season to taste with salt and pepper. Serve immediately, with extra cheese at the table.

Quick-Pickled Chanterelles with Huckleberries and Herbs

Have you ever seen a batch of small button chanterelles that are so adorable you can't imagine cutting them or hiding them in a risotto? That's when you should pull out this recipe. It's not that you can't use bigger chanterelles for this (just cut them into quarters or halves), but when pickled, these munchkin chanterelles look adorable on a cheese platter, in a salad, or alongside charcuterie. While the huckleberries are great in this pickle, if you don't have access to any, the chanterelles are still nice on their own (though I'd recommend using ⅓ cup sugar instead of the ¼ cup). If you know how to can, then by all means go ahead and can these and store them in your pantry. I've developed this recipe as a refrigerator pickle and it will keep for a month, and probably longer, but you'll have eaten them by then.

MAKES: 2 pint jars or 1 quart jar | **PAIRING:** French Champagne Blanc de Blancs

1 pound fresh small chanterelle mushrooms (caps less than 1 inch)

4 thyme sprigs

2 to 4 dill or fennel flower tops (optional)

2 ounces huckleberries (about ¼ cup)

2 cups distilled white vinegar

½ cup water

¼ cup sugar

1 tablespoon fine sea salt

Heaping ¼ teaspoon red pepper flakes

2 dried bay leaves

Heat a large skillet over medium-high heat. Add the chanterelles to the dry pan (in 2 batches) and sauté them until they release their liquid and soften up, about 5 minutes. Clean 1 quart jar or 2 pint jars. Place the thyme sprigs and flower tops, if using, in the bottom of the jar(s). In a medium bowl, toss together the chanterelles and huckleberries. Add the mixture to the jar(s). Tamp the jar down by tapping it on a towel on the counter.

In a medium saucepan, add the vinegar, water, sugar, salt, red pepper flakes, and bay leaves. Bring to a boil. Simmer, stirring, until the sugar and salt are dissolved. Pour the hot liquid on top of the mushrooms to fill the jar. Close the jars and store in the refrigerator.

Roasted Chanterelles and Bacon with Sweet Corn Sauce

This dish would make a great first course for a multicourse dinner served sometime in September, right when the chanterelles start popping and the corn is waning. If you happen to have a couple of garden tomatoes lying around, chop them up and spread them on the toast to serve on the side, or even better, serve this dish with a panzanella salad with basil, tomato, croutons, and mozzarella.

SERVES: 4 | PAIRING: Sonoma Chardonnay

9 ounces chanterelles, large ones split in half, small ones left whole

¼ pound bacon, small diced

3 ears fresh corn

⅔ cup Mushroom Stock (page xxiii)

1 tablespoon butter, melted, plus more for drizzling

Tabasco sauce (or hot sauce of your choice; optional)

¼ teaspoon sea salt, plus more as needed

4 ounces piquillo chile peppers from a jar (or roasted red peppers), thinly sliced

Freshly ground black pepper

1 tablespoon chopped fresh basil

4 slices toasted crusty bread

Line a baking pan with aluminum foil and spread out the chanterelles and bacon on it. Pop in a cold oven and set the temperature to 400°F. Set a timer for 10 minutes. When the timer goes off, mix the mushrooms and bacon and place back in the oven for another 5 minutes (making sure they are spread out). Mix again, and return to the oven for another 5 to 10 minutes, until the bacon is rendered and crisp and the mushrooms are tender and caramelized. When they are done, remove from the oven and cover with foil until everything else is finished.

Meanwhile, cut the corn off the cobs. Add half of the corn kernels to a blender. Then, putting the blender in the sink, hold the cobs over the blender and, using a spoon, scrape down the cobs into the blender to get all the corn "milk" from the cobs. Add the stock, melted butter, and Tabasco to the blender as well. Puree until smooth (adding a little water if necessary to get the blender to work). Pour the puree through a fine-mesh strainer into a small saucepan. Use a rubber spatula to press as much as you can through the strainer. Season with ⅛ teaspoon of the salt, plus more if needed.

In a sauté pan over medium-high heat, put 1 tablespoon of the bacon fat from the baking pan. Add the remaining half of the corn kernels, the piquillo peppers, the remaining ⅛ teaspoon salt, and black pepper and sauté for 5 minutes, until you get a little color on the corn. Add the basil, sauté for another minute, season to taste (keep in mind the bacon is salty), and reserve. Right before serving, heat up the corn sauce over medium heat, mixing carefully with a rubber spatula so that the natural cornstarch doesn't burn on the bottom of the pot. It should thicken and coat the back of a spoon in just a few minutes.

To serve, pour an equal amount of corn sauce into each of 4 shallow bowls. Spoon a portion of the corn and pepper mixture in the middle. On top of that, serve equal portions of the chanterelles and bacon. Serve with the toasted bread.

Sautéed Chanterelles and Pears with Crispy Herb-Infused Duck Breast

Being a cooking teacher, I'm constantly on the lookout for what I call "input opportunities" to refresh my knowledge and add to it, so I can turn around and give it back to my students. When I met Chef Lynne Vea and got the opportunity to watch her teach, I hatched a plan: convince her to co-teach an Iron Chef–type class called Dueling Divas; while she was teaching, I could not-so-secretly learn from her. Five years later, we're still teaching this class together and I have added many new skills and flavor combinations to my repertoire, as well as a wonderful friend. Lynne's stunning recipes mirror her generous and sparkling personality. I've adapted her recipe only slightly, so it sings with the flavors and balance that Lynne is famous for.

SERVES: 4 | PAIRING: French red Burgundy (Pinot Noir)

4 boneless, skin-on duck breasts, silver skin trimmed off

2 teaspoons minced fresh thyme

2 teaspoons minced fresh sage

2 teaspoons minced fresh rosemary

1 teaspoon fine sea salt

Freshly ground black pepper

½ cup hard pear cider or apple cider

½ cup thickly sliced shallot

½ pound chanterelle mushrooms, torn in half or quarters lengthwise

1 semi-ripe pear, sliced (see Note)

1 teaspoon maple syrup

1 teaspoon sherry vinegar

Fried Sage Leaves (page 99), for garnish

Nasturtium flowers, for garnish

Score the skin of each duck breast in a crosshatch pattern with the tip of a sharp knife. Sprinkle the meaty side of the breasts with half of the thyme, sage, rosemary, and salt. Add ground pepper to your taste.

Preheat a large sauté pan over medium heat and add the duck, skin/fat side down. Cook for 15 to 18 minutes, until the skin is dark golden brown and crispy and has rendered a great portion of its fat. You'll know it's ready when you can no longer see white streaks of fat in the lines of the crosshatches you scored. Turn the breasts over and cook for 2 to 4 minutes longer for a nice pink interior (125°F to 130°F on a thermometer for medium-rare). Remove the breasts from the pan and tent loosely with aluminum foil to rest for at least 10 minutes.

Pour the fat from the pan into a heatproof vessel and place the pan back over medium-high heat. Pour the pear cider into the pan and bring to a simmer. Scrape up any lovely bits of caramelization and remove the pan from the heat. Pour the cider into a different small vessel and reserve.

Return the same pan to the stove over medium-heat and add 1 tablespoon of the duck fat. (If you are making the sauté without the duck, use butter for this step.) Add the shallot and sauté for about 1 minute, and then add the chanterelles. Cook, stirring frequently, for about 5 minutes, or until the mushrooms and shallot are starting to become tender and lightly caramelized. Add the pear, the remaining half of the herbs, the remaining ½ teaspoon salt, and a generous amount of black pepper. Sauté this mixture for 2 minutes. Add the reserved pear cider and cook until reduced by half, about 2 minutes. Stir in the maple syrup, sherry vinegar, and any juices that have pooled on the plate with the duck and toss to coat. Taste for seasoning and add additional salt and/or pepper as needed.

Slice the duck breasts into thin slices and serve each, fanned on a plate, with the chanterelles and pear. Garnish with fried sage leaves and nasturtium flowers. Lynne's note: "I love this dish accompanied by soft polenta or smashed garnet yams."

NOTE: Red Bartlett pears make a lovely contrast in this dish, but Anjou are also wonderful for their taste and texture. Choose a pear that is barely soft to the touch. Too ripe and it won't hold up to the heat. To prep the pear, cut it in quarters lengthwise and cut the core from each quarter. Cut each quarter into fat slices on the diagonal to approximate the length of the chanterelles.

Chapter 10

Hedgehog

LATIN: *Hydnum spp.*

Fact Sheet:
Hedgehog

FLAVOR, TEXTURE, AND AROMA NOTES: Hedgehogs can be tangy, spicy, and slightly bitter when older. Their texture is best described as firm, though when pushed they can crumble into pieces. Some describe the aroma of hedgehogs as peppery.

GENERALLY SPEAKING: While folks are fawning all over the ubiquitous chanterelle or spring porcini, I'm saving my adoration for the mushroom that's too cute to mess with pedestrian gills. Hedgehogs have comical fungi-quill equivalents where gills would normally be. They are sometimes referred to as teeth. It might actually be true that the sillier and uglier a food is, the better it seems to taste (for example, celery root, rambutan, truffles, geoduck). This is truer than ever when it comes to the hedgehog mushroom. The hedgehog is so friendly that it seems to be in a symbiotic relationship with every kind of tree and, in a nod to beginning foragers, has no dangerous lookalikes. There are two main varieties of hedgehog mushrooms: *Hydnum repandum* ("spreader" or "sweet tooth"), which can be large, up to 2 pounds and very meaty, and *Hydnum umbilicatum* or "belly buttons," which are smaller, with an indentation in the middle of the cap, naturally.

AKA: Hedgehogs are also known as *pied de mouton*, sweet tooth, hogs, belly button, spreader hedgehog, hedgies, wood urchin, pig's trotter, and wood hedgehog.

SEASON: They can be found from August to March. (They will keep growing even through snow!)

BUYING TIPS: Check the teeth—make sure they are dry and not sticking together. The cap edges should be intact, not torn. Look for smaller, younger mushrooms. The older/bigger they get, the more likely they are to be bitter. Bonus: There are almost zero worm problems to deal with when it comes to this type of mushroom.

CLEANING: Trim the stems. Brush any dirt out of the teeth and wipe the top of the caps, if dirty, with a damp cloth. If the mushroom is less than 1 inch, don't bother cutting or tearing it in half as you would a chanterelle. If they are really filthy, the easiest way to deal with them would be to use a spoon to scoop out the teeth and discard, then wash and dry them (refer to page xxvi).

STORAGE: Hedgehogs can be stored for up to 1 week. As with all mushrooms, store them in the refrigerator in a brown paper bag. Second choice would be to store them in a basket or box with a dry piece of paper towel or newsprint on top of them (replace this each day).

PRESERVATION:

DRYING: Not recommended for hedgehog mushrooms; they don't hold their shape well when dried and have little flavor when rehydrated.

FREEZING: See page xxxi.

LOVES: Hedgehogs add great flavor to stews, soups, and curries. They are fantastic when pickled or smoked.

COOKING NOTES: Most of the teeth will break off while you are sautéing, which is why hedgehogs are best used in stuffings, gravies, or any dish where their shedding teeth won't mar the look of the dish.

SUBSTITUTE: Chanterelles are often considered interchangeable with hedgehogs because of their color, but the tangy, lightly bitter aspect of hedgehogs (bitter in a good way) put them in their own unique category. I think beech mushrooms, though very different in appearance, have some of that tangy-bitter thing going on and would make a better substitute for hedgehogs.

NERDY FACTOIDS:

- Red squirrels love hedgehogs, too.

- Hedgehogs are hardy and capable of surviving light freezes.

Hedgehog Mushrooms and Cheddar Grits with Fried Eggs and Tabasco Honey

I will always think of my friend Ashlyn when I reach for the ever-present bottle of Tabasco in my kitchen. We share a mutual admiration for the hot sauce stemming from our childhood. In fact, she thinks of it so fondly that she named her red-coated Golden Retriever after it. Ashlyn was born in the South but has lived and cheffed all over the world, including Spain. We often put our heads together to discuss food, and this simple Southern-style breakfast has her name all over it. She served me a version of this when I stayed at her bed-and-breakfast on Whidbey Island. If you are ever in the Pacific Northwest, you should go stay at the Whidbey Island Bed & Breakfast. You'll love your room, the acreage, the free-running chickens, and the Southern hospitality, but you will never stop talking about Ashlyn's breakfasts. Not ever.

SERVES: 4 | PAIRING: Bloody Marys

CHEDDAR GRITS
3 cups water

½ teaspoon fine sea salt, plus more as needed

1 cup white corn grits (preferably Bob's Red Mill)

1 cup grated good-quality cheddar (preferably Beecher's Flagship Cheddar)

TABASCO HONEY
¼ cup water

2 tablespoons honey

1 teaspoon Tabasco sauce

SAUTÉED MUSHROOMS
2 tablespoons unsalted butter

½ pound hedgehog mushrooms, broken into bite-size pieces

¼ teaspoon fine sea salt

FRIED EGGS
1 tablespoon unsalted butter

4 large eggs

¼ teaspoon salt

Freshly ground black pepper

To make the grits, bring the water and salt to a boil in a large saucepan over high heat. Gradually whisk in the grits and decrease the heat to medium-low. Cook for 5 to 10 minutes, stirring from time to time. Add the cheese and stir it in until it melts. Season to taste with salt and keep warm.

To make the Tabasco honey, add the water and honey to a small saucepan and bring to a boil. Lower to a simmer and stir until the honey has dissolved into the water. Take it off the heat, let it cool for a few minutes, and then stir in the Tabasco. Set aside.

To cook the mushrooms, heat a large skillet over medium-high heat, and add the butter. Once the foam dies down, add the hedgehog mushrooms and salt and sauté until the mushrooms are browned and tender, 5 to 7 minutes. Transfer to a plate and keep warm while you fry the eggs.

To fry the eggs, reheat the skillet over medium-high heat. Add the butter and carefully crack the eggs into the pan. Season with the salt and pepper and throw a lid on top of the skillet to cook the eggs faster. Remove from the skillet when they are cooked the way you like them, though I recommend a firm white and a runny yolk for this dish.

To serve, spoon a portion of grits in the middle of each plate. Top the grits with the fried egg and then the mushrooms. Drizzle the Tabasco honey around the outside of the plate.

Hedgehog and Cashew Chili

I've been making versions of this chili since my college days, when I had something like it at a restaurant called the Cabbagetown Café in Ithaca, New York. Their cookbook of the same name was my very first. It is so used and loved that duct tape is the only thing currently holding it together. This recipe is infinitely adaptable. Sometimes I'll make it with beef, other times pork. If I'm feeling really crazy I'll make it with beef and pork. However, in keeping with the peace, love, and hippie beads spirit of the cafe, we'll keep this version vegetarian. It's great served with corn bread.

SERVES: 4 | PAIRING: California Zinfandel or a lager such as Negra Modelo

SPICE BLEND
1 tablespoon cumin seeds

1 tablespoon coriander seeds

2 teaspoons ancho chili powder (substitute pure chili powder of your choice), plus more as needed

1 teaspoon dried oregano

½ teaspoon black peppercorns

¼ teaspoon cayenne pepper

½ cup raw unsalted cashews

3 tablespoons extra-virgin olive oil

1 large yellow onion, small diced

2 stalks celery, small diced

2 red bell peppers, seeded and medium diced

1 teaspoon fine sea salt

½ pound hedgehog mushrooms, broken into bite-size pieces

1 (28-ounce) can Muir Glen fire-roasted diced tomatoes, with juices

2 (15-ounce) cans black beans, rinsed and drained

1 tablespoon red wine vinegar

Freshly ground black pepper

FOR SERVING
1 cup sour cream

1 cup grated cheddar

¼ cup minced fresh flat-leaf parsley or cilantro

Preheat the oven to 350°F.

Grind all the spice blend ingredients together in a spice grinder. Set aside.

Toast the cashews (see page xxiv).

In a large soup pot, heat 2 tablespoons of the oil over medium-high heat. Sauté the onion, celery, and peppers with the salt until starting to get soft and light brown, 5 to 7 minutes. Scrape them to the side of the pot, add the remaining 1 tablespoon oil, and then add the mushrooms. Sauté until they release their liquid and start to brown, 5 to 6 minutes. Add the spice blend and sauté everything together for 1 to 2 minutes longer, stirring frequently so the spices don't burn.

Add the tomatoes with their juices and the beans and cook for 15 to 20 minutes more. Add the toasted cashews to the chili along with the vinegar. Season to taste with salt, pepper and chili powder, and serve topped with the sour cream, cheese, and parsley.

Khao Soi Noodles with Hedgehog Mushroom Curry and Crispy Egg Noodles

Soon after I graduated from culinary school, I treated myself to a month-long culinary adventure in Thailand. I ate only street food (both to save money and because it was incredible) and by far, khao soi noodles, the regional dish of Chiang Mai, was my favorite dish. Traditionally you'd see this served with chicken or beef, but I like this meatless version, and it is no less satisfying a meal. Panang curry paste is milder than some of the other jarred Thai curry pastes you might be familiar with. If for some reason you can't find panang curry paste, feel free to substitute Thai yellow curry paste.

SERVES: 4 | PAIRING: **German dry Riesling**

3 tablespoons coconut oil

2 tablespoons panang curry paste (or use 3 for a stronger, spicier curry)

1 pound hedgehog mushrooms, broken into bite-size pieces

1 teaspoon yellow curry powder

1 (14-ounce) can unsweetened coconut milk

1 cup Mushroom Stock (page xxiii)

2 limes, 1 juiced, the other cut into wedges

2 teaspoons fish sauce

2 cups peanut oil

1 pound fresh fettuccine or linguine

1 tablespoon kosher salt

GARNISH

1 package pickled mustard greens, sliced (sold at Asian markets; or to make your own, see page 64)

1 small shallot, sliced paper-thin (about ¼ cup)

1 bunch cilantro

Bring a large pot of water to a boil. Preheat the oven to 400°F.

To prepare the mushrooms, line a baking pan with aluminum foil. Melt 1 tablespoon of the coconut oil and brush it onto the pan. In a bowl, mix 1 tablespoon of the coconut oil into 1 tablespoon of the curry paste (add a little water if necessary if it's very thick) and then toss with the mushrooms. Lay them out on the baking pan and roast until they are caramelized and tender, 10 to 15 minutes. Transfer to a plate and cover loosely with foil.

Prepare the curry by heating a large skillet over medium-high heat and then adding the remaining 1 tablespoon coconut oil. Add the remaining 1 tablespoon curry paste and cook, stirring, until it turns a nice dark rust color, about 2 minutes. Add the curry powder and cook for 30 more seconds, then add the coconut milk and stock. Bring to a boil and then simmer for 10 minutes. Taste and adjust the curry with the lime juice and fish sauce.

To fry the noodles, line a plate with power towels. Heat a small deep pot with the peanut oil to 350°F over medium-high heat. Be careful when you add the noodles, as they will sputter and puff up quickly. Fry 1 cup of the noodles in the oil until brown and crispy (you may need to flip them over to brown them evenly on both sides). They will brown fairly quickly, so be ready! Drain on the paper towels.

Add the salt to the boiling water. Boil the rest of the noodles for 3 to 4 minutes, until tender. Don't overcook.

To assemble the dish and garnishes, add the boiled noodles to the curry and toss with the sauce. Arrange the mushrooms, crispy noodles, mustard greens, shallot, cilantro, and lime wedges on a platter and allow your guests to garnish their own bowls of curry noodles. Serve immediately.

Hog and Bacon Omelette

It's impossible for me to make a French omelette without thinking about Julia Child. That one episode on *The French Chef* where she just cranked out one after another? Truly impressive. "Here is the standard, classic omelette, it's flat and French and it's very lovely and tender and soft," she warbled in classic Julia style. She made it look very, very easy. The truth is that it takes practice. I've explained the basic procedure, though I encourage you to look for clips of Julia herself making her omelette to fine-tune your technique. Bon appétit!

SERVES: 4 | PAIRING: Mimosas or Bloody Marys

½ cup small-diced bacon

½ pound hedgehog mushrooms, broken into bite-size pieces

2 ounces fresh goat cheese

8 large eggs

Fine sea salt and freshly ground black pepper

4 tablespoons unsalted butter

¼ cup minced fresh flat-leaf parsley

Lay some paper towels on a plate. In a large sauté pan over medium heat, render the fat out of the bacon until the bacon crisps up. With a slotted spoon, transfer the bacon to the paper towels, leaving the bacon fat in the pan. Add the hedgehog mushroom pieces and, over medium-high heat, sauté until the mushrooms are browned and tender, 5 to 7 minutes. Pour the mushrooms into a bowl and add the crispy bacon bits (reserving about 1 tablespoon of bacon to garnish the omelettes). Add the goat cheese to the mushroom-bacon mixture and stir until the cheese melts.

For each of the 4 omelettes you are making, beat 2 eggs in a bowl, and add a pinch of salt and some black pepper. Heat a small nonstick skillet (about 7 or so inches) with sloping sides over medium-high heat. Add 1 tablespoon of the butter per omelette. When the bubbles die down on the butter, add the eggs and with your dominant hand quickly use the back of a fork to stir the eggs, while with your non-dominant hand you rapidly shake the pan back and forth. (Alternatively, you can just swirl the pan over the heat while shaking the pan back and forth, which will begin to firm up the eggs.) The eggs will very quickly set up. As soon as this happens, stop stirring. This whole process takes 20 seconds or less. The goal is to cook the eggs fast and furious without browning or overcooking. Jerk the pan toward you to slide the eggs toward the far end. Tilt the pan up on the side closest to you and slide or push the omelette into the opposite end of the pan. Spoon one-quarter of the filling in a horizontal line across the middle of the omelette. Grab the pan at the end of the handle, placing your thumb on the top of the handle. Fold the edge closest to you over the filling and shimmy the omelette further down the pan so it's almost off the far edge. Hold a plate with your other hand and gently turn the pan over onto the plate—with practice, the omelette will roll over onto itself, onto the plate. Garnish with the reserved bacon and the parsley. Make sure to watch Julia do this on YouTube a few times before you attempt it.

Pizza with Smoked Hedgehog Mushrooms, Slow-Roasted Tomatoes, and Fontina

I don't know why I don't make pizza at home more often. I'm always pleasantly surprised at how good it comes out without any of the stuff that they say you need to make the perfect pizza at home, like a wood-burning pizza oven. I don't have that or a peel to transfer the pizza, either. I don't even have a pizza stone. It's ghetto pizza here at my house, and guess what? It still comes out pretty damn good. For the best-tasting crust, it pays to let it rise twice and then rest it in the fridge overnight. Smoking the hedgehogs really adds something special to this pizza, though it's still good with straightforward sautéed hedgehogs on top.

SERVES: 4 (makes two 14-inch or four 7-inch pizzas)

PAIRING: Italian Chianti Classico

DOUGH
1 (¼-ounce) package active dry yeast (or 2¼ teaspoons fresh yeast)

1½ cups warm water (110°F)

3½ cups unbleached all-purpose flour

2 teaspoons fine sea salt

2 tablespoons extra-virgin olive oil

SLOW-ROASTED TOMATOES
1 pound plum tomatoes, quartered

2 tablespoons extra-virgin olive oil

1 teaspoon balsamic vinegar

2 teaspoons minced fresh rosemary

½ teaspoon fine sea salt (use truffle salt if you have some)

Freshly ground black pepper

SMOKED HEDGEHOGS
1 charcoal briquette (I recommend using a natural hardwood charcoal)

1 pound fresh hedgehog mushrooms, left whole if small, halved or quartered if large

1 teaspoon vegetable oil

¼ cup extra-virgin olive oil

1 tablespoon minced garlic

1 teaspoon red pepper flakes

10 ounces fontina, shredded (3 cups)

To make the dough, add the yeast to the water in a small bowl and mix well. Leave it for at least 5 minutes or until you see the yeast proof. You should see a mini mushroom cloud develop. If you don't see any yeast activity, start over with new yeast (make sure to check the expiration dates on your yeast). Put the flour and salt in a food processor or large bowl. Pulse or mix to combine. With the food processor running, add the yeast water plus the olive oil, or mix by hand in a bowl. When the dough comes together, dump it out onto a lightly floured board (you may need to add up to another ½ cup flour) and knead until silky, about 10 minutes.

Turn the oven to 400°F for 2 minutes and then turn it off. Place the dough in a lightly oiled bowl and cover with plastic wrap. Let rise in the oven until doubled in size, 45 minutes to 1 hour. Lightly punch the dough down. (If you have time, let it rise a second time and then store in your fridge overnight. The next day, let it rise a bit at room temperature, punch down, and use.)

To roast the tomatoes, preheat the oven to 300°F. Line a baking pan with aluminum foil. Spread the tomatoes out on the pan and then drizzle the olive oil and vinegar over them. Lightly toss until they are coated and then spread them out into a single layer. Sprinkle with 1 teaspoon of the rosemary, the salt, and black pepper. Bake for 1 hour, or until they have shrunk in size and started to dry out.

Pizza with Smoked Hedgehog Mushrooms, Slow-Roasted Tomatoes, and Fontina

CONTINUED

To smoke the mushrooms, light the charcoal briquette outside (in your grill or other suitable place). Once it's covered with white ash, carefully bring it in the kitchen, and place it in a small heatproof dish in the middle of a skillet (that you have a lid for). Add the hedgehog mushrooms around the dish. Pour the vegetable oil over the briquette. It will smoke up, so place the lid on quickly and let the smoke infuse the mushrooms with its magic. Allow the mushrooms to smoke, off the heat, for 10 minutes.

Divide the dough into 2 equal pieces (or 4 for personal pizzas). Keep the one(s) you are not working with covered with plastic wrap so they don't dry out. Roll each dough ball into a 14-inch circle (or 7-inch circles for personal pizzas). Spread each pizza with an equal amount of olive oil, garlic, tomatoes, mushrooms, red pepper flakes, and fontina, making sure to leave at least a ¼-inch border around the edges. Bake until done to your liking, usually 10 to 15 minutes. Garnish with the remaining 1 teaspoon rosemary.

HERE IS A SELECTION OF THINGS TO BAKE A PIZZA ON AND WAYS TO GET IT INTO THE OVEN.

IF YOU HAVE:

A PIZZA STONE AND A PEEL *(a wooden board with a handle to slide the pizza into the oven):* Preheat the stone on the bottom rack of a 500°F oven for at least 20 minutes. Lay the circle of dough onto a cornmeal-dusted peel, top with your ingredients, and then slide the pizza off the peel onto the preheated stone.

A PIZZA STONE BUT NO PEEL: Lay the pizza round onto a parchment paper–lined rimless baking pan and top with your ingredients. Use the edge of the parchment paper to slide the pie off the baking pan and onto the preheated stone. You can cook the pizza on the parchment (on the stone) with no problem, though I recommend you cut the paper into a circle no wider than an inch beyond the circumference of the pizza to prevent the paper from catching fire in the hot oven.

NO PIZZA STONE AND NO PEEL: Hi, we're in the same boat! Preheat a rimless baking pan on the bottom rack of a 500°F oven for at least 20 minutes. Lay the pizza round onto a parchment paper–lined rimless baking pan. Use the edge of the parchment paper to slide the pie off the cold baking pan and onto the preheated baking pan. If you don't have 2 rimless baking pans, you can use the back side of a baking pan to cook your pizza or transfer it.

Chapter 11
Porcini

LATIN: *Boletus edulis*

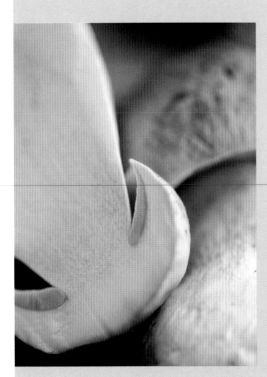

Fact Sheet:
Porcini

FLAVOR, TEXTURE,
AND AROMA NOTES:
The flavor of porcini is reminiscent
of hazelnuts. They are firm and
finely textured, with a succulent
and luscious aspect when roasted
or grilled. They smell earthy,
slightly nutty, musky, and rich,
and one taste is enough to know
why they are highly coveted.

GENERALLY SPEAKING: Porcini (porcino is the singular and means "piglet" in Italian) are one of the most highly prized mushrooms in the world. The cap looks like a hamburger bun and the stem is often short and round in the middle. Porcini is the kind of mushroom you could imagine Santa being into; it's jolly looking, with a round belly (in Mexico, porcini is called *panza*, meaning "belly"); some say porcini look like big Champagne corks growing in the woods. Instead of gills, porcini have pores, little tubules that the spores travel through on their way to the ground below. They are found throughout Europe and North America, and in parts of China and Mexico, and they are associated with the following trees: pine, chestnut, hemlock, and spruce, among other mycorrhizal partners.

AKA: King bolete (from the Greek word for "lump," because when porcini first emerge, they push up the duff and make little "mushrumps" that eagle-eyed foragers can see); cèpe (from the French word meaning "trunk"); the King; penny bun; and *steinpilz* (German, meaning "stone mushroom," which refers to its firm flesh).

SEASON: They are found from May to December.

BUYING TIPS: Porcini are graded according to quality: #1 are buttons—they are firm, have tight caps, and the pores/tubes are white to cream colored; #2 can be a bit softer, the cap has started to open, the pores/tubes have darkened to yellow; and #3 are typically used for drying (I don't buy them fresh), the pores/tubes are darker yellow to brown. #1 porcini are the most expensive. If I don't plan on chopping the porcini (in other words, if I'm wanting to use the whole porcini for aesthetic reasons), I'll spend the money on #1, but most of the time #2 porcini are perfectly wonderful, and the cost savings are appreciated.

Worms love porcini just as much as everyone else. I haven't seen fresh porcini sold in many supermarkets, so you're going to find them fresh either at a farmers' market, through mail order, or if you're lucky as a gift from a forager friend or on one of your own foraging trips. Check the stem for worm damage. If it feels firm, that's excellent. A hollow or squishy stem is a sign that there is significant insect damage. If you're buying it at a farmer's market, you might find that the seller has sliced them in half from the cap down through the stem to show you that it's not too worm-eaten. Also touch the pores; they should be firm. Once the gills have turned green, they are really on their way out and you have likely lost the battle to the worms. If you're buying dried porcini, make sure the mushrooms aren't crumbly. (They are likely very old and lacking in flavor, if so.) Dried porcini should be light in color. Also check the dried mushrooms for worm holes.

CLEANING: A damp towel is all that you'll need to wipe off any dirt or needles. A thin cut off the bottom of the stem and a vegetable peeler to take off any really dirty stem bits are helpful.

STORAGE: It's best to use fresh porcini mushrooms within a few days after you get them. Buttons (younger specimens) will keep longer than older mushrooms. As with all mushrooms, store them in the refrigerator in a brown paper bag. Second choice would be to store them in a basket or box with a dry piece of paper towel or newsprint on top of them (replace this each day).

PRESERVATION:

DRYING: See page xxix. For a description of rehydrating mushrooms, see page xxx.

FREEZING: See page xxxi. Porcini (along with morels) freeze pretty well when raw. Best to use a vacuum sealer to get all the air out of the plastic bag prior to long-term freezing. Roast them in a very hot oven from a semi-frozen state.

LOVES: Porcini mushrooms love everything and are one of the best eating mushrooms out there. Any mushroom recipe you have would be made better by substituting some porcini into the mix. Like the best steak of the mushroom world, it can simply be grilled with salt and pepper, but also can play a strong behind-the-scenes role when used dried in soups, sauces, and braises.

COOKING NOTES: Some differences exist based on at what stage you are getting the fresh porcini. Young buttons are milder in flavor and are great sautéed, shaved, or pickled; middle-age porcini have developed their pores and have an earthier flavor and are great grilled; the oldest specimens are also the strongest, and some can be musky; these are best used dried or in stews and sauces.

SUBSTITUTE: King trumpet mushrooms, plus some dried porcini or porcini powder (see page xxiii) used somewhere in the recipe, make a good substitute.

NERDY FACTOIDS:

- Porcini are considered one of the safer mushrooms to pick, as no poisonous species look similar to porcini.

- Porcini can grow very large; some tip the scales at around 7 pounds.

Porcini Salad with Pine Nuts and Lemon Salt

This is a deceptively simple composed salad that really highlights the versatility of porcini. When thinly sliced and roasted—but not overly so—porcini can be subtle, delicate, and sublime. The heat is applied lightly here, so that you can appreciate the subtlety of the dish, while the pine nuts echo the nuttiness and depth of the porcini and the lemon zings it up an octave.

SERVES: 4 as an appetizer | **PAIRING:** Austrian Grüner Veltliner

Extra-virgin olive oil, as needed

1 pound fresh porcini mushrooms, sliced ¼ inch thick (cap-through-stem slices)

1¼ teaspoons fine sea salt

¼ teaspoon red pepper flakes

Finely grated zest of 1 lemon (save lemon halves for squeezing on salad)

¼ cup pine nuts, toasted (page xxiv)

1 stalk celery (see Note), shaved paper-thin into half-moons on a mandoline (leaves cut into chiffonade and reserved for garnish)

About ¼ cup shaved Parmigiano-Reggiano (use a vegetable peeler)

Fresh chervil leaves, for garnish (substitute small flat-leaf parsley leaves)

Preheat the oven to 450°F. Line 2 baking pans with parchment paper and brush with olive oil.

Lay the porcini slices on the parchment. Brush with more olive oil. Sprinkle 1 teaspoon of the salt over the top. Roast until lightly browned in spots, 15 to 25 minutes, flipping once after 10 minutes.

In a spice grinder, pulse the red pepper flakes, lemon zest, pine nuts, and the remaining ¼ teaspoon salt to a chunky consistency.

Arrange the cooked porcini slices on plates. Sprinkle the celery over the mushrooms. Drizzle olive oil over the salads (1 to 2 teaspoons, but you don't need to measure), followed by a squeeze of lemon juice. Sprinkle the pine nut mixture over the top. Garnish with cheese shavings and celery and chervil leaves.

NOTE: Try to take off as many celery strings as you can prior to shaving the stalk on the mandoline (otherwise, they get caught in the blade). Use a paring knife—starting at the top, grab the strings between your thumb and the side of the knife and pull downward, stripping them off. If you don't have a mandoline, use a very sharp knife and cut the celery as thinly as you can manage.

Grilled Porcini with Toasted Shallot and Balsamic Vinaigrette

My father used to be an engineering manager who worked for a company that contracted with the Defense Department through the 1970s and '80s. I remember one day while I was creating some ridiculously complicated art project, he taught me the KISS principle. I thought it had to stand for something especially affectionate. But no, he told me, it stands for: Keep it simple stupid. Used in his world, it's a principle that has stood the test of time for all kinds of engineering. Simpler design equals less work, fewer broken parts, and typically greater reliability. It turns out that many things in life benefit from a little KISS, including recipe development. Especially if your goal is to take great ingredients and not muck them up. Porcini are a grand gift from nature, and the smartest thing a cook can do is get out of the way. This simple but elegant recipe was developed with you in mind, Dad.

SERVES: 4 | PAIRING: French Côtes du Rhône

TOASTED SHALLOT AND BALSAMIC VINAIGRETTE

¼ cup extra-virgin olive oil

1 tablespoon thinly sliced shallot

½ teaspoon fine sea salt or smoked salt

¼ teaspoon red pepper flakes

¼ teaspoon honey

Freshly ground black pepper

1 teaspoon Porcini Powder (page xxiii)

1 tablespoon balsamic vinegar

½ pound fresh porcini mushrooms

1 tablespoon vegetable oil

½ teaspoon fine sea salt

1 cup fresh flat-leaf parsley leaves

Start a medium-hot fire going in the grill. Make sure the grill grate is clean and oiled.

To make the vinaigrette, heat the oil in a medium sauté pan over medium heat. Add the shallot, salt, red pepper flakes, honey, black pepper, and porcini powder and cook until the shallot gets deeply browned and toasty, 7 to 10 minutes. Stir often and make sure the shallot browns but doesn't burn. Transfer to a small glass jar with a lid and add the vinegar. Shake well and let it hang out at room temperature while you cook the porcini.

To grill the mushrooms, cut the porcini in half from the cap through the stem (if whole to start with). Brush with the vegetable oil and sprinkle with the salt. Grill cut side down, flipping over when you get good grill marks on one side, about 2 minutes. Move the marked porcini off the direct heat and cover to finish the cooking, 3 to 5 minutes more depending on how hot your fire is. You want the mushrooms to be tender on the inside and caramelized on the outside. Cut into one and taste if you're unsure of doneness. Alternatively, you can pan-sear the porcini. Heat a large skillet over medium-high heat and add the oil to the pan. Place the porcini in the pan, cut side down, and sprinkle with the salt. Cook until you've got great color on the mushrooms and they are tender, 2 to 3 minutes on each side.

In a small bowl, mix the parsley leaves with 2 teaspoons of the dressing. Place equal portions of the parsley salad on each plate, top with the cooked porcini, and drizzle more of the dressing over the top, about 1 tablespoon per person.

Porcini in Broth with Parmesan Passatelli and Lemon

Once again, the Italians amaze me with their thrifty dishes that are flavorful enough to serve to royalty. I learned about this dish when I worked in a restaurant that specialized in the cuisine of Emilia-Romagna. The dish employs the rind of Parmigiano-Reggiano, a waste-not want-not strategy that pays off in flavor. Stale bread is turned into crumbs (that's the passatelli, which are quite similar to spätzle), and a humble stock is distilled from mushrooms and vegetables. It's traditionally made with a meat broth, but I really love the mushroom flavor the homemade broth adds to the dish. Adding porcini raises the cost, of course, but not if you happen to find them in the woods. I recommend using grade #1 here, as the small, tight, and firm slices look and taste great. You will need a special tool for this dish called a ricer. It's not costly and it also makes the best mashed potatoes ever, so it's a good tool to have around.

SERVES: **4 as a first course** | PAIRING: **Italian Orvieto or Soave**

2 quarts Mushroom Stock (page xxiii)

1 (¼-pound) Parmigiano-Reggiano rind

Fine sea salt, as needed

PASSATELLI DOUGH
2 large eggs

1 large egg yolk

1 teaspoon finely grated lemon zest

1 tablespoon Porcini Powder (page xxiii)

¾ cup plain bread crumbs

1 cup freshly grated Parmigiano-Reggiano, plus more for serving

Extra-virgin olive oil, as needed

½ pound grade #1 fresh porcini mushrooms, sliced ¼ inch thick (cap-through-stem slices)

½ teaspoon fine sea salt

½ lemon

Fresh flat-leaf parsley or chervil leaves, for garnish

Preheat the oven to 450°F.

In a large soup pot, bring the stock to a boil. Add the cheese rind and turn the heat down to maintain an active simmer. Reduce it to 1½ quarts. Add up to 1 teaspoon of salt after it's been reduced. Keep in mind the passatelli dough has cheese in it, which is salty.

In a medium bowl, make the dough by whisking the eggs, egg yolk, lemon zest, and porcini powder together. Stir in the bread crumbs and cheese. Refrigerate until firm, at least 30 minutes (or overnight).

Line a baking pan with parchment paper and brush with olive oil. Lay the porcini slices out on the parchment. Brush with more olive oil. Sprinkle the salt over the top of the mushrooms. Roast until lightly browned in spots, 15 to 25 minutes, flipping once after 10 minutes. Keep warm.

In a large saucepan, bring the reduced broth back to a gentle boil. Working in batches, transfer one-quarter of the dough at a time to a potato ricer with a ¼-inch hole disk. Squeeze 1-inch lengths of the dough into the simmering broth, cutting the dumplings with a knife flush against the ricer. Stir and cook gently just until the passatelli float to the surface and are tender, about 2 minutes. Using a skimmer, transfer the passatelli to a large bowl. Drizzle each batch with about a teaspoon of olive oil, tossing it around to keep from sticking. Repeat with the remaining dough.

Pass the broth through a fine-mesh strainer and reheat before serving. Spoon the passatelli into 4 bowls, and drizzle with extra-virgin olive oil and a little squeeze of lemon per bowl. Pour the hot broth on top, along with a portion of the porcini. Garnish with some parsley leaves. Serve right away, passing the grated cheese at the table.

Hanger Steak with Porcini, Blue Cheese Butter, and Truffled Sweet Potato Frites

When porcini are caramelized in a hot skillet, they become amazingly meat-like, complementing a gorgeous piece of hanger steak. But wait, there's more: How about some slowly melting blue cheese butter coating the steaks, porcini-dusted sweet potato frites, and a Bordeaux pan sauce? Hanger steak is at its best (and most tender) at medium-rare. Too rare and it's slippery in a not-so-good way. Use a thermometer for best accuracy and pull the steak from the oven or pan when it registers in the range of 125°F to 130°F.

SERVES: 4 | PAIRING: French red Bordeaux
(blend of Cabernet Sauvignon and Merlot)

1 pound hanger steaks, any silver skin trimmed off

1 heaping teaspoon truffle salt, plus more as needed

1 tablespoon Porcini Powder (page xxiii)

Freshly ground black pepper

2 ounces blue cheese, softened

4 tablespoons unsalted butter, softened

2 pounds orange-fleshed sweet potatoes, cut in half crosswise and lengthwise, then each quarter sliced lengthwise into wedges

3 tablespoons vegetable oil

¼ teaspoon red pepper flakes (optional)

¾ pound fresh porcini mushrooms, small ones halved, large ones quartered

¼ teaspoon fine sea salt

¼ cup red Bordeaux wine

¼ cup Mushroom Stock (page xxiii)

Preheat the oven to 500°F.

Bring the steaks out 30 minutes before you want to cook them and season all over with a heaping ½ teaspoon of the truffle salt, 1 teaspoon of the porcini powder, and plenty of black pepper.

In a small bowl, using a fork, mash up the blue cheese with the butter until they are well mixed. Put the blue cheese butter onto a small piece of plastic wrap or parchment paper and roll it, forming it into a ½-inch cylinder. Refrigerate until solid.

Line a baking pan with aluminum foil and place an oiled cooling rack on top of it. Toss the sweet potato wedges with 1 tablespoon of the vegetable oil, along with the remaining heaping ½ teaspoon truffle salt, red pepper flakes, if using, and the remaining 2 teaspoons porcini powder. Mix well and lay out on the cooling rack. Roast in the oven until browned and lightly crisp around the edges, 25 to 30 minutes. Flip the sweet potatoes after 15 minutes.

Heat a cast-iron skillet over high heat. Add 1 tablespoon of the vegetable oil. Add the hanger steaks and sear until deeply caramelized on all sides to medium-rare (125°F to 130°F). Set aside to rest for 10 minutes, lightly covered with aluminum foil. In the same pan, add the remaining 1 tablespoon vegetable oil. Add the porcini pieces, cut side down. Sprinkle with the sea salt. When you get nice caramelization on one side, flip them over and cook for another minute or two. Add the red wine and stock and simmer for a few minutes. Pull the porcini out of the pan and add to the plate with the resting meat. Tip the plate into the pan sauce to use all of the accumulated juices. Reduce the sauce, scraping up any stuck bits on the bottom of the pan, until it thickens enough to coat the back of a spoon, 3 to 5 minutes. Taste and season with truffle salt.

Slice the steak against the grain and serve with the mushrooms, sweet potato *frites*, and a drizzle of the pan sauce. Cut the blue cheese butter into ¼-inch disks and lay on top of the steak. Serve extra truffle salt and black pepper at the table.

Skillet-Seared Lamb Chops and Porcini with Porcini-Pistachio Cream and Cumin-Roasted Carrots

Recipe inspiration can come from anywhere, whether the cuisine of countries halfway around the globe or the cooking and conversation of friends around the corner. This recipe assembled itself in my brain from cogs and wheels both near and far: A sunset dinner on Whidbey Island of grilled shrimp with smoked paprika merged with a dinner of chicken with grilled lemon halves; colorful chats with a friend from Morocco living in the Pacific Northwest who is passionate about food; a successful recipe test where pine nuts combined so well with porcini, accentuating the nuttiness of the mushrooms (see page 131), which led me to try pistachios with porcini; a chef friend who tosses carrots with olive oil and cumin seeds and roasts them—the perfect combination of sweet and earthy and a natural pairing with lamb. But let's cut to the chase: If porcini and lamb were lovers, this recipe would be the story of their tryst in Morocco.

SERVES: 4 | PAIRING: French Crozes-Hermitage (Syrah)

8 large lamb rib chops or 4 roughly ¾-inch-thick bone-in lamb leg steaks

1¾ teaspoons fine sea salt, plus more as needed

½ teaspoon hot or smoked paprika, your choice

Freshly ground black pepper (or red pepper flakes, if you like heat)

2½ tablespoons extra-virgin olive oil

¾ pound fresh porcini mushrooms

1 pound carrots, peeled and cut on the bias into large pieces

2 lemons, halved

1 teaspoon cumin seeds

¼ cup pistachios, plus 2 tablespoons toasted and halved

1 teaspoon minced garlic

¼ cup dry (white) vermouth

½ cup heavy cream

½ cup Mushroom Stock (page xxiii)

½ teaspoon sherry vinegar

1 tablespoon vegetable oil

Parsley oil (recipe follows)

Fresh flat-leaf parsley leaves, for garnish

Preheat the oven to 450°F.

Bring the lamb out onto the counter 30 minutes before cooking. Sprinkle 1 teaspoon of the salt, paprika, and black pepper on both sides of the lamb and let sit while you prepare the roasted porcini and carrots.

Line a baking pan with aluminum foil. Brush it with some olive oil. Pick out the prettiest ½ pound of the porcini, and cut them in half from cap through the stem if they are whole. In a medium bowl, carefully toss the ½ pound porcini, carrots, and lemon halves with 1½ tablespoons of the olive oil, ½ teaspoon of the salt, and plenty of black pepper. Lay the carrots, porcini, and lemons, cut sides down, on the baking pan. Roast for 15 minutes, then leave the mushrooms where they are, but toss around the carrots. Cook for 10 more minutes. Flip the mushrooms over, sprinkle the cumin on the carrots, and roast for another 2 minutes, or until the porcini and carrots are brown in places, the carrots are tender, and the lemon is caramelized on the cut side. Depending on the size of your carrots or porcini, you may need to remove one before the other is done.

Cut the remaining ¼ pound porcini into medium dice. In a large ovenproof skillet over medium heat, add the remaining 1 tablespoon olive oil. Add the porcini and the remaining ¼ teaspoon salt. Cook until caramelized and all the water has been released, 5 to 7 minutes. Add the untoasted pistachios and garlic and sauté until the nuts toast a bit and the garlic is aromatic. Deglaze the pan with the vermouth, making sure to scrape up any bits stuck to the pan. Reduce until no liquid is left. Add the cream and mushroom stock and reduce by half. (You should be able to coat the back of a spoon with the reduction when it's ready. In other words, you should be able to draw your finger through the coated spoon and the line will remain and not fill in.) Transfer the sauce to a blender. Blend well, then add the sherry vinegar, and season to taste with salt and black pepper. Keep warm.

Clean and reheat the skillet over high heat (if using rib chops, you may need to use 2 skillets). Add the vegetable oil to the pan(s) and sear the lamb until browned on one side, then flip over and pop in the oven. Check with an instant-read thermometer every 5 minutes. Pull them out when the thermometer reads 125°F to 130°F for medium-rare lamb (which I recommend). Let rest on a plate lightly covered with foil.

To serve, place a circle of porcini-pistachio cream in the middle of each plate. Top with the lamb. (If using lamb rib chops, serve them whole. If you are using leg steaks, cut the bone out, slice, and serve.) Serve a portion of carrots and 1 large piece (or several smaller pieces) of porcini next to the lamb. Garnish with the parsley oil (drizzled around the outside edge of the plate), some parsley leaves, and the toasted pistachios.

Parsley Oil

¾ cup packed fresh flat-leaf parsley

½ cup extra-virgin olive oil

Pinch of fine sea salt

In a blender, combine the parsley, olive oil, and salt. Blend until the oil turns a vibrant green color, about 3 minutes. You can strain the oil through a fine-mesh strainer, if you like, or leave it with some texture. Transfer the oil to a bowl, or feel free to transfer it to a squeeze bottle. Store the leftovers (and you will be left with some) in the fridge. It will keep for several weeks, eventually losing its vibrancy. Use the oil in vinaigrettes or to coat vegetables for roasting.

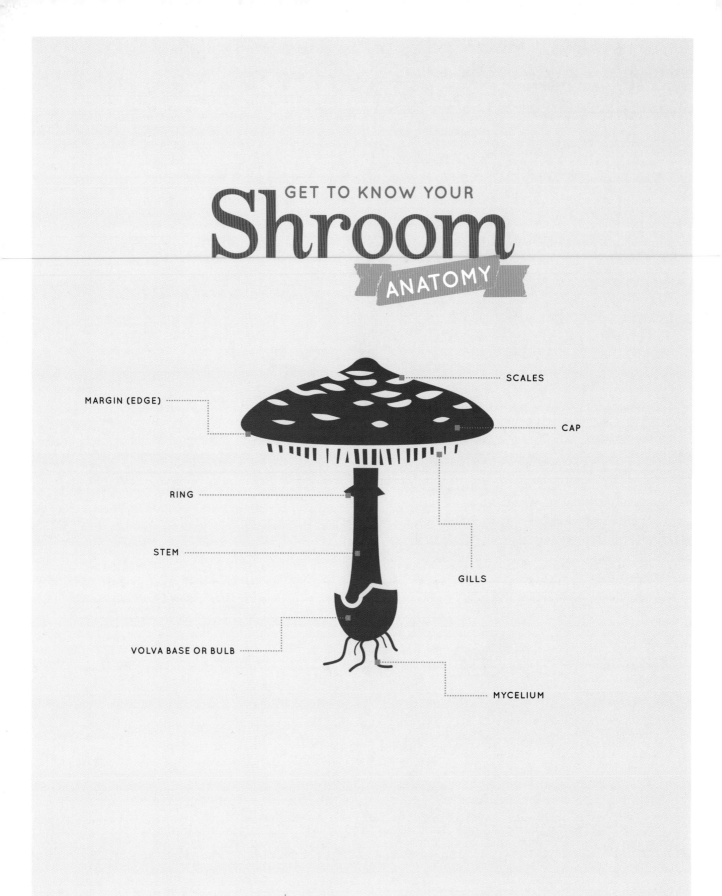

GET TO KNOW YOUR

Shroom

ANATOMY

SCALES

MARGIN (EDGE)

CAP

RING

STEM

GILLS

VOLVA BASE OR BULB

MYCELIUM

Chapter 12

Lobster

LATIN: *Hypomyces lactifluorum*

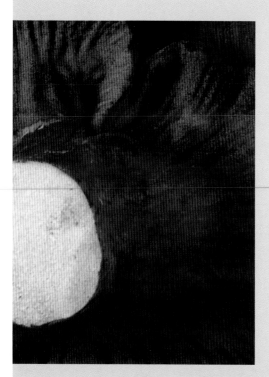

Fact Sheet:
Lobster

FLAVOR, TEXTURE, AND AROMA NOTES: Some say lobster mushrooms taste like seafood (I think they may be swayed a little by the name and the color). Some lobster mushrooms can be peppery or slightly bitter. Prized for their texture, they are dense, snappy, and chewy, with an unusual aroma that makes me think of tomatoes and corn chips. In a nod to those who find the lobster mushroom to be shellfish-like, sometimes I detect a faint aroma of ocean brininess.

GENERALLY SPEAKING: Proving that we are not really alone in this world, enter the lobster mushroom, not one but two different entities sharing the same real estate. Culinarily speaking, the first (the host) is typically *Russula brevipes* (though it can also be a member of the genus *Lactarius*). *Russula brevipes* is a meaty but flavorless mushroom. Enter stage left a parasitic fungus called *Hypomyces lactifluorum*, spreading itself all over the host, transforming it in color (red) and flavor (oddly seafood-like). Mushroom expert Tom Volk calls it "mycological cannibalism." Lobster mushrooms are found in abundance in the Pacific Northwest near old-growth fir-dominant forests, but they also can be found from Alaska to Mexico and among oak trees on the East Coast of the United States.

AKA: Lobster mushrooms don't have as many nicknames as some others (see Morels, page 90, for example). Perhaps they are universally known as "lobsters" because the name is already so spot-on descriptive.

SEASON: They can be found from July to October.

BUYING TIPS: Ideal lobster mushrooms are firm, with no dark spots or squishiness. While many are intense red-orange, others are lighter in color. On each mushroom, however, look for a consistent coloration on the top and a pinkish to tomato red color on the bottom. Avoid very dark-colored lobsters, as darkening is typically a sign of age. Occasionally you'll see lobsters with a white dust; these are spores and they wash off easily. It's also common that you'll find a secondary mold on the mushroom that's harmless and looks like cobwebs; simply wipe this off.

CLEANING: Lobsters can get quite dirty, especially on their concave tops; use the tip of a knife and a brush (the pros use toothbrushes to clean the mushrooms, and you can too). The knife and brush will get the lion's share of the dirt off, but you might still need a wipe with a damp towel or a quick rinse with the faucet's spray attachment to get rid of the rest. Trim off any small brown or dark reddish spots.

STORAGE: Unlike many other mushrooms, lobsters have a decent shelf life, perhaps due to the tougher exterior (thank you, parasitic fungus). As with all mushrooms, store them in the refrigerator in a brown paper bag. Second choice would be to store them in a basket or box with a dry piece of paper towel or newsprint on top of them (replace this each day).

PRESERVATION:

DRYING: See page xxix. For a description of rehydrating mushrooms, see page xxx.

FREEZING: See page xxxi.

LOVES: Lobster mushrooms pair well with fish (shellfish, in particular) and because of their firm texture hold up well on the grill. Other loves include: chowders, butter, stews and braises, risotto, and paella (as a bonus, it colors the rice).

COOKING NOTES: Lobster mushrooms have a firm texture that takes some getting used to. They readily absorb the flavors of foods you cook them with, so capitalize on that by adding those flavors while they are cooking. Lobster mushrooms are fabulous when braised because their density stands up well to long cooking. Unlike most other mushrooms, they barely kick off any liquid when you cook them.

SUBSTITUTE: Because of their slight brininess and affinity for seafood, the best stand-in for lobster mushrooms would be king trumpet or oyster mushrooms.

NERDY FACTOIDS:

- The red color makes a good dye, so keep that in mind when adding to cream-based dishes.

- Eventually, the parasitic fungus twists the mushroom into odd shapes, nothing like what the original species looked like.

Lobster Mushroom Tempura with Daikon-Dashi Dipping Sauce and Fried Basil

When polling my cooking students, I'm told that the number-one reason people don't deep-fry at home is that they're afraid they'll start a fire. But when pushed, they'll also offer that they fear their cardiologist will lecture them, or that they have no idea what to do with the oil when they're done. These are all valid concerns. Let me address them one by one. First, never fill your pot more than halfway with fat and don't superheat it (keep it under 400°F). Second tell your cardiologist that life is short and tempura every once in a while is a thing of beauty, and appreciating beauty is good for your soul, so it follows that a happy soul is better for your health. In summary: tempura = better health. Last, you can strain the oil through a fine-mesh strainer, label it as fry oil, and store it in your fridge for numerous reuses, so there's no waste, at least in the short run. You'll have time to look into whether you need to throw it out or whether your locality recycles fry oil, as some do. So you can stand there and clutch your heart and your pearls and worry about burning your house down or you can go make lobster mushroom tempura.

SERVES: 4 to 6 | PAIRING: Italian extra-dry Prosecco

DAIKON-DASHI DIPPING SAUCE

½ cup Mushroom Dashi (page xxiii; see Note)

2 tablespoons finely grated daikon radish (see Note)

2 tablespoons mirin

2 tablespoons soy sauce

1 tablespoon seasoned rice vinegar

TEMPURA BATTER

½ cup unbleached all-purpose flour

½ cup rice flour

1 teaspoon baking powder

½ teaspoon fine sea salt

⅛ teaspoon cayenne pepper

1 large egg yolk

1½ cups ice-cold water

Peanut oil, for frying

1 tablespoon toasted sesame oil

½ cup fresh basil leaves

½ pound fresh lobster mushrooms, cut into ¼-inch-thick slices

To make the dipping sauce, mix all of the ingredients together in a medium bowl. Pour into individual small cups for each diner and set aside.

To make the tempura batter, mix both flours, baking powder, salt, and cayenne together in a medium bowl using a whisk. In another medium bowl, whisk up the egg yolk and then whisk in the ice-cold water (literally have ice cubes in the measuring cup with the water). Using chopsticks or a fork, add the dry ingredients to the wet ingredients. The key here is to not mix very much at all. Lumps are good. Any energy in really mixing the batter will develop gluten, making your tempura batter bready and heavy, the opposite of great tempura. The batter should be the consistency of thin pancake batter with lots of lumps.

To fry, heat 2 inches of peanut oil to 360°F in a Dutch oven or heavy sauce pot. Have a paper towel–lined plate or a brown paper bag at the ready to drain the tempura. When the oil reaches that temperature, carefully add the sesame oil. Have a splatter guard ready. Quickly put the basil leaves in the oil, covering it with the splatter guard so you don't get burned by the popping of the leaves. After the popping dies down, lift the splatter guard and stir the leaves around. They are done as soon as they firm up (this takes no more than 30 seconds). Pull the leaves out and place on the paper towels to drain. They should be a stunning shade of light forest green.

Dip the lobster mushroom pieces into the batter and, using chopsticks or tongs, add to the oil. Fry in a few batches (fewer with a big pan, more with a smaller capacity pan). When the pieces are in, dip the fingers of one hand into the batter and carefully spray the excess into the oil. This will deposit little balls of batter into the oil, creating wispy bits on the mushrooms. They are yummy. Fry, flipping over once while cooking, until the mushroom pieces are light brown, 3 to 4 minutes total cooking time. Use a skimmer to remove the mushrooms and any stuck-on little batter balls from the pan and allow to drain before eating. In between batches, use the skimmer to pull out any sediment floating in the oil. Make sure the temperature is between 350° and 360°F before you fry another batch.

NOTE: You can substitute ½ cup rehydrated Hondashi brand instant dashi, though it contains MSG. You'll have to use less salt in the rest of the sauce, substitute regular rice wine vinegar for the seasoned, and also use a low-sodium soy sauce.

NOTE: An interesting daikon factoid is that the vegetable has 3 different flavor zones. The top (closest to the leaves) is the mildest. The middle section is the sweetest. The tip (closest to the roots) is the spiciest.

Grilled Lobster Mushrooms, Tandoori-Style

Most cooks can look to one or two chefs who, either overtly or through quiet example, educated and inspired them to become better at their craft. Jerry Traunfeld, chef-owner of Poppy restaurant in Seattle and the James Beard Award–winning former chef of The Herbfarm restaurant, is one of those people to me. I cooked for Jerry for three years at The Herbfarm, but it has been our thirteen-year friendship that has inspired me to expand my culinary horizons in food and writing and enthusiastically embrace the world of herbs and spices. I've adapted his dish, made at Poppy in the tandoor oven, to work in a home kitchen, either on your grill or under your broiler.

SERVES: 4 as an appetizer or side dish | PAIRING: German dry Riesling

YOGURT SAUCE

½ cup whole-milk plain yogurt

½ teaspoon ground roasted cumin

2 tablespoons chopped fresh cilantro

½ teaspoon kosher salt

½ teaspoon honey

2 teaspoons freshly squeezed lemon juice

MARINATED MUSHROOMS

1 tablespoon garam masala

1 teaspoon fine sea salt

½ teaspoon cayenne pepper

½ teaspoon ground turmeric

¼ teaspoon ground nutmeg

2 teaspoons garbanzo bean flour (or unbleached all-purpose flour)

2 teaspoons grated fresh ginger

2 teaspoons minced garlic

2 teaspoons minced jalapeño chiles (seeds and membranes too, if you like the heat)

2 teaspoons freshly squeezed lemon juice

¼ cup whole-milk plain yogurt

⅓ cup chopped fresh cilantro (stems are okay)

¾ pound fresh lobster mushrooms, cut into ½-inch-thick slices

Preheat a grill to medium heat and oil the grate with coconut or vegetable oil. Alternatively, set an oven rack in the middle of the oven and preheat your broiler to high; line a baking pan with aluminum foil and brush the foil with the oil.

To make the yogurt sauce, whisk all of the ingredients together in a bowl. Set aside.

To marinate the mushrooms, grab a medium bowl and stir together the garam masala, salt, cayenne, turmeric, nutmeg, and garbanzo flour. Stir in the ginger, garlic, jalapeño, lemon juice, yogurt, and cilantro. Once the marinade is well mixed, add the mushrooms to the bowl and, using your fingers, make sure each mushroom is well coated with the marinade. Grill the mushrooms until browned and cooked through, 7 to 10 minutes. Or if you are broiling them, place the mushrooms on the prepared baking pan. Broil for 10 minutes, flip them over, and broil for another 5 minutes. Serve with the yogurt sauce.

Squid Ink Pasta with Lobster Mushrooms and Squid

This dish makes me think of Spain, a country I have yet to visit, so more appropriately this dish makes me think of the Spain of my dreams. When I close my eyes, the streets are lined with endless bottles of olive oil and sherry vinegar. There are overflowing baskets of oranges, heaping tabletops are mounded with chiles and peppers, and fresh fish abounds. Everywhere I turn, people are eating something amazing. The topping is key to the balance of this dish, with the panko's lightness and crunch combined with the bright citrus notes of the orange zest and the earthy, rich porcini powder. As with all recipes, but especially with this one, this dish excels in direct proportion to the quality of the ingredients.

SERVES: 4 | PAIRING: Italian Vermentino

¼ pound fresh lobster mushrooms, medium diced, or ¼ ounce dried

1 heaping tablespoon kosher salt

¼ cup plus 2 tablespoons extra-virgin olive oil

1 cup panko bread crumbs

2 tablespoons Porcini Powder (page xxiii)

1 orange, zested and juiced (about 1 tablespoon finely grated zest)

⅛ teaspoon plus ¼ teaspoon fine sea salt

1 tablespoon minced fresh flat-leaf parsley

½ pound dried squid ink linguine

¼ cup minced shallot

2 cloves garlic, minced

1 teaspoon red pepper flakes

4 ounces sliced, drained jarred piquillo peppers (substitute roasted red peppers)

½ pound cleaned squid (tubes sliced crosswise into ¼-inch rings, tentacles left whole if small, halved if large; see Note)

1 tablespoon sherry vinegar

If you're using dried lobster mushrooms, rehydrate as directed on page xxx and then cut into medium dice. Save the rehydration liquid. If you're using fresh lobster mushrooms, clean as directed on page 141 and cut into medium dice.

Bring a large pot of water to a boil. Add the kosher salt.

In a large skillet over medium heat, add 2 tablespoons of the olive oil and, after a moment, add the panko, porcini powder, and orange zest and sauté until golden brown, 3 to 5 minutes. Transfer to a bowl and stir in the ⅛ teaspoon sea salt and parsley. Season to taste—this is the crunchy topping for the pasta.

Wipe the skillet out with a paper towel and add 2 more tablespoons of olive oil. Turn the heat to medium-high. Add the lobster mushrooms and the remaining ¼ teaspoon sea salt. Sauté for 6 to 8 minutes, until they start to brown on the edges. If you are using rehydrated dried mushrooms, you can now add the rehydration liquid and cook the mushrooms until all the liquid has been absorbed. If you are using fresh mushrooms, simply proceed with the next step.

Drop the pasta into the boiling water, and give it a stir or two.

Add the remaining 2 tablespoons olive oil to the skillet with the mushrooms, along with the shallot, garlic, red pepper flakes, and piquillo peppers. Sauté for 2 to 3 minutes over medium-high heat, until the shallot is translucent. Add the squid, vinegar, and orange juice and cook for 1 to 2 minutes, just until the squid turns white and firms up. Remove the pan from the heat and wait for the pasta to be cooked just a little bit less than al dente. You will finish cooking the pasta with the sauce to better absorb the flavors.

When the pasta is just a minute or two shy of al dente, reserve ½ cup of the cooking water, and then drain the pasta. Taste the sauce and, if it needs salt, add some of the pasta water to the sauce skillet. Add the pasta to the skillet, return the skillet to medium-high heat, and, using tongs, keep turning the pasta over in the sauce until it has absorbed some of it. If it still needs more salt, stir in some or all of the remaining pasta water.

Serve the pasta in wide bowls (white ones for dramatic effect) and top generously with the crunchy panko-porcini topping. Put the excess topping in a bowl to serve at the table.

NOTE: If you can't find already cleaned and sliced squid tubes and tentacles, buy them whole. You can refer to my how-to video online for assistance on cleaning and cutting squid at www.goodfishbook.com.

Thai Sweet and Sour Soup with Lobster Mushrooms, Lemongrass, and Shrimp

This soup is based on the classic Thai dish known as tom yum goong; the secret to making a great one is to put all your effort and love into making a great stock. I encourage you to use dried lobster mushrooms here, as their rehydration liquid, along with the toasted shrimp shell stock, makes a fine base for the soup. Extra bonus: The rehydrated lobster mushrooms retain a touch of chewiness that makes for a great textural contrast.

SERVES: 4 | PAIRING: French Gewurztraminer

1 ounce dried lobster mushrooms (or ½ pound fresh)

3 tablespoons coconut oil (or vegetable oil)

½ pound sustainable shrimp, peeled and deveined (save the peels)

1 small carrot, small diced

1 stalk celery, small diced

½ small yellow onion, small diced

¼ cup dry white wine

2 stalks lemongrass

1 bunch cilantro, stems and leaves separated

5 kaffir lime leaves

3 serrano chiles, 2 split in half, leaving the stem intact, 1 thinly sliced, seeds and all

3 (⅛-inch) coins fresh ginger

6 cups water

1 scant teaspoon fine sea salt, plus a pinch

1 tomato, medium diced (about 1 cup), or 1 whole canned tomato

2 to 3 tablespoons freshly squeezed lime juice

2 to 3 tablespoons fish sauce

1 teaspoon sugar

¼ cup fresh Thai basil, stemmed and torn into bite-size pieces

If using dried lobster mushrooms, rehydrate as directed on page xxx. Save the rehydration liquid and chop the rehydrated mushrooms into medium dice. Clean fresh lobster mushrooms as directed on page 141 and cut into medium dice.

Place 2 tablespoons of the coconut oil in a soup pot over high heat. Add the shrimp shells and toast until lightly browned and nutty smelling, about 5 minutes. Add the carrot, celery, and onion and sauté until lightly browned, 8 to 10 minutes more. Deglaze the pot with the white wine, making sure to scrape up any bits stuck to the pot. Prep your lemongrass. If the stalks are whole, chop off the top two-thirds and compost them (they're tough and don't have the intense flavor of the bottom third). Smash the bottom third with the side of a knife to help release the essential oils. To the stock, add the smashed lemongrass, cilantro stems, kaffir lime leaves, 2 split serrano chiles, and ginger. Add the lobster mushroom rehydration liquid, if using dried mushrooms, and enough of the water to equal 6 cups of liquid total. Bring the stock to a boil over high heat, then lower to a simmer and cook for 30 minutes.

Strain the stock through a fine-mesh sieve into a container, pressing on the ingredients. Clean the soup pot and return to the stove over medium-high heat. Add the remaining 1 tablespoon coconut oil to the pot along with the lobster mushrooms. Add the pinch of salt and sauté until brown and caramelized, 8 to 10 minutes. It's OK to get a little bit of char on the mushrooms; the flavor adds a lovely smokiness to the broth. Add the diced tomato and stock. Bring back to a boil over medium-high heat. Simmer for 10 minutes to infuse the flavor of the mushrooms into the soup. Add the raw shrimp and immediately turn off the heat and cover (the shrimp will poach using this technique and won't overcook). After 2 minutes, lift the lid and add the lime juice, fish sauce, remaining 1 teaspoon salt, and sugar. Adjust the amounts of these final seasonings to your taste. Garnish each bowl with sliced serrano chiles, basil, and cilantro leaves.

Lobster Mushroom Chawanmushi with Lobster

Chawanmushi is Japanese for "steamed in a tea bowl." You'll need 4 (1-cup) heatproof teacups, ramekins, or small bowls for this recipe with a diameter of 3 to 3½ inches. This is a subtle dish that is all about texture and beauty and, like the best Japanese food, is intimately tied to the seasons. The feeling of slicing through that top layer of custard with your spoon and pulling it back to reveal the infused liquid is not unlike coming to the edge of a barely frozen pond with a thin layer of crystal-clear water on top. Make this dish when you want to woo someone.

SERVES: 4 | **PAIRING:** Washington or California Viognier

LOBSTER POACHING LIQUID
¼ cup Mushroom Dashi (page xxiii) or Mushroom Stock (page xxiii)

2 tablespoons sake

½ teaspoon soy sauce

1 tablespoon unsalted butter

2 ounces fresh lobster mushrooms

1 (¼-pound) uncooked lobster tail, shelled and cut into 8 bite-sized pieces (save the shell for shellfish stock)

4 large eggs (since this is all about the custard, use the best eggs you can find)

2½ cups Mushroom Dashi (page xxiii)

½ teaspoon fine sea salt

½ teaspoon mirin

1 tablespoon soy sauce

4 carrot flowers, blanched for 2 minutes in salted water (see Note)

4 curls lemon zest

4 tarragon sprigs

Prepare the poaching liquid by combining all of the ingredients in a small bowl. Set aside.

Set up a steamer with at least 2 inches of water in the bottom (you can use an insert inside your pasta pot as a steamer if you don't have a metal or bamboo steamer).

To poach the lobster and lobster mushrooms, first cut 4 pretty garnish slices of lobster mushroom that show the pretty orange color but will fit in the serving vessels you are using. Then cut the rest into small dice.

In a medium sauté pan over medium heat, put the poaching liquid. Cook until the butter is melted, then decrease to a bare simmer and add the lobster meat. Tilt the pan slightly and, using a spoon, baste the lobster meat with the liquid. Cook the lobster meat until it just starts to firm up, 1 to 3 minutes. Transfer the lobster meat to a small bowl. Raise the heat to medium-high and add the lobster mushrooms (both garnish pieces and the small-diced pieces). Cook until they have absorbed all of the liquid, 4 to 5 minutes.

Pull out 4 nice garnish pieces of lobster meat from the bowl and set aside along with the reserved 4 slices of lobster mushroom (this dish is *ALL* about pretty). Divide the rest of the lobster pieces and the diced, cooked lobster mushrooms evenly among 4 (1-cup) heatproof ramekins.

Lobster Mushroom Chawanmushi with Lobster

Break the eggs into a medium bowl. Use chopsticks (or a fork) to carefully break up the eggs. You want to completely mix up the eggs but prevent too much froth from developing (bubbles will mar the glassy texture of the dish). Once the eggs are carefully mixed, pour in the dashi while slowly stirring with chopsticks. Gently mix in the salt, mirin, and soy sauce. Strain this mixture through a fine-mesh strainer into a container with a spout. Divide the liquid evenly into the 4 ramekins, on top of the lobster meat and lobster mushrooms, leaving ½ inch headspace at the top. (If you end up with bubbles on top of the custards, use a spoon to gently scoop them out.)

To steam the custards, bring the water in the steamer to a boil. Cover each ramekin with either a lid or aluminum foil. Place into the steamer, put the lid on the steamer, and cook over a full boil for 1 minute. Turn the heat down to low so that the water is lightly simmering and cook for another 7 minutes. Open the pot and pull a lid off of one of the ramekins. If the custard looks like it has set on the top (enough to support the weight of the garnish pieces), add a pretty piece of lobster, lobster mushroom, carrot flower, and lemon curl; repeat for each ramekin. Re-cover, turn the heat back to high, and steam for 30 seconds. Then turn the heat back down to its lowest setting and steam for a final 5 minutes. Open the lid and shake each ramekin gently; the custard should jiggle just a bit, without being runny. It's a looser custard than you might be used to. Add a tiny sprig of tarragon to each ramekin and serve immediately.

NOTE: To make carrot flowers, cut out a 3-inch section of carrot that is roughly equal in diameter from top to bottom. Holding your thumb and pointer finger on the round edges of carrot, hold the carrot flat as can be on a cutting board. Make 5 lengthwise triangular notches in the carrot roughly equidistant apart. If you want to be even fancier, using a paring knife cut the rough edges off at an angle where the triangular notch meets the carrot. Now, cut the carrot crosswise into ⅛-inch pieces. Or you could buy a flower stamp and stamp them out of carrot rounds, but then you'd feel like a cheater and where's the pride in that? I mean, really, you've already committed to doing one of the fussiest recipes in the book.

Chapter 13
Black Trumpet

LATIN: *Craterellus spp.*

Fact Sheet:
Black Trumpet

GENERALLY SPEAKING: The black trumpet mushroom is both saprotrophic and mycorrhizal. They can be found in the woods of Europe, North America, Korea, and Japan. They are associated with oak, beech, or other broad-leaved trees. They grow on moist spots on heavy calcareous (that is, chalky) soils. Variations in color range from all black to gray to brown. They are thin, somewhat brittle, and pretty hard to find, blending in easily with the leaves and shadows on the forest floor. Foragers advise beginners to look for the black holes in the ground. They are in the same family as chanterelles (*Cantharellaceae*).

FLAVOR, TEXTURE, AND AROMA NOTES:
The flavor of the black trumpet rivals that of a morel mushroom. While it's related to a chanterelle, I liken it more to a morel, with its deep woodsy, nearly smoky flavor. The texture is thin, feathery, supple, and velour- or suede-like when fresh. Because of their thin walls, over high heat they can cook up to a nearly crunchy texture, like mushroom bacon. The aroma is musky and just faintly sweet or fruity.

AKA: Alternate names are black chanterelle, horn of plenty, *trompette de la mort* (French), poor man's truffle, and trumpet of the dead. Common lore says that the dead send up the mushrooms around the grave to play the black trumpets for the living—a little morbid for such a delicious edible, perhaps, but don't let that stop you from seeking them out. David Aurora, in his must-have book *Mushrooms Demystified*, calls them black petunias—I call them one of my favorite mushrooms in the world.

SEASON: They are in season on the U.S. East Coast and in the Midwest from June to October. On the West Coast, they can be found from November to April.

LOVES: Because of the light smokiness I detect, I especially love black trumpets paired with anything smoked (Scotch, smoked chiles, bacon, smoked fish). They also love being teamed up with eggs, cream, and dill.

BUYING TIPS: Look for black trumpets that are sturdy and as much as possible free of sand; when dried out (I'm talking about fresh mushrooms here), they can become brittle. If they smell pungent or unpleasant, they are past their prime. Bonus: There are almost zero worm problems to deal with when it comes to this type of mushroom.

CLEANING: If you see a closed end at the bottom of the stem, you'll want to cut or snip it off. This stem bit traps the grit and sand. Often, though, the mushroom will have been cut above this end, so look before you cut. Then split the trumpets lengthwise to expose any grit, dunk in a bowl of water, swish around, and gently squeeze the water out; repeat in a fresh bowl of clean water. Lay them on a towel to dry or put a towel in the bottom of a salad spinner, lay the mushrooms on top of the towel, and spin them dry. Dried black trumpets require extremely careful cleaning: The grit and sand can really get wedged in the crevices. See page xxvi for a detailed explanation of how to clean dried wild mushrooms.

PRESERVATION:

DRYING: See page xxix. For a description of rehydrating mushrooms, see page xxx. Black trumpets dry very well, with no loss in flavor (and perhaps even acquire improved flavor).

FREEZING: See page xxxi.

COOKING NOTES: The liquid that fresh black trumpets kick off in the pan is really flavorful, so it can be used almost as a braising liquid; once the mushrooms are tender, you can increase the heat and spread them out to get some browning, deepening the already complex flavors. Keep in mind that seeing the browning on a black mushroom is nearly impossible. Listen for the snap and crackle sound and a reduction in steam, which will signify that caramelization has begun and the water has evaporated. Let your nose also guide you—the mushrooms will smell toasty when ready. Black trumpets can bleed some of their black color onto other foods, so when combining with eggs or fish, for example, you may want to cook them separately and add them at the end.

STORAGE: Fresh trumpet mushrooms have a very good shelf life, akin to chanterelles. As with all mushrooms, store them in the refrigerator in a brown paper bag. Second choice would be to store them in a basket or box with a dry piece of paper towel or newsprint on top of them (replace this each day).

SUBSTITUTE: If you can't find black trumpet mushrooms, look for morels (fresh or dried). The rich, woodsy savoriness and faint smokiness of both mushrooms make them interchangeable in my mind, flavorwise if not in texture or shape. Another substitution possibility would be to use a mixture of fresh chanterelles and a little dried porcini.

NERDY FACTOIDS:

- The aroma of black trumpets is lightly fruity (some say it reminds them of apricots), and they are sometimes used to flavor dry white wines that need a little flavor lift.

- There are no poisonous lookalikes.

Smoky Squash Soup with Black Trumpet Mushrooms and Scotch

I adore this simple weeknight soup. It's comforting, complex, and takes so little time to make. It feels a little like cheating to put "Scotch" into a recipe title. On the other hand, unless you abstain from drinking, why wouldn't you want to justify your drinking habit by claiming it was your dinner? You don't need a fancy Scotch for this; something you would enjoy drinking but don't go crazy and buy a single malt just to cook with it. More and more stores are selling specialty salts. The smoked salt called for just adds to the smokiness of the mushrooms and Scotch, but it is certainly not a crucial ingredient.

SERVES: 4 | **PAIRING:** French Crozes-Hermitage (Syrah)

¼ pound fresh black trumpet mushrooms or ½ ounce dried

2 tablespoons extra-virgin olive oil

1 teaspoon smoked salt (substitute fine sea salt), plus more as needed

1 medium yellow onion, small diced (about 2 cups)

¼ teaspoon cayenne pepper

1 tablespoon chopped fresh sage

1 dried bay leaf

4 cups peeled and large-diced butternut squash

¼ cup Scotch whisky

4 cups Mushroom Stock (page xxiii if using purchased, taste before adding more salt at the end)

Freshly ground black pepper

Crème fraîche (substitute sour cream), for garnish

Fresh flat-leaf parsley leaves, for garnish

Clean the fresh black trumpet mushrooms as directed on page 155 and cut into bite-size pieces. If you're using dried black trumpet mushrooms, clean and rehydrate as directed on page xxx (saving 1 cup of strained rehydration liquid as part of the amount of stock needed) and cut the rehydrated mushrooms into bite-size pieces.

In a soup pot over medium heat, place 1 tablespoon of olive oil. Add the mushrooms and ½ teaspoon of the smoked salt. Sauté for 4 to 5 minutes to release any water and start the browning process. Pull the mushrooms out and keep them warm. Add the remaining 1 tablespoon olive oil, onion, and the remaining ½ teaspoon smoked salt, and sauté for 8 to 10 minutes, until the onion is soft and starting to brown. Add the cayenne, sage, bay leaf, and butternut squash. Sauté for 2 to 3 minutes, deglaze the pan using the Scotch, making sure to scrape up any bits stuck to the pan. Add the mushroom stock/rehydration liquid. Bring to a boil, then decrease the heat to a simmer and cook, partially covered until the squash is tender, about 20 minutes. Remove the bay leaf. Using a masher or an immersion blender, mash/blend half of the soup to give it some body (or alternatively, you can puree the whole thing). Season to taste with black pepper and more smoked salt. Divide the soup among 4 bowls and top each with one-quarter of the sautéed black trumpet mushrooms. Garnish with a dollop of crème fraîche and some parsley leaves.

Black Trumpet Pâté with Sage and Marsala

I don't like telling people which recipe in my cookbooks is my favorite because it sort of feels like choosing your preferred child or pet. However, this recipe right here? It's my favorite: It's like the foie gras of vegetarian dishes. It's an umami-blasting, all-night-long flavor machine of a dish, and it's relatively easy to make and even more flavorful using dried trumpets rather than fresh. Use a ½-cup to ¾-cup capacity ramekin or tapas dish.

SERVES: 4 as an appetizer　｜　PAIRING: French Champagne

½ ounce dried black trumpet mushrooms

3 tablespoons unsalted butter

1 cup small-diced yellow onion

½ teaspoon fine sea salt, plus more as needed

¼ teaspoon smoked salt, plus more for garnish

1 teaspoon tomato paste

1 teaspoon minced fresh sage, plus a few tiny sage leaves for garnish

1 teaspoon minced fresh thyme

1 teaspoon freshly squeezed lemon juice

½ teaspoon soy sauce

¼ teaspoon freshly ground black pepper

⅛ teaspoon cayenne pepper (less if you want it pretty mild)

2 tablespoons Marsala

Rehydrate the black trumpet mushrooms as directed on page xxx, reserving 1 cup of the rehydration liquid.

In a medium skillet over medium-high heat, melt 1 tablespoon of the butter and add the onion and sea salt. Turn the heat down to medium and cook the onion, stirring occasionally, for 15 minutes, until the onion is very soft and lightly caramelized. Add the black trumpets and sauté for 3 to 4 minutes. Remove 1 or 2 mushrooms to use as garnish; set them aside. Add the smoked salt, tomato paste, minced sage and thyme, lemon juice, soy sauce, black pepper, and cayenne to the ingredients in the pan and sauté for 1 more minute. Deglaze the pan with the Marsala and then, 30 seconds later, add the reserved 1 cup strained mushroom soaking liquid. Reduce the mushroom mixture by about half (you should be left with roughly ¾ cup). Transfer the mixture to a blender and puree until very smooth. Season to taste with fine sea salt.

Fill a ½- to ¾-cup capacity serving dish with the pâté. Use a spatula to smooth out the surface. Melt the remaining 2 tablespoons butter in a small sauté pan, skimming the top with a spoon to scoop out the white milk solids. You can discard or spread the milk solids onto a piece of bread as a snack. Pour the clarified butter evenly over the top of the pâté. Refrigerate until chilled and the butter is set. Garnish with a scant sprinkle of smoked salt, the reserved pieces of mushroom, and some tiny sage leaves.

NOTE: You can easily double the recipe and freeze one ramekin (just wrap it really well in plastic wrap and then foil); thaw in the refrigerator overnight before serving. I like to eat the pâté with a spoon, while blocking other diners from it with my arm; however, if you are feeling more charitable, it is lovely served with fresh bread, crostini, brioche toast points, or any cracker of your choice. The pâté can also be used as a spread on a sandwich, in combination with a slab of roasted eggplant, perhaps, or a slice of tomato, or both.

Black Trumpet and Roasted Poblano Chilaquiles with Crema

Most of the chilaquiles dishes I've had in Mexico featured the tortillas stewed into the sauce, whether it was green or red. The result was a soft (some might say soggy) tortilla dish, somewhere between polenta and nachos. I make my chilaquiles by frying my own tortillas (you can easily substitute purchased tortilla chips) and quickly dunking them in the red sauce, and then tapping off any extra and putting them right onto the plates, moments before serving the dish. This is the best of both worlds, as the fried tortillas have crispy parts and soft parts and soak up the flavorful sauce without becoming soggy. Black trumpet mushrooms are a little smoky, so pairing them with charred sliced poblanos was a no-brainer. You will have leftover chili sauce, feel free to freeze it for another round of chilaquiles at a different date, or use it with cheddar cheese in an egg scramble the next day.

SERVES: 4 | PAIRING: Pilsner

¼ pound fresh black trumpet mushrooms or ½ ounce dried

2 dried ancho chiles (use only 1 if you want a really mild sauce), stems and seeds removed

3 tablespoons extra-virgin olive oil

1 small yellow onion, small diced (about ¾ cup)

⅛ teaspoon fine sea salt, plus more for sprinkling

2 large red tomatoes, cored and quartered

½ teaspoon honey

1 poblano chile

1 cup vegetable oil

20 corn tortillas, cut into triangles (or good-quality tortilla chips)

TOPPINGS
1 lime, sliced into wedges

Queso fresco (substitute queso cotija)

Mexican crema (substitute sour cream)

1 avocado, pitted, peeled, and sliced right before serving

1 bunch cilantro

4 large eggs, fried over easy

Clean the fresh black trumpet mushrooms as directed on page 155. If you're using dried black trumpet mushrooms, clean and rehydrate as directed on page xxx.

In a dry medium cast-iron skillet or frying pan over medium-high heat, toast the ancho chiles by spreading them out and toasting them for a few minutes on each side. They will become aromatic and pliable. Transfer them to a small saucepan and cover them with water. Bring to a boil. Remove them from the heat, making sure they are submerged under the water, and rehydrate them for 10 minutes.

Meanwhile, heat 1 tablespoon of the olive oil over medium-high heat in the same skillet you used for the ancho chiles. Add the onion and salt and sauté for 8 to 10 minutes. Add a tablespoon or two of the chile rehydration liquid from the saucepan if the onion starts to stick or gets too dried out. Transfer the onion to a blender when soft and lightly browned. Scoop out the anchos from the liquid and add them to the blender, along with the tomatoes and honey. Blend into a smooth puree and season to taste with salt and honey. (Go light on the salt if you will be using already salted purchased tortilla chips in the dish.) Pour the chili sauce into the small saucepan, bring to a boil, lower the heat to a simmer, and cook for 10 minutes.

Black Trumpet and Roasted Poblano Chilaquiles with Crema

CONTINUED

Blacken the poblano chile by either setting it directly over a gas flame (and turning as needed) or broiling right under the heating element, turning it occasionally until it is completely black. Place the blackened poblano in a paper bag or in a bowl covered with plastic wrap. Let it steam for 10 minutes.

Meanwhile, add the remaining 2 tablespoons olive oil to the skillet (no need to clean it) and turn the heat to medium-high. Add the black trumpet mushrooms and a pinch of salt. Sauté for 5 to 7 minutes, until they are browned around the edges and cooked through. Remove most of the blackened poblano skin with your fingers, a knife, or by rubbing the pepper between 2 pieces of paper towel (it's totally okay if some charred skin remains, and definitely don't wash it, as that would remove much of the flavor). Slice it into thin strips. Mix the poblanos into the mushrooms, and keep warm in a bowl. Wipe out the skillet with a paper towel.

Add the vegetable oil to the skillet and heat to 350°F. Set up a baking pan with several layers of paper towels on it. Working in batches, slip as many tortilla triangles as will fit and not overlap into the skillet. Flip them over with tongs when they start to brown. Remove from the oil with a slotted spoon or grab a bunch with your tongs, letting as much oil as possible drain back into the skillet. Spread them out on the paper towels. Repeat until all the tortillas are fried. Sprinkle salt, to your liking, on the fried tortilla chips.

To prepare each plate, dunk one-quarter of the chips into the sauce, turning them all around with your tongs. Knock off any extra sauce and place on the plate. Add on any or all of the toppings, including a portion of the black trumpet–poblano mixture, and serve.

Braised Chicken Thighs with Black Trumpet Mushrooms, Frizzled Leeks, Sweet Potato Puree, and Vermouth Gravy

This is one of those dishes that looks harder than it actually is. You can braise the chicken thighs a day or two before serving. Ditto for the sweet potato puree. Fry the leeks the same day you are serving the meal. As with many braises, it tastes great several days later. While black trumpet mushrooms are my favorite, this dish would still be worthy of your table if you substituted cremini mushrooms in place of the black trumpets. If you don't like sweet potatoes, you could easily make a parsnip or celery root puree in its place, following the same procedure but substituting the different root vegetable.

SERVES: 4 | PAIRING: French red Burgundy (Pinot Noir)

½ pound fresh black trumpet mushrooms or 1 ounce dried

1 rosemary sprig

3 thyme sprigs

1 fresh bay leaf or 2 dried

4 bone-in, skin-on chicken thighs (1½ to 2 pounds total)

½ teaspoon plus ⅛ teaspoon fine sea salt, plus more as needed

Freshly ground black pepper

2 tablespoons extra-virgin olive oil

1 tablespoon unsalted butter

1 medium leek, dark green part trimmed for use in stock, white part cut into thin half-moons, light green part cut into thin julienne (for frizzled leeks, see right)

1 medium carrot, peeled and small diced

2 stalks celery, small diced

1 cup dry (white) vermouth

2 cups chicken stock

1 teaspoon champagne vinegar (substitute white wine vinegar)

BROWN BUTTER– SWEET POTATO PUREE

2 orange-fleshed sweet potatoes (1½ to 2 pounds), peeled and cut into large chunks

1 tablespoon kosher salt

4 tablespoons unsalted butter

1 teaspoon minced fresh rosemary

2 or 3 dashes Tabasco sauce (or your favorite hot sauce)

½ teaspoon fine sea salt, plus more as needed

FRIZZLED LEEKS

¼ cup vegetable oil

Light green julienned leek (see left)

Pinch of fine sea salt

Braised Chicken Thighs with
Black Trumpet Mushrooms, Frizzled Leeks,
Sweet Potato Puree, and Vermouth Gravy

CONTINUED

Preheat the oven to 325°F.

Clean the fresh black trumpet mushrooms as directed on page 155. If you're using dried black trumpet mushrooms, clean and rehydrate as directed on page xxx. Save the rehydration liquid and use as part of the chicken stock amount. Check to make sure the mushrooms are in bite-size strips (you can most likely leave them as they are, especially if you followed the instructions to split them from cap through stem for cleaning). Tie up the rosemary, thyme, and bay leaf with a small piece of kitchen string.

Season the chicken with ½ teaspoon of the salt and as much black pepper as you prefer. Heat 1 tablespoon of the olive oil in an ovenproof braising pan or pot over medium-high heat. Place the chicken into the pan, fat side down. Cook until the skin crisps up and browns, 6 to 8 minutes. Transfer from the pan onto a plate without cooking the other side.

Add the remaining 1 tablespoon olive oil and the butter to the pan. Add either the rehydrated mushrooms or the fresh mushrooms and the ⅛ teaspoon of salt. Sauté for 5 to 7 minutes, until they smell toasty. Remove the mushrooms from the pan and add them to the chicken. Add the leek half-moons, carrot, and celery to the pan and sauté until soft and lightly browned, about 10 minutes. Deglaze the pan with the vermouth, making sure to scrape up any bits stuck to the pan. Add the chicken, skin side up, and mushrooms back in and pour the stock over the top. Tuck in the herb bundle. Bring to a boil, then decrease the heat to a gentle simmer, put a lid on slightly ajar, and transfer to the oven. Cook until the chicken is very tender and when prodded with 2 forks nearly falls off the bone, about 1 hour. Transfer

the chicken to a platter. Remove and discard the herb bundle. Keep the chicken warm on the side while you reduce the mushroom braising liquid on the stovetop until it's a thick and glossy gravy, 10 to 15 minutes. Add the champagne vinegar and taste for seasoning. If it needs more brightness, add more vinegar. Otherwise, season to taste with salt and freshly ground black pepper. Keep warm.

To prepare the sweet potato puree, bring a medium saucepan of water to a boil. Add the potatoes and kosher salt. Bring back to a boil, decrease the heat to a simmer, and cook until knife-tender, about 20 minutes. Drain off the water.

While the sweet potatoes are cooking, melt the butter in a separate saucepan (easiest to see the butter brown in a stainless pan versus black cast iron). When the bubbles diminish, add the rosemary and cook until the butter browns and smells nutty, 3 to 4 minutes. Add the browned butter, Tabasco, sea salt, and sweet potatoes to a blender or food processor. Puree until satiny smooth (add a tiny bit of water or stock if necessary). Season to taste and keep warm.

To prepare the leeks, heat the oil to 350°F in a small pot over medium-high heat. Lay out some paper towels on a plate. Carefully add the leeks to the hot oil, tucking them under the surface of the oil, and fry until light brown and crisp. Transfer from the oil using a slotted spoon to drain on the paper towels. Sprinkle a pinch of salt on the leeks.

To serve, scoop a generous ½ cup sweet potato puree onto each plate. Top with a piece of chicken, pour the mushroom gravy over the top, and garnish with the frizzled leeks.

Black Trumpet Mushroom Tarts with Camembert, Leeks, and Port-Soaked Cherries

I'll be honest with you: This is one of the fussiest recipes in this whole book. But—stay with me—the satisfaction of serving this up to your friends and loved ones will be worth the effort. The flaky crust is ridiculously awesome, and what more can I say than bacon, black trumpets, fried sage, and boozy cherries? This is an appetizer to serve when you really want to impress someone. Oh, and for those other nights, I give you permission to buy frozen puff pastry and follow the directions on the package. A few important things to keep in mind: This is a free-form tart meant to be baked on a flat baking pan (look at the photo on page 165); if you use a traditional tart pan, the edges won't keep their shape (due to the high butter content). To make the dish a bit easier to execute the day you want to serve it, feel free to make the tart dough a few days ahead and keep it in the fridge. You can even bake the crust the day before and, when completely cool, wrap it up and leave it at room temperature. The cheese and leek filling and the mushrooms can be cooked ahead of time and rewarmed to spread on the tart the next day.

SERVES: 4 | PAIRING: New Zealand Sauvignon Blanc

TART DOUGH
1 cup unbleached all-purpose flour

½ cup (1 stick) unsalted butter, cut into ½-inch cubes

¼ teaspoon fine sea salt

3 tablespoons ice-cold water, plus more as needed

CHERRIES
½ cup ruby port

¼ cup dried, unsweetened cherries

3 fresh sage leaves, plus a scant ¼ cup more for frying

⅛ teaspoon fine sea salt

¼ pound fresh black trumpet mushrooms or ½ ounce dried

FILLING
¼ pound bacon, small diced

1 leek, light green and white parts, dark green parts reserved for stock, thinly sliced (about 2 cups)

Scant ⅛ teaspoon fine sea salt

½ cup water

7 to 8 ounces Camembert, cut into chunks

1 large egg, beaten

Vegetable oil, as needed

⅛ teaspoon fine sea salt, plus more as needed

1 cup pomegranate seeds

Black Trumpet Mushroom Tarts with Camembert, Leeks, and Port-Soaked Cherries

CONTINUED

To prepare the dough, place a rack in the middle of the oven and preheat the oven to 350°F. Place the flour, butter, and salt in a food processor and pulse about 30 times. Check the consistency of the dough. You want to see the butter in small pieces (the size of small peas or large grains of rice). You can also do this with a pastry cutter or your fingers. When you have reached that consistency, dump the contents into a wide bowl. Add the 3 tablespoons ice water to the bowl and with one hand, with fingers in a claw shape, mix the dough. Squeeze the dough in your hands. It should start to form a ball without crumbling. If it crumbles, add a little more ice water and gently mix until it's ready. Mix again with your hand. Lay out some parchment paper. Turn the contents out onto the paper. Pull up the sides of the paper, using it to help form a disk out of the pastry. Cover and chill in the refrigerator for at least 10 minutes, and preferably 20.

To infuse the cherries, heat the port in a small saucepan over medium-high heat until hot. Add the cherries, the 3 sage leaves, and salt. Turn off the heat, cover the pot, and let the cherries soften in the liquid for 30 minutes. Drain the cherries and sage, reserving the liquid, and discard the sage. Reduce the liquid by half, and then pour it back over the cherries. Let sit at room temperature until you are ready to use.

To finish the dough, divide it in half. Rewrap and chill one half while you work with the other. Roll out each disk on a lightly floured surface until ⅛ inch thick (roughly 10 inches in diameter). Transfer the dough to a baking pan lined with parchment paper. Fold the sides of the dough in to form a rustic edge. Poke the bottom of the tart with the tines of a fork. Repeat with the other piece of dough. Chill both tarts for 10 minutes. Bake the tarts in the middle of the oven for 15 to 20 minutes, until nicely browned. Lift each tart carefully and make sure the bottom is light brown in spots. It should lift up in one solid piece when done, with no bending or flopping. Let cool.

Clean the fresh black trumpet mushrooms as directed on page 155. If you're using dried black trumpet mushrooms, clean and rehydrate as directed on page xxx.

Black Trumpet Mushroom Tarts with Camembert, Leeks, and Port-Soaked Cherries

CONTINUED

To make the filling, heat a medium skillet over medium heat, add the bacon, and then lower the heat slightly. Render the fat from the bacon, occasionally stirring it to prevent sticking. When it is nicely browned and crisp, transfer it with a slotted spoon to a paper towel–lined plate. Pour the fat out, reserve, and add 1 tablespoon bacon fat back to the pan. Add the leek to the fat in the pan and add the sea salt (the bacon will be salty). Sauté for 5 minutes, until the leek softens, then add the water and simmer over low heat until all the water has evaporated and the leek is very tender, about 10 more minutes. Lower the heat and then add the cheese. Let the cheese melt into the leek. Transfer to a bowl, let cool for 5 minutes, and stir in the bacon. Taste and add more salt if you'd like. Mix in the egg until you have a nice spreadable consistency.

To sauté the black trumpets, rinse out the skillet and heat over medium-high heat. Add another 1 tablespoon bacon fat to the skillet (or use vegetable oil if you don't have enough bacon fat). Add the black trumpet mushrooms and the ⅛ teaspoon salt and sauté for 6 to 7 minutes, until tender, cooked through, and a little browned around the edges (though, being black, that might be a little hard to see so use your nose to detect when they start smelling toasty). Set the mushrooms aside and keep warm, covered with aluminum foil. Add ¼ cup more bacon fat or vegetable oil (or a mixture of both) to the pan and, when hot, fry the sage leaves until they crisp up, 30 seconds to 2 minutes. Pull one out and place on a paper towel–lined plate to check for crispness. When they are all done and transferred to the plate, sprinkle very lightly with sea salt.

To assemble, preheat the oven to 375°F. Using a thin spatula, carefully spread the leek-bacon-cheese-egg mixture over the bottom of the tart shells, dividing the filling equally over the 2 tarts. Put the tarts in the oven to set the egg, 5 to 7 minutes. Remove from the oven. Let cool for a few minutes, and then slice each tart into 8 equal pieces. Garnish each tart with a scant amount of port-soaked cherries, black trumpet mushrooms, fried sage leaves, and pomegranate seeds. Serve immediately.

Chapter 14
Truffle

LATIN: *Tuber spp.*

Fact Sheet:
Truffle

FLAVOR, TEXTURE, AND AROMA NOTES: The flavor of a truffle entirely follows the aroma—so let's start with aroma. In attempting to qualify the aroma of a truffle, I fear I might get into some trouble. You know that movie *Scent of a Woman*? Poets have struggled to put the perfect word on the scent of a truffle. At their ripest and best, they are beguiling, lusty, earthy, musty, floral, garlicky, otherworldly yet strangely familiar.

An ideal truffle smells like the perfect lover in your most elaborate fantasy, only better. The texture of a truffle strikes a fine balance between slightly chalky (though not in an unpleasant way) and creamy.

GENERALLY SPEAKING: Named from the Latin term tuber, meaning "lump," which then became *tufer* and variants (*trufa* in Spanish) all the way to "truffle" in English, truffles are the underground fruiting bodies of a fungus (ascomycete). They are mycorrhizal with the roots of many types of trees (oak, birch, poplar, hazelnut, and beech, among others). They are being cultivated in orchards in several places around the world, with varying degrees of success. Truffle growers are essentially tasked with re-creating an entire ecology to produce the still somewhat mysterious conditions under which truffles fruit. Several truffle species are highly valued as a luxury food, the "diamonds of the kitchen" according to the French gourmand Jean Anthelme Brillat-Savarin; and with Italian white truffles costing upward of $10,000 per pound, you might as well eat diamonds. There are many kinds of truffles not mentioned here; I've listed the ones you are most likely to see in the marketplace and that I have personally tried. I'm curious to try the "pecan" truffles found in the American South (*Tuber lyonii*), especially as the price of the European truffles keeps going up.

AKA: The following are some of the many types of truffles you might come across: Italian white truffle (*Tuber magnatum*), Piedmont or Alba truffle, *trifola d'Alba* (Italian), Perigord black winter truffle (*Tuber melanosporum*), winter truffle, black summer truffle (*Tuber aestivum*), Burgundy truffle (*Tuber uncinatum*), Oregon black truffle (*Leucangium carthusianum*), and Oregon white truffle (*Tuber oregonense* and *Tuber gibbosum*).

SEASON:

ITALIAN WHITE ALBA TRUFFLES:
September through November.

PERIGORD BLACK WINTER TRUFFLE:
November through March.

BLACK SUMMER TRUFFLE:
May through August.

BURGUNDY TRUFFLE:
September through January.

OREGON BLACK AND WHITE TRUFFLES:
November to April.

BUYING TIPS: Make sure you are buying truffles from a reputable supplier. Because truffles are a high-money game, sometimes chicanery is afoot. Truffles can be mislabeled such that a lesser species with no aroma is sold as a French Perigord. And while I'm here, truffle oil is the biggest underhanded game in town. Made from petroleum-based products, the truffle "aroma" or truffle "flavor" isn't actually from truffles. If you see the words "truffle essence" on the packaging, you're actually eating 2, 4-dithiapentane. I won't cook with this stuff, just as I wouldn't offer someone a "tomato" made from tomato "essence" crafted in a lab. There are products, however, that contain real truffle, such as truffle salt and truffle butter (no "essence" or "aroma" but actual truffles mixed with salt or butter). In our household, this is the standard delivery system when we want a truffle fix.

CLEANING: Personally, the few times I've had an Alba or Perigord truffle in my hands, the last thing I would want to do would be to potentially wash any of that aroma away with chlorinated tap water. This is the one time where, no matter how dirty it is, no matter how many pig or dog snouts have touched it, I will wipe it with a lightly damp cloth rather than wash it under water. If you have to peel the truffle (I don't really recommend it), save these peelings and infuse them into sauces and braises. After you use the damp cloth, use the tip of a knife to flick out any dirty areas in crevices. A soft toothbrush is also handy to remove stubborn dirt.

STORAGE: Best to use ripe truffles within a day or two after you get them. Wrap them in dry paper towels and seal them in a closed container, replacing the paper towels each day. My friend Langdon Cook likes to seal them in a container with a stick of butter; as the truffles off-gas, the butter is flavored with the truffle scent. If you purchased your truffles when they are underripe (no discernible aroma), it's best to "cure" them in your refrigerator wrapped in dry paper towels in a sealed container until they ripen—check them every day and let your nose guide you. When ripe, the truffle interior darkens and slightly softens, but more notably, the aroma grows stronger. If the truffle ever smells off, like ammonia, pitch it. It's gone too far.

PRESERVATION: Truffles are best eaten fresh. Preserving them is an interesting concept because, truly, if you are in the position to have so much truffle that you need to preserve them, you could probably just have fresh ones FedExed to you at a moment's notice. But just for argument's sake, you could surround them with melted butter or oil and vacuum-seal them and freeze them, or just vacuum-seal them. You could make a compound butter with them and then vacuum-seal that. If you have lots of little bits of truffle left over, you can infuse them in a jar of bourbon in your fridge and then use that for a pan sauce. Or you could sell them and donate the money to your local food bank.

LOVES: Fresh truffles are so special that it would be criminal to not feature them. Pair them with eggs, rice, and cheese. Mix them into pâtés and foie gras. Truffle salt and popcorn is a match made in heaven. Truffles love rich people, most of all.

COOKING NOTES: Since the truffle is all about the aroma, it's best preserved through minimal cooking. Shaving raw truffles over foods to pick up the heat and carry the aroma on the steam is always a good idea, especially if you only have a very small amount. For this you should use a mandoline or a truffle slicer.

SUBSTITUTE: Find richer friends, or in a pinch, use black trumpet mushrooms (often known as poor man's truffles) along with truffle salt.

NERDY FACTOIDS:

- In Eugenia Bone's excellent book *Mycophilia*, she writes that there are 300 "serious" truffle orchards in the United States.

- The little bumps on the outside of a truffle are called warts.

- The substance in truffles, both white and black, that people find irresistible is a compound similar to testosterone called testosterase.

Silken Scrambled Eggs with Shaved Alba White Truffles

Unless you are fabulously wealthy or work in fine dining, you may not get to experience the famous Italian white Alba truffle. But let's just say someone buys you one or you're walking down the street and you trip and fall face first into one; read this recipe and consider yourself prepared. In my opinion, there is no better way to experience one of the world's most expensive foods than shaved on top of creamy, custardy scrambled eggs. Because of their cost, Alba truffles don't have a line item on my household grocery budget, so it's good to know that black truffles, far cheaper, can be used as a substitute. Don't have any truffles? Use truffle salt. Don't have truffle salt? Eat some nice creamy scrambled eggs!

SERVES: 4 | PAIRING: French white Burgundy (Chardonnay) or Champagne

3 tablespoons unsalted butter (use real black truffle butter, if you can find it)

6 large eggs

½ cup half-and-half (or ¼ cup heavy cream plus ¼ cup whole milk)

1 teaspoon fine sea salt

Alba truffle (or black truffle)

Heat a large pan (pick one that doesn't have a bad reputation as a "sticker") over medium-high heat. Add the butter. Let it bubble, then turn the heat down to medium-low. Crack the eggs into a medium bowl; whisk the half-and-half and salt into the eggs, and pour the mixture into the pan. Grab a wooden spoon or heat-proof rubber spatula and start stirring. You will be tempted to turn the heat up, but don't. If you keep stirring the eggs at a medium-low temperature they will produce the creamiest, most delicious eggs you've ever had. It should take 8 to 10 minutes before they start to set into small curds, but they will still have lots of moisture. Look for creamy, barely set eggs. Remove the pan from the heat and stir for 20 seconds or so more—the residual heat in the pan will continue cooking them. Spoon the eggs into 4 bowls. Bring the bowls to the table and with great pomp and circumstance (I mean, it's a white truffle, after all!) shave as many slices per bowl as you can afford (the worth of which would feed a small family for a year).

Truffle Gougères

Gougères are like fancy French Cheetos, and I haven't even gotten to the truffles yet. The night I tested this recipe, a bunch of us stood around sipping Champagne, delicately and politely nibbling on them. There were a lot of gougères and many more recipes to sample, so I broke the seal, snatched two, and said, "C'mon, dig in!" In a grabby, gluttonous sort of way, we dug in. It was a pretty undignified thing to do with such a luxury item, but perhaps you haven't met my friends (hi, Marc!). You can make the dough ahead and then bring it out to warm up a bit before baking them right before your guests arrive.

SERVES: 4 | **PAIRING:** French Champagne, natch

1 cup milk

4 tablespoons unsalted butter

¼ teaspoon fine sea salt

1 cup unbleached all-purpose flour

3 large eggs

½ cup grated Parmesan

1½ cups grated Swiss cheese (Emmenthaler or Gruyère)

Coarse sea salt (fleur de sel or Maldon salt), for sprinkling

White Alba truffle, or any other kind of truffle

Preheat the oven to 375°F.

Bring the milk, butter, and salt to boil in a medium saucepan. Remove from the heat, add the flour all at once, and mix vigorously with a wooden spoon until the mixture forms a ball. Return the pan to the heat and cook over medium heat, stirring occasionally, for about 1 minute to dry the mixture a bit. Transfer to the bowl of a food processor, let cool for 5 minutes, then process for about 5 seconds.

Add the eggs to the processor bowl and process for 10 to 15 seconds, until well mixed. Transfer the dough to a medium bowl, and let cool for 10 minutes.

Line a baking pan with a nonstick baking mat or parchment paper. Reserve 1 tablespoon of the grated Parmesan cheese, then add the remainder and all the Swiss cheese to the dough. Stir just enough to incorporate. Using a tablespoon (or a pastry bag), scoop out a level 1 tablespoon of the *gougères* dough, and push it off the spoon onto the baking pan. Continue making individual *gougères*, spacing them about 2 inches apart on the sheet. Sprinkle a little of the reserved Parmesan cheese and a few grains of coarse salt on each *gougère*. Bake for 20 to 30 minutes, until nicely browned and crisp.

Serve lukewarm, split open, with as many shaved white truffles in the middle as you can afford.

Homemade Fettuccine with Shaved Truffle

I got to experience a fresh white Alba truffle being shaved over my fettuccine in the town of Orvieto, Italy. So precious and expensive is this ingredient that restaurant management typically weighs the truffle before and after the waiter shaves it tableside. It was a magical experience, only marred by the fact that I grabbed the whole truffle from the waiter, popped it in my mouth, and had to spend two years in an Italian prison. I joke. It was more like three years. The good news? I learned how to roll pasta in that Italian prison.* People are always shocked when they realize that making pasta dough takes ten minutes, tops. I, for one, didn't much care how long it took me, as all I had was time. The skill comes with the rolling of the dough, and here, practice makes perfect. There are two tips that will help your experience. First, you can always add flour to a slightly wet dough, but it's much harder to add moisture back to a dry dough. Second, never clean your hand-crank pasta machine with water. The moisture will trap flour bits that will tear your dough or make it stick when you roll it out. Dust your machine with flour and clean with a brush before storing. One more note: You can roll your dough out by hand and eschew the machine. I've done this once and in that experience I understood why Italian mommas (and prison guards) could crush my little pea-head in their massive biceps.

SERVES: 4 | PAIRING: French white Burgundy (Chardonnay)

PASTA DOUGH
4 cups unbleached all-purpose flour

6 large eggs

½ teaspoon fine sea salt

1 tablespoon extra-virgin olive oil

2 tablespoons water

Heaping 1 tablespoon kosher salt

6 tablespoons unsalted butter

Block of Parmigiano-Reggiano, for shaving

White or black truffle

Freshly ground black pepper

Using a food processor: Add the flour, eggs, salt, olive oil, and water to the processor. Pulse until the mixture comes together into a ball. If it should appear a bit dry, add small amounts of water until it comes together. Knead for a few minutes, and then wrap in plastic wrap and let it rest for at least 10 minutes.

By hand: Mix the flour with the salt and pour out onto a wooden board. Make a well in the center, add the eggs and olive oil to the well, and with a fork, gently beat the eggs and olive oil in the middle. Slowly start incorporating flour from the edges until you have a thick paste, and then scrape up the mixture and knead with your hands on the board until it comes together into a ball. Wrap in plastic wrap and let it rest for at least 10 minutes.

* *I didn't really go to an Italian prison for stealing a truffle. The prison was in Istanbul.*

Using a hand-crank pasta machine (I own an Atlas), divide the dough into 3 or 4 workable pieces (keep the others wrapped when not in use). Run through the machine on #1 (or whatever the widest setting is on your machine), fold it into 3 pieces (like a letter), and run through again (inserting the narrow end first). Set the machine to #2 and repeat the process, dusting with flour as necessary. Do the same on #3. After this point, you don't need to fold the dough. Keep running it through each number down to #7 or #8, depending on how thick you want the dough. I usually use #7 for pappardelle and fettuccine and #8 for when I want it thinner for ravioli.

Cut the dough into sheets 12 to 14 inches long. Let these sheets sit on a wooden board or floured linen for 10 minutes on each side to slightly dry out (making it easier to cut). Run the sheets through the fettuccine cutter or cut by hand.

To cook the pasta, bring a large pot of water to a boil and add a heaping tablespoon of salt. Boil the pasta until it is just barely al dente, about 3 minutes. Drain the pasta through a colander, reserving at least ½ cup of pasta cooking water. Put the pasta back in the pot (off the heat), add the butter, and gently toss with tongs until the butter has melted. Taste the pasta and use the pasta cooking liquid to salt it, as needed. For each portion of pasta that you serve, shave the cheese over the top (have more at the table) and then shave (at the table) a copious amount of truffle over the pasta, white or black. Offer black pepper at the table.

Black Cod with Truffled Potatoes and Beurre Rouge

This dish is a riff on something I learned from working at The Herbfarm. I've been making a form of it on and off for more than ten years. Sometimes I make it with duck or squab (see page 100), but it goes equally well with a rich, buttery fish such as black cod. The truffles just send the whole thing over the top, in the best possible way. Grab your Lipitor for this one—it's not shy with the butter. You can make the sauce reduction days ahead and you can roast the fennel the day before; simply finish the sauce and reheat the fennel just before serving.

SERVES: 4 | PAIRING: Oregon Pinot Noir

BEURRE ROUGE

¼ cup sliced shallot

2 cups Pinot Noir

2 cups chicken or Mushroom Stock (page xxiii)

Bones from black cod (see right)

¼ cup medium-diced fennel stems and core

1 dried bay leaf

¼ teaspoon fine sea salt

ROASTED FENNEL

2 tablespoons extra-virgin olive oil

1 pound fennel, stems and core removed (used for sauce), cut into thin wedges, fennel fronds reserved for garnish

Heaping ½ teaspoon fine sea salt

Freshly ground black pepper

10 thyme sprigs

TRUFFLED POTATOES

1½ pounds potatoes (mixture of russet and Yukon Gold), peeled, halved or quartered if medium or large

1½ teaspoons kosher salt

¾ to 1 cup whole milk (less for a denser mashed potato, more for a creamier puree)

5 tablespoons unsalted butter

1 teaspoon fine sea salt (if you don't have truffles, substitute this sea salt for truffle salt)

Black Perigord truffle, or any other kind of truffle

½ cup (1 stick) plus 3 tablespoons unsalted butter

1 pound black cod, skinned, bones removed (and saved), cut into 4 equal portions

Olive oil, for brushing on the pan

¼ teaspoon fine sea salt

Preheat the oven to 400°F.

Start the beurre rouge reduction in a wide, high-sided pan (10 to 12 inches) by combining the shallot, wine, stock, black cod bones, fennel stems and core, bay leaf, and salt. Bring to a boil and then lower the heat to a simmer. Cook the sauce, letting it reduce in volume, until you have ¾ cup left, 30 to 45 minutes. Strain it prior to measuring, discarding the solids but pressing on them first to get all the goodness out (it's important that you measure the reduction after you've strained it for best accuracy). Set aside.

To roast the fennel, line a baking pan with aluminum foil and pour the olive oil onto the pan. Add the fennel, toss with the oil, season with the salt and pepper, and then tuck the thyme sprigs underneath the fennel wedges so they don't burn. Cover with aluminum foil and roast for 20 minutes. Uncover and roast for an additional 15 to 20 minutes, until the fennel is caramelized and tender (start the potatoes while you wait). Cover tightly with foil to keep warm while you cook the fish.

To make the truffled potatoes, cover the potatoes with cold water in a medium saucepan. Add the kosher salt to the water and bring to a boil. Decrease the heat to a simmer and cook until a knife can be easily inserted, about 20 minutes. While the potatoes cook, heat the milk, butter, and 1 teaspoon sea salt together in a small saucepan. When hot, turn off the heat and shave about 2 tablespoons of truffles into the milk. Cover and let infuse for 10 minutes. Drain the potatoes, run through a ricer (or use a masher), and then stir in the infused milk. Season to taste with sea salt and keep warm.

To finish the sauce, pour it into a saucepan set over medium-low heat. Whisk the butter into the sauce, melting just 1 tablespoon at a time, and keep warm over very low heat. Taste and add salt as needed. (If you used boxed stock, which I don't recommend, it's very important that you taste before adding salt, or you could easily oversalt the sauce). If you're using homemade stock, start by adding ¼ teaspoon fine sea salt.

To cook the fish, turn the oven temperature down to 325°F. Line a baking pan with parchment paper. Brush with a little olive oil. Place the fillets on the pan. Season with ¼ teaspoon sea salt. Bake for 10 to 12 minutes, until a small amount of liquid collects at the bottom of the fillets and the fish begins to flake when gently nudged with your finger.

To serve, scoop some truffled potatoes onto each plate. Top with a piece of black cod. Place some fennel pieces around the fish. Spoon the sauce over the fish and potatoes, and garnish with more shaved truffles and the fennel fronds.

Braised Rabbit with Truffle-Stuffed Rabbit Loin, Chanterelle Cream, Roasted Root Vegetables, and Shaved Truffles

This is the kind of recipe that some people just scratch their heads over and happily subcontract to the professionals. Anything that starts with "Day 1" usually quickly weeds out the Rachael Ray crowd. For the rest of you: Are you up for the challenge? I think it's worth it. First, locate a rabbit and a truffle. Second, cut it up and marinate it overnight (the rabbit, not the truffle). Make the chanterelle cream. Day 2: Braise the legs, roast the vegetables, stuff the loins with truffles, and sear them. Open up an old and awesome Barolo and present your two-day project with truffles shaved all over the top. Don't let anyone wipe that proud grin off of your face. You deserve to be happy, for now at least, because turn around and look at that filthy kitchen. Day 3: Clean it up.

SERVES: **4** | PAIRING: Italian Barolo

MARINADE

½ teaspoon fine sea salt

¼ teaspoon freshly ground black pepper

3 rosemary sprigs

1 thin peel from a lemon

1 tablespoon apple cider vinegar

2 tablespoons extra-virgin olive oil

2 rabbits, loins, forearms, and legs removed (bones saved for stock, liver fried up as a chef snack, ditto for kidneys and heart)

CHANTERELLE CREAM

1 tablespoon extra-virgin olive oil

¼ pound fresh chanterelle mushrooms, medium diced

½ teaspoon fine sea salt

¼ cup dry (white) vermouth

½ cup heavy cream

½ cup Mushroom Stock (page xxiii)

¼ teaspoon apple cider vinegar

DAY 1: To prepare the marinade, combine the salt, pepper, rosemary, lemon, vinegar, and olive oil in a bowl. Mix well and pour the marinade over the rabbit legs and forearms, coating well. Cover and refrigerate overnight.

To prepare the mushroom cream, heat a large skillet over medium-high heat. Add the oil, then the mushrooms and salt, and sauté until the chanterelles release their liquid and begin to brown, 5 to 6 minutes. Deglaze the pan with vermouth, making sure to scrape any bits stuck to the pan, and cook until all the liquid is evaporated. Add the cream and mushroom stock and cook for another 1 to 2 minutes. Transfer to a blender or food processor and add the vinegar. Process until very smooth and then season to taste with salt. Transfer to a small saucepan, cover, and refrigerate until ready to serve.

Braised Rabbit with Truffle-Stuffed Rabbit Loin, Chanterelle Cream, Roasted Root Vegetables, and Shaved Truffles

CONTINUED

BRAISING INGREDIENTS

2 tablespoons extra-virgin olive oil

2 ounces pancetta, small diced

1 medium yellow onion, small diced

1 medium carrot, small diced

1 stalk celery, small diced

1 cup dry (white) vermouth

3 cups Mushroom Stock (page xxiii) or chicken stock

6 sage leaves

6 thyme sprigs

2 dried bay leaves

¼ teaspoon red pepper flakes

DAY 2: Arrange a rack in the middle of the oven and preheat the oven to 275°F. Heat 1 tablespoon of the olive oil in a wide Dutch oven or other ovenproof pot over medium heat. Add the pancetta and allow the fat to render out of the pancetta, about 5 minutes. Remove the pancetta with a slotted spoon, reserving the fat in the pot. Set the pancetta aside. Add another tablespoon of the olive oil to the pancetta fat in the pan.

Remove the legs and forearms from the marinade (reserving the marinade) and sear them on both sides in the pancetta fat until brown. Remove the rabbit pieces from the pot and set aside. Add the onion, carrot, and celery to the pot and cook until caramelized, stirring frequently with a wooden spoon, about 15 minutes. Deglaze the pan with the vermouth, making sure to scrape up the bits stuck to the pan. After the vermouth has reduced by one-quarter, about a minute or two, add the stock, sage, thyme, bay leaves, and red pepper flakes. Return the legs, forearms, reserved marinade, and pancetta to the pot and bring to a boil. Immediately remove from the heat, cover the inside of the pot with a parchment paper lid just big enough to sit on the food (see Note on page 182), and bake in the center of the oven for 1 hour and up to 2 hours, or until the meat is silky and tender.

Remove the meat from the pot and let cool. Skim the fat from the braising liquid and strain the liquid through a fine-mesh sieve. Reduce the braising liquid by half or until thickened to your liking. Add the rabbit pieces back to the sauce. Season to taste with salt. You can keep warm until you serve it, or refrigerate and reheat at a later time.

ROASTED VEGETABLES

2 tablespoons extra-virgin olive oil

1 pound fingerling potatoes, halved

½ pound carrots, cut into large chunks

½ pound parsnips, peeled, halved, cut into chunky half-moons

1 teaspoon fine sea salt

Freshly ground black pepper

Turn the oven up to 400°F.

Line a baking pan with aluminum foil. Pour the olive oil onto the pan and then add the potatoes, carrots, and parsnips. Mix well and season with the salt and pepper. Cover with aluminum foil and bake for 20 minutes. Uncover and bake for another 20 to 30 minutes, until caramelized and tender. Re-cover with foil to keep warm while you sear the loins.

Braised Rabbit with Truffle-Stuffed Rabbit Loin, Chanterelle Cream, Roasted Root Vegetables, and Shaved Truffles

CONTINUED

TRUFFLE-STUFFED RABBIT LOIN

Pinch of fine sea salt

Freshly ground black pepper

Shaved truffle (any kind)

8 paper-thin prosciutto di Parma slices

1 tablespoon vegetable oil

Refer to the technique photo on page 181 when working with the loins. Try to preserve the belly flap when you cut the loins from the rabbit backbone. Flip the thinner end of each loin onto itself to make the loin uniformly thick. Cut the flap to resemble a square piece equal to the length of the loin. Season the loins with salt and pepper. Shave the truffles onto the belly flap and then roll up the loins. For each loin, lay out 2 pieces of prosciutto slices, one slightly overlapping the other with the narrow side facing you. Lay the loin roll on the far edge of the prosciutto and trim the sides of the prosciutto so that they are flush with the loin. Use the scrap for another purpose. Holding the loin firmly, roll the prosciutto up and over the loin (jelly-roll style).

Place the loin rolls on a plate, seam side down, while you heat a cast-iron or similarly heavy sauté pan over high heat. Add the oil and, when hot, add all of the loins seam side down and brown well on both sides, cooking no longer than 2 minutes on each side so that the rabbit is a rosy medium when done. Slice crosswise into 2-inch pieces.

To serve, reheat the rabbit pieces and their braising liquid if necessary. Divide the rabbit meat equally among 4 plates. Tuck the vegetables next to the rabbit pieces. Coat with the braising sauce. Place a few pieces of rabbit loin on each plate. Shave truffles over the top. Refer to page 179 to see one way to plate this dish.

NOTE: Google "parchment paper lid" to learn how to easily make one of these.

Chapter 15

Matsutake

LATIN: *Tricholoma spp.*

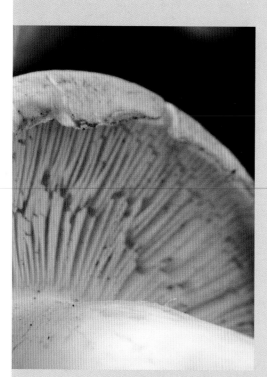

Fact Sheet:
Matsutake

FLAVOR, TEXTURE, AND AROMA NOTES: David Arora famously describes matsutakes as smelling like "wet socks and red hots." And, well, he is pretty spot-on. The flavor mirrors this aroma nearly perfectly. The texture is firm, almost crisp, and the aroma has this explosively perfumed and spicy woodsiness.

GENERALLY SPEAKING: One of the most amazing species of edible mushrooms and historically one of the more expensive (though prices have really dropped in the past ten years), matsutakes are found wild in Europe, North America, and Asia, as well as Mexico, Guatemala, Brazil, and Sweden (among other places). They are often given as gifts in Japanese culture and revered as a symbol of power and virility. Matsutake in Asia are mycorrhyizal with pine trees (pine and fir in the Pacific Northwest and with hardwoods in California). They are notoriously hard to find, as most of their growth occurs hidden under the forest duff. The height of the matsutake commercial foraging craze in the United States was during the late 1980s and early '90s, when perfect specimens rewarded pickers with hundreds of dollars before being sold for far more in the Japanese market.

AKA: Matsutakes are also known as *Tricholoma matsutake* (Japanese matsutake), *Tricholoma magnivelare* (American matsutake), ponderosa mushrooms, white matsutake, matsies, matsu, pine mushrooms.

SEASON: They are in season in the Pacific Northwest from September to November.

BUYING TIPS: Matsutake buttons (young, gills not yet exposed) make for the prettiest slices in soups and broths. Avoid any mushrooms that appear worm-eaten, soft, or dried out. Matsutakes are categorized into seven grades (with 1 being an unopened button all the way to 7, an over-the-hill fully open cap). Matsutakes are all about the aroma; make sure it smells heavenly before you buy it.

CLEANING: A damp towel is all that you'll need to wipe off any dirt or needles on the unopened buttons. A thin cut off the bottom of the stem is necessary and perhaps some trimming of any dirty or damaged spots. Matsutakes that have open caps likely have very dirty gills. Scrape or cut the gills out before using.

STORAGE: Best to use matsutake mushrooms within a week after you get them, especially specimens where the veil has broken and the caps are spread out. As with all mushrooms, store them in the refrigerator in a brown paper bag. Second choice would be to store them in a basket or box with a dry piece of paper towel or newsprint on top of them (replace this each day).

PRESERVATION:

DRYING: See page xxix. See page xxx for a description of rehydrating mushrooms. Many people think matsutakes should never be dried, claiming that all the flavor will be lost. I disagree. While they are certainly less aromatic than their fresh counterpart, in my testing I found that the aroma of rehydrated matsutakes can still be appreciated, especially if trapped in the cooking process, such as in the matsutake popovers on page 191.

FREEZING: See page xxxi. Matsutakes can be individually quick frozen and then vacuum-sealed.

LOVES: Because of their intense flavor, matsutakes should be the star ingredient of any dish; simple is usually the best way to prepare them. Infuse them into broths, skewer and grill them, or pair them with rice or butter.

COOKING NOTES: Chefs in the West are just starting to play around with the deeply perfumed matsutake. For years (due to a pine nematode destroying Japanese forests) we exported almost all of our mushrooms to Japan. Japanese youth are less interested in maintaining the traditions of their parents and grandparents, so more (but still very little) of the matsutake harvest is being sold in the United States to chefs curious to try the unusual mushroom. Most dishes keep things simple to maximize the flavor and aroma. Keep your pot covered, wrap them in parchment, and bake them into things. Trap the magical scent as best as you can and try not to overwhelm it with spice or hide it behind even stronger flavors. The flavor is powerful; a little goes a long way in a dish.

SUBSTITUTE: Honestly, there are no great substitutes for the matsutake; it's simply that unique. All of the recipes in this chapter would be good with other mushrooms (the popovers on page 191 would be great using truffles), but they won't be the same.

NERDY FACTOIDS:
- Confusion of matsutakes with *Amanita smithiana* has led to serious poisonings.
- Deer love matsutakes.
- Matsutakes have not been successfully cultivated.

Grilled Matsutakes with Rosemary, Salt, and Lemon

This is one of the simplest and most satisfying ways to enjoy this unique mushroom. If you don't have a grill, you can still manage this in a skillet (I recommend using smoked salt in place of the regular salt to approximate the smoke you'd get on the grill). If you can't find woody rosemary branches to use as skewers, Douglas fir branches would work really well here.

SERVES: 4 | **PAIRING:** French white Burgundy (Chardonnay)

½ pound fresh matsutake mushrooms, cut into ⅓-inch slices

12 (6- to 8-inch) sections of mature rosemary (with sturdy stems), leaves stripped off except for a little tuft at the top

2 tablespoons extra-virgin olive oil

1 teaspoon minced fresh rosemary

⅛ teaspoon fine sea salt

Freshly ground black pepper

1 lemon, cut into wedges

Maldon salt or fleur de sel, for garnish

Preheat a grill so that one side is very hot and the other side is cooler. Carefully thread the matsutake onto the rosemary skewers (refer to the photo to see how to skewer the pieces). Pour the olive oil over the mushrooms and coat them really well. Sprinkle with the rosemary and salt. Grind black pepper over the top, to your taste. Let the mushrooms sit at room temperature to marinate for at least 20 minutes while the grill heats up.

Grill the skewers (hanging the rosemary-leaved end of the skewer away from the heat) on both sides until the mushrooms are browned and tender, about 3 minutes per side. You may have to move them over to the cooler side of the grill to finish cooking. Test one to be sure of doneness; they shouldn't be tough or woody at all, but tender and juicy. Serve with lemon wedges and Maldon salt.

Roasted Brussels Sprouts with Matsutakes and Lemon

Most folks advise to keep dishes using matsutakes as simple as possible to allow the unique perfume of this special mushroom to waft, untethered to other strong scents, to the diner's nose. Then along came ThuyLieu Hoang, who cooked at Poppy, one of my favorite restaurants in Seattle, with a simple, off-the-cuff dish taking the very bold, often maligned Brussels sprout and pairing the vegetable with the equally bold, spicy, and ethereal matsutake. This can't work, I thought. I was wrong. I think this dish would hold up well tossed with butternut squash gnocchi to make it more of a main course or served as a side dish with pan-seared halibut or striped bass, or even a pork loin.

SERVES: 4 | PAIRING: Austrian Grüner Veltliner

1 pound Brussels sprouts, stems and any brown bits trimmed off and quartered

¼ cup extra-virgin olive oil

1 teaspoon honey

2 tablespoons freshly squeezed lemon juice

1½ teaspoons fine sea salt

Freshly ground black pepper

¼ pound fresh matsutake mushrooms, stems medium diced, caps thinly sliced

¼ pound fresh maitake mushrooms, medium diced

1 tablespoon lemon zest

¼ cup Mushroom Stock (page xxiii)

1 lemon, cut into wedges

Preheat the oven to 425°F. Line a baking pan with aluminum foil and brush with some olive oil. Pile the sprouts on the pan, and drizzle 2 tablespoons of the olive oil and the honey on top, as well as the lemon juice. Mix well and then add 1 teaspoon of the salt. Mix again and spread out on the pan. Grind some black pepper over the top. Pop the pan into the oven and set a timer for 15 minutes. Stir them when the timer goes off and then roast for another 10 to 20 minutes, until brown, tender, and a little crispy at the edges.

Meanwhile, heat 1 tablespoon of the olive oil in a large skillet over medium heat and sauté the mushrooms, along with the remaining ½ teaspoon salt, until they are tender and lightly browned. Stir in the lemon zest, and some black pepper, and when the sprouts are done, mix them in. Moisten with the stock and the remaining 1 tablespoon olive oil. Serve with lemon wedges.

Aromatic Matsutake Broth

The first time I had a matsutake mushroom I wasn't exactly sure what was happening in my mouth. You know how a mullet haircut is described as "business in the front, party in the back," right? Now work with me through this terrible analogy: The first sensations to hit my brain were the spiciness and intense perfume, almost an affront to my senses, but these soon faded to the party in the back: a long lingering, good-time walk in the woods; the pleasure you get from smelling your jacket after a camping trip and detecting the faded scent of pine woods and smoke. This broth is the purest essence of matsutake. Don't make this dish unless you already know you like matsutakes. It's something special and completely unadulterated by the hand of a chef or a hairdresser, tempted though they both may be. You might not appreciate a mullet at first, but maybe you're just seeing one side of it.

SERVES: 4 | PAIRING: French white Burgundy (Chardonnay)

4 cups Mushroom Dashi
(page xxiii; substitute vegetable stock)

1 tablespoon sake

1 tablespoon soy sauce (1½ teaspoons
if using store-bought broth)

1 small carrot, cut into thin carrot
flowers (page 152) or thinly sliced

¼ pound fresh matsutake
mushrooms, stems trimmed and
cut into ⅛-inch-thick slices

Fine sea salt

1 lemon, cut into wedges

1 lime, cut into wedges

In a saucepan over medium heat, reduce the dashi to 1 cup to concentrate the flavor. Add the sake, soy sauce, carrot, and matsutakes to the dashi and bring to the barest wisp of a boil. Then turn the heat to its lowest setting, cover, and cook, infusing the broth with the perfume of the matsutake, 6 to 8 minutes. Taste a mushroom and a carrot for tenderness. Season the broth to taste with salt.

To channel a more traditional way of serving matsutake broth, you can serve in a teapot and offer chopsticks to guests to pick pieces of mushroom and carrot out of the communal pot. If you have covered teacups or even miso cups, use those. Offer lemon and lime wedges at the table and encourage each guest to squeeze a few drops of each into their bowls. The broth is best appreciated when you lift the lid off of your cup or bowl and inhale the aroma. If you're feeling really decadent, serve this broth with matsutake popovers (page 191) on the side.

Fragrant Matsutake Chicken Rice (Gohan)

This is a classic Japanese dish that signals the coming of fall. I don't know this for sure, but I'm imagining this is extreme comfort food for those Japanese lucky enough to get their hands on matsutake mushrooms. The rice captures the alluring aroma of a pine forest, and the kelp in the dashi and as garnish brings the sea into the mix. The freshness of the rice is important for this dish to be a success; this is not the dish for using up that sushi rice that's been in your pantry for three years. Whatever brand of sushi rice you end up using, make sure to read the ratio. They all seem to be close to 1-to-1, with just a little bit more liquid than rice, but defer to the package if there is any discrepancy.

SERVES: 4 | PAIRING: French white Burgundy (Chardonnay)

2 cups Mushroom Stock (page xxiii)

1 (3 by 5-inch) piece kombu (kelp), wiped with a damp paper towel

1½ cups Japanese short-grained rice

½ pound boneless, skinless chicken thighs, medium diced

1½ tablespoons soy sauce

2 tablespoons mirin

1 tablespoon sake

¾ teaspoon fine sea salt

¼ pound fresh matsutake mushrooms, smallest one cut into 4 thin slices for garnish, the rest medium diced

2 scallions, dark and light green parts cut thinly on an angle

Pea shoots or daikon sprouts, for garnish

To make the dashi, bring the stock and kelp slowly to a boil in a stockpot. It should take about 10 minutes. Remove the kelp and mince a 2-inch section of it for garnish. Set aside.

Rinse the rice 3 times, until the water runs clear, then drain and add to a rice cooker pot or a saucepan. Add the chicken to the rice, along with the soy sauce, mirin, sake, and salt. Add 1½ cups plus 3 tablespoons of the freshly made dashi. (If there happens to be any dashi left over, add salt to taste and drink it.) If there's not enough dashi, add water to make up the amount. Add the diced matsutake, and let the rice, dashi, mushrooms, and all the other seasonings sit for 20 minutes (this helps the rice soften for better results).

If you are using a rice cooker, lay the 4 slices of matsutake on the top of all the other ingredients and follow the manufacturer's instructions to cook the rice.

If you are cooking the rice on the stovetop, lay the 4 slices of matsutake on the top of all the other ingredients, bring the pot to a full boil, and let it cook for 2 to 3 minutes. Cover the pot, decrease the heat to the lowest setting, and cook for 20 minutes. When the timer goes off, take the pot off the heat without lifting the lid and let it steam for 10 minutes.

Serve the rice garnished with the scallions, pea shoots, and minced kelp.

Matsutake Popovers with Scallion Butter

This recipe capitalizes on the matsutake's storied mystique, trapping it in the steamy interior of crusty, eggy popovers. The scent, released when you split the popover open, carries you from a well-appointed Victorian parlor to the stacks of an old library, filled with turn-of-the-century manuscripts. The aroma is both older than time and tantalizingly spicy. For a decadent appetizer, split the popovers open, add scallion butter, and then fill them with a little crab or lobster salad.

SERVES: 8 (makes 24 mini popovers or 8 regular)

PAIRING: Spanish Cava

POPOVER DOUGH
¼ pound fresh matsutake mushrooms or ½ ounce dried

1 cup unbleached all-purpose flour

1 tablespoon unsalted butter, plus 1 tablespoon, melted

¾ teaspoon fine sea salt

1¼ cups whole milk

SCALLION BUTTER
4 tablespoons unsalted butter, at room temperature

3 scallions, minced (about ⅓ cup)

¼ teaspoon fine sea salt, plus a pinch

2 large eggs, lightly beaten

Arrange a rack in the center of the oven and preheat the oven to 450°F. Prepare mini muffin tins, standard muffin tins, or a popover pan by generously buttering and flouring them, then knocking out any excess flour. If your matsutakes are dried, rehydrate and strain as directed on page xxx, using 1 cup boiling water (save soaking liquid for stock). Mince the fresh or rehydrated mushrooms.

To prepare the dough, place the flour in a large bowl and set aside. Melt the butter in a small saucepan over medium heat. Decrease the heat to medium-low and add the minced matsutakes and salt. Sauté for 3 to 5 minutes. Add the milk, and bring to a boil over medium-high heat. Turn off the heat, cover the pan, and let steep for 10 minutes. Transfer the milk and mushroom mixture to a separate bowl to let cool. Clean and dry the saucepan.

To make the scallion butter, use the same pan you used for sautéing the mushrooms. Over medium-high heat, melt 1 tablespoon of the butter. Add the scallions and the pinch of salt, decrease the heat to medium-low, and sauté for 5 to 7 minutes, until tender, but do not let them brown. Let cool, and then mix in the remaining 3 tablespoons softened butter and the ¼ teaspoon salt. The butter can be made ahead, covered, and refrigerated for up to 1 week. Remove and let soften before serving.

To finish the popovers, beat the eggs in a medium bowl and, when the milk mixture has cooled off a bit, stir into the eggs, whisking as you pour. Using a large spoon, gently mix the egg and milk mixture into the flour until no more lumps show, but don't overmix. Fill the prepared muffin or popover cups two-thirds full.

Place in the oven on the middle rack. For mini popovers, bake for 15 minutes and then turn the oven off and leave in for another 5 minutes. For regular popovers, bake for 25 minutes, then turn off the oven and leave in for 10 minutes. Remove from the oven, immediately remove from the cups, and serve with the scallion butter.

Why Eating Random Wild Shrooms Is a Really, Really Bad Idea

It's unlikely that I needed to put this section into the book, but 10,000 out of 10,000 hypothetical lawyers told me it's probably a good idea. I could write a long-winded explanation of how you need to be able to positively ID any mushroom you find in the wild before eating it. I could go on and on about the importance of consulting guides and experts and, when you're done with the guides and experts, revisiting them to doubly confirm. I could tell you that your life is valuable and foraging is not a beginner's game. I could wrap it all up with a skull-and-crossbones bow and inform you that, while there are only a handful of known deadly mushrooms, there are many more that would make you wish you were dead.

I am not a mushroom-foraging expert. There are only three mushrooms I will pick in the wild, take home, cook up, and feel comfortable about not consulting an expert. Those are chanterelles, hedgehogs, and morels. They happen to be mushrooms that don't have deadly lookalikes, and I have had experts show them to me in the woods and tell me exactly what to look for.

I highly recommend that if you are interested in foraging, you join your local mycological society or suck up to a mushroom expert. Foraging is an incredibly exciting and fun hobby; it's free, it's good exercise, and when you have a good day, it's delicious. Be safe.

THANK YOU.

Other Shrooms Worth Eating

- **THE PRINCE** *(Agaricus augustus)*: Often a forager favorite, the prince mushroom is known for its almond-anise aroma and flavor.

- **BLEWIT** *(Clitocybe nuda* or *Lepista nuda* or *Tricholoma nudum)*: A gaudy purple-pink color and firm and chewy in texture. I don't recommend eating any mushroom raw, but definitely not this one, as it could make you quite ill.

- **CAULIFLOWER** *(Sparassis spp.)*: This mushroom looks like someone dumped cold egg noodles out of a colander onto the forest floor. They taste a lot better than that.

- **SHAGGY MANE** *(Coprinus comatus)*: But really, the best alternative common name is "lawyer's wig," because that's exactly what it looks like. Best in its youngest stage, especially considering it auto-digests at a certain stage, turning itself into an inky, nasty mess. Mushrooms are crazy.

- **YELLOWFOOT** *(Craterellus tubaeformis)*: These skinny little winter mushrooms are in the black trumpet family and make a good stand-in for chanterelles after the fall season is over. They are hollow and thin, lacking the substance of chanterelles but still packing in some flavor.

Bibliography

BOOKS

Arora, David. *Mushrooms Demystified*. Ten Speed Press, 1986.

____. *All That the Rain Promises and More*. Ten Speed Press, 1991.

Bone, Eugenia. *Mycophilia*. Rodale Books, 2011.

Cook, Langdon. *The Mushroom Hunters*. Ballantine Books, 2013.

Czarnecki, Jack. *A Cook's Book of Mushrooms*. Artisan, 1995.

Emanuelli, Philippe. *A Cook's Initiation into the Gorgeous World of Mushrooms*. Chronicle Books, 2013.

Farges, Amy. *The Mushroom Lover's Mushroom Cookbook and Primer*. Workman, 2000.

Green, Connie, and Sarah Scott. *The Wild Table*. Viking Studio, 2010.

Grigson, Jane. *The Mushroom Feast*. Alfred A. Knopf, 1975.

Nims, Cynthia. *Wild Mushrooms*. WestWinds Press, 2004.

Schwab, Alexander. *Mushrooming with Confidence*. Skyhorse Publishing, 2012.

Stamets, Paul. *Mycelium Running*. Ten Speed Press, 2005.

Weil, Andrew. "Is it Safe to Eat Raw Mushrooms?" Article on Prevention.com, February 2013.

WEB SITES

FAT OF THE LAND: www.fat-of-the-land.blogspot.com

MARX FOODS: www.marxfoods.com

HUNTER ANGLER GARDENER COOK: www.honest-food.net

Mail-Order Resources

D'ARTAGNAN: www.dartagnan.com

FORAGED AND FOUND EDIBLES: www.foragedandfoundedibles.com

FOODS IN SEASON: www.foodsinseason.com

OREGON MUSHROOMS: www.oregonmushrooms.com

WINE FOREST: www.wineforest.com

Metric Conversions and Equivalents

TO CONVERT	MULTIPLY	TO CONVERT	MULTIPLY
Ounces to grams	Ounces by 28.35	Cups to milliliters	Cups by 236.59
Pounds to kilograms	Pounds by .454	Cups to liters	Cups by .236
Teaspoons to milliliters	Teaspoons by 4.93	Pints to liters	Pints by .473
Tablespoons to milliliters	Tablespoons by 14.79	Quarts to liters	Quarts by .946
Fluid ounces to milliliters	Fluid ounces by 29.57	Gallons to liters	Gallons by 3.785
		Inches to centimeters	Inches by 2.54

Approximate Metric Equivalents

WEIGHT

¼ ounce	7 grams
½ ounce	14 grams
¾ ounce	21 grams
1 ounce	28 grams
1¼ ounces	35 grams
1½ ounces	42.5 grams
1⅔ ounces	45 grams
2 ounces	57 grams
3 ounces	85 grams
4 ounces (¼ pound)	113 grams
5 ounces	142 grams
6 ounces	170 grams
7 ounces	198 grams
8 ounces (½ pound)	227 grams
16 ounces (1 pound)	454 grams
35.25 ounces (2.2 pounds)	1 kilogram

LENGTH

⅛ inch	3 millimeters
¼ inch	6 millimeters
½ inch	1¼ centimeters
1 inch	2½ centimeters
2 inches	5 centimeters
2½ inches	6 centimeters
4 inches	10 centimeters
5 inches	13 centimeters
6 inches	15¼ centimeters
12 inches (1 foot)	30 centimeters

VOLUME

¼ teaspoon	1 milliliter
½ teaspoon	2.5 milliliters
¾ teaspoon	4 milliliters
1 teaspoon	5 milliliters
1¼ teaspoons	6 milliliters
1½ teaspoons	7.5 milliliters
1¾ teaspoons	8.5 milliliters
2 teaspoons	10 milliliters
1 tablespoon (½ fluid ounce)	15 milliliters
2 tablespoons (1 fluid ounce)	30 milliliters
¼ cup	60 milliliters
⅓ cup	80 milliliters
½ cup (4 fluid ounces)	120 milliliters
⅔ cup	160 milliliters
¾ cup	180 milliliters
1 cup (8 fluid ounces)	240 milliliters
1¼ cups	300 milliliters
1½ cups (12 fluid ounces)	360 milliliters
1⅔ cups	400 milliliters
2 cups (1 pint)	460 milliliters
3 cups	700 milliliters
4 cups (1 quart)	0.95 liter
1 quart plus ¼ cup	1 liter
4 quarts (1 gallon)	3.8 liters

Oven Temperatures

To convert Fahrenheit to Celsius, subtract 32 from Fahrenheit, multiply the result by 5, then divide by 9.

DESCRIPTION	FAHRENHEIT	CELSIUS	BRITISH GAS MARK
Very cool	200°	95°	0
Very cool	225°	110°	¼
Very cool	250°	120°	½
Cool	275°	135°	1
Cool	300°	150°	2
Warm	325°	165°	3
Moderate	350°	175°	4
Moderately hot	375°	190°	5
Fairly hot	400°	200°	6
Hot	425°	220°	7
Very hot	450°	230°	8
Very hot	475°	245°	9

Common Ingredients and Their Approximate Equivalents

1 cup uncooked white rice = 185 grams

1 cup all-purpose flour = 140 grams

1 stick butter (4 ounces • ½ cup • 8 tablespoons) = 110 grams

1 cup butter (8 ounces • 2 sticks • 16 tablespoons) = 220 grams

1 cup brown sugar, firmly packed = 225 grams

1 cup granulated sugar = 200 grams

Information compiled from a variety of sources, including *Recipes into Type* by Joan Whitman and Dolores Simon (Newton, MA: Biscuit Books, 2000); *The New Food Lover's Companion* by Sharon Tyler Herbst (Hauppauge, NY: Barron's, 1995); and *Rosemary Brown's Big Kitchen Instruction Book* (Kansas City, MO: Andrews McMeel, 1998).

Index

OTHER BOOKS BY BECKY SELENGUT

*GOOD FISH: SUSTAINABLE SEAFOOD RECIPES
FROM THE PACIFIC COAST*

*THE WASHINGTON LOCAL
AND SEASONAL COOKBOOK*

Andrews McMeel Publishing, LLC
an Andrews McMeel Universal company
1130 Walnut Street, Kansas City, Missouri 64106

WWW.ANDREWSMCMEEL.COM

14 15 16 17 18 TEN 10 9 8 7 6 5 4 3 2 1

ISBN: 978-1-4494-4826-4

Library of Congress Control Number: 2014931303

DESIGN: Diane Marsh
PHOTOGRAPHY: Clare Barboza
FOOD STYLIST: Becky Selengut
PROP STYLIST: Clare Barboza

WWW.SHROOMTHECOOKBOOK.COM

ATTENTION: SCHOOLS AND BUSINESSES

Andrews McMeel books are available at quantity discounts with bulk purchase for educational, business, or sales promotional use. For information, please e-mail the Andrews McMeel Special Sales Department: specialsales@amuniversal.com.